THE WORLD
OF
JOHN LARDNER

EDITED BY ROGER KAHN

WITH A PREFACE BY WALT KELLY

SIMON AND SCHUSTER   NEW YORK   1961

FIRST PRINTING

LIBRARY OF CONGRESS CATALOG CARD NUMBER: 61-12847

MANUFACTURED IN THE UNITED STATES OF AMERICA BY GEO. MCKIBBIN &
SONS, NEW YORK, N. Y.

Permission to reprint the following pieces is gratefully acknowledged:

Newsweek: "What They Did to Jack" (1959); "Docker the Knocker" (1956); "Dixie Deposit" (1957); "No Scar, No Memory" (1957); "Death of a Simian and Scholar" (1949); "The Rangers' Beachhead Alamo" (1944); "The Frontier Down Under" (1942).

Sport: "They Walked by Night" (1950); "The Roller Derby" (1949); "Cockfighting Is Here to Stay" (1950); "Babe Herman" (1952).

The Saturday Evening Post: "The Great Spring Training Nonsense" (1953).

True: the Man's Magazine: "Titanic Thompson" (1951); "Down Great Purple Valleys" (1954).

The following articles originally appeared in *The New Yorker*—"D Day, Iwo Jima" (1945); "Lieutenant Lemick-Emden" (1946); "Battling Siki," in different form (1949); "A Happy Sullivan Day" (1958); "Thoughts on Radio-Televese" and "Small World" (1959)—and were copyrighted ©, in the respective years shown, by The New Yorker Magazine, Inc.

Parts of "Battling Siki" appeared in *The New Yorker.* The expanded version, included here, is reprinted from the book *White Hopes and Other Tigers,* J. B. Lippincott Co., 1951. "The Lindbergh Legends" first appeared in *The Aspirin Age,* edited by Isabel Leighton, Simon and Schuster, 1949. The selections on American drinking are from an unfinished book and, of course, have not been published before.

The editor is grateful for the counsel and assistance of Ring Lardner, Jr., who was not only John's brother but his friend. He appreciates, too, research work done by Barry Gottehrer and Richard Schaap of Newsweek Magazine, and extends his thanks to Don McKinney of True: the Man's Magazine, Robert Fuoss of The Saturday Evening Post, and Edward Fitzgerald, former editor of Sport.

CONTENTS

WAR CORRESPONDENCE

DRINKING IN AMERICA—
An Unfinished History

Preface

by WALT KELLY

To be alone with John Lardner was to enjoy solitude in the best of company. The quiet of the man's presence was like the silence of a forest, where the lack of noise does not indicate a lack of life. In some measure his pages here should bring again a sense of his liveliness, a hint of his virility, a bar of the music that made the man.

The approach to Lardner was somewhat more backward than is common. Knowing him did not necessarily lead to liking. It was the other way around. To love him was to know him. He did not confuse chatter with conversation; he was not the cocktail-party type. Thus he gave many the impression of being withdrawn. It is significant that he liked cats, and had several around the house, all of them generally reserved but given to sporadic bursts of imaginative activity. In this he was somewhat like them, although, where a cat stares, John gazed. A lady in Rome once remarked, when John took off his glasses, that he had the most kindly eyes she had ever seen. The removal of my own glasses did nothing to change her mind.

Lardner may have seen with his heart, for he missed nothing; but he had been given a pair of eyes which must have been spare parts from a previous model. On the one occasion in any man's memory when he was roused to attempt physical combat he agreed to proceed outdoors with his fellow combatant for the event. Once outside the bar, each had to take off his glasses. Neither was able to see the other, and the group decided to move back into Bleeck's and defend honor with a match game.

Very simply, he was a brave man who, during World War II, as Joe Liebling points out, "walked toward the bomb flashes in order to see better." Such was the way he walked through life. Despair, dismay, fright never walked with him, despite wrenching internal tragedies that would have slowed, in fact, stopped, other men. You will see no sign of anguish in his work. Much of what is here was written against a background of tuberculosis, the pain of heart disease, multiple sclerosis, personal troubles too private for anyone else to reveal, and a gnawing, understandable premonition that he would not live to be forty-eight years of age. He had just about a month to go.

A suggestion of his modesty lies in the fact that he never slugged his copy with a capital "L" for Lardner. It was always lower case. Yet his stature grew to such a point that friends and editors with whom he worked came to call him by a single name. His father, to them, had not been eclipsed, merely set aside. John was the Lardner. The quality implicit in his height, his mind, and the resultant point of view became the name.

Contempt was an emotion beneath his abilities, but his deep and burning scorn for the panic-driven dullards of the Fifties who imprisoned his brother, a man filled with nothing but respect and love for humanity, bordered on contempt. His attachments were strong and his loyalties firm. He loved his family in a way that did not seem to go hand in hand with a man who liked to stay up all night, sing, drink Scotch whisky and gamble on the flick of an eyelash.

Some have said that he was apolitical. This opinion can have been reached only because there were no soap boxes in his luggage. He was, in fact, a fierce partisan. There was an occasion when a man, unabashed at the proximity of a mind better than his own, stoutly avowed that he was an honest conservative. Lardner advised him to get himself stuffed and go up to the Museum of Natural History. "You're the only one of your kind," he said.

Though he was a man of deep sentiment (his regard for yesterday and its songs, sports records, and poetry was unique), he left to others the more usual expressions of the sentimental. A companion who so admired him as to wish to name a son after him asked permission for the use of the name. "I guess so," said John, touched and embarrassed, "so long as I get the usual space rates and royalties."

His leave-taking was as might have been expected, quiet and without fuss. A friend who had traveled many places in his company sat through the last Saturday morning with him at a New York funeral home, smoking a cigar and reading the Times. Asked how he could do such a thing, he replied, "Well, actually it wasn't very much different than other mornings on the road. He didn't usually wear his glasses to bed and he never said much in the morning anyway." This kind of gentle, affectionate disregard for the normal seemed to be bred in Lardner's friends. One of them slipped three matches into his hand for any game he might get into elsewhere, and another put two dollars into his pocket in the event there might be a horse running anyplace. All of this, of course, was an unconscious reenactment of man's long inability to say goodbye. In any other circumstances, Lardner, who knew how to clip a farewell to a minimum with a quick "See ya," would not have held still for any of it.

PEOPLE

Titanic Thompson

1951

ONE DAY not long ago, a St. Louis hotel detective tipped off a cop friend of his that there was a fellow in a room on the eighth floor who packed a gun. They decided to do a little further research. They went into the room without knocking, and it didn't take long to find the gun. It was pointing at them. The man who held it was tall, dark, thin, well dressed and fiftyish.

"Take it easy," he said. Then, observing the cop's uniform, he set down the gun, a small Army model, on a table, and smiled pleasantly. "I thought it might be a stick-up," he said. "I have to be careful."

Down at the station house, where the man was taken to explain why he was armed and why he drew his hardware so quickly, they got a polite and possibly a truthful answer. He happened to have $3,930 on him. He was expecting to claim a race horse with it. When he carried cash, he liked to feel protected. He had a license for the gun. His name was Alvin C. Thomas. At this point, the police lost interest in the details of the story and merely sat looking at the speaker with the frank curiosity of zoo-goers looking at a duck-billed platypus—for Alvin C. Thomas, as they knew and as he readily confirmed, is also Titanic Thompson. All the cops in the house took a good, long stare. Then they released him, and he went on his way.

On a small scale, Titanic Thompson is an American legend. I say a small scale, because an overpowering majority of the public has never heard of him. That is the way Titanic likes it. He is a professional gambler. He has sometimes been called the gamblers' gambler. He does not resent his fame among fellow hustlers as a "man with a million propositions," as a master of percentage, but he likes to have it kept within the lodge. In the years of his early manhood, no one knew of him except gamblers, a few rich suckers, a few golf pros, and, by rumor, the police of New York City, the Middle West, and California, his favorite bases of operation. The cops had heard that he clipped people at everything, from golf to throwing quarters at a crack in the floor. But the people he clipped were mostly members of his own profession. Those outside it, honest suckers, did not complain. Suckers seldom do. Besides, they believed—and often they were right—that they had been beaten by pure skill.

One night in 1928, the most celebrated card game in American criminal history took place. As a result of it, Arnold Rothstein, a so-called underworld king, was murdered. And then it turned out that someone named Titanic Thompson had sat in on the game, and might know something about the killing.

That was the end, for a while, of Titanic's obscurity. Members of the Grassy Sprain Country Club, near New York City, blurted out a story that had been on their minds for a month. One day, some time between the Rothstein killing and Titanic's arrest as a material witness, Leo P. Flynn, a big-time fight manager and matchmaker who once handled Jack Dempsey, had brought a stranger out to the club. Leo was known there as a sport and a pretty fair golfer. This time, though, he didn't want to play golf himself. He wanted to match the stranger, whom he called Titanic, against the club professional, George McLean.

A side bet of $2,500 was arranged, with Flynn backing Thompson and several members pooling their funds in support of the local pride. That day, McLean won. He won with ease—the stranger, though he hit some good shots, did not seem to be in George's class. Besides, he was left-handed, and top-notch left-handed golfers are almost as rare as left-handed catchers. The McLean faction listened to Flynn's talk of a return match. McLean listened to the stranger's mild appeal for a ten-stroke handicap.

"I'm not in your league," said the unknown, running his hand through his floppy dark hair, "but I think I can do better than I did today. Give me a real edge in strokes, and we'll bet real dough."

The handicap, after some needling back and forth, was fixed at eight strokes. The real dough, supplied mostly by Mr. Flynn and another golfing sport, a Mr. Duffy, was $13,000, and the members covered every dime of it in behalf of their pro. Mr. Duffy, it happened, was Big Bill Duffy, a jolly henchman of Owney Madden, the racketeer. The members did not know this, but it would probably have made no difference if they had. They did not see how you could fix a golf match, and they did not see how an amateur could beat a good pro. It may not have occurred to them that for $13,000 Titanic was not, strictly speaking, an amateur.

The stranger shot much better, or luckier, golf this time than he had in the first match, but at the end of sixteen holes he had used up his eight-stroke advantage. The match was dead even, and McLean prepared to close in. On the short seventeenth, his tee shot stopped six feet from the pin. Titanic studied the distance and dropped one four feet closer. Perhaps that shot unnerved McLean. At any rate, he missed his putt. The stranger sank his. Titanic stood one up. He halved the last hole in par, and Mr. Flynn and Mr. Duffy picked up the $13,000—of which they gaily gave Mr. Thompson his share—and called for drinks for the house. The members went home to brood on the fact that a golf match can indeed be fixed—"fixed upward," as gamblers say—if the fixer is a talented athlete who knows how to hide the symptoms until the price is right.

On the day the news broke of Titanic's arrest in the Rothstein case, Grassy Sprain started the legend rolling. It has been gathering strength ever since. Generally speaking, New York newspaper readers forgot Thompson soon after the trial of George A. McManus for Rothstein's murder (Titanic was a state witness who gave the state no help at all). To most of the rest of the world, he was then, and still is, unknown. But in the small circle in which his name is famous, Titanic Thompson stories have been collected, pooled, and warmed over slow fires for nearly a quarter of a century, till now they amount to a kind of saga—the sharpshooter's Adventures of Robin Hood.

Rothstein's death reminded Broadway story-swappers of what

might on other levels be called the Adventure of the White Horses. The horse-playing set to which Titanic and Rothstein belonged had formed the habit of spotting white horses from the train that took them to the Belmont or Jamaica track. One morning, some twenty of these smoking-car handicappers made up a pool, of $50 each, on the number of white horses that would be counted on the trip that day. Rothstein's estimate was surprisingly high; Titanic studied the tycoon thoughtfully before he made his own guess, just one horse above Rothstein's. There was an outburst of white horsemeat along the Long Island Rail Road tracks that day—a batch of fifteen animals at one crossing, a batch of twelve at another. The first batch had been planted by Titanic, the second by Rothstein.

"That will teach you not to be close with your money," said Titanic to Rothstein, as he pocketed the pool. "For thirty bucks, you could have had a whole livery stable."

Bear in mind that if Titanic had taken from the rich to give to the poor, as Robin Hood and Jesse James are said to have done, the legend-makers of the gambling world would want no part of him. He would be the wrong kind of hero. But Mr. Thompson has always taken very frankly to give to himself, or to split with the people who stake him. He has seldom made a bet he wasn't sure of winning. He always carries a gimmick—sometimes his hidden athletic skill, sometimes his trained knowledge of percentage, and occasionally a little something extra.

Here are some of the tales they tell:

1. Titanic once bet a peanut vendor $10 he could throw a peanut across Times Square in New York. He took a peanut from the vendor's stack, palmed a loaded one in its place, and pitched the phony goober up against the marquee of the Hotel Astor, across the street.

2. Billy Duffy once backed Titanic in a bet against a powerful amateur golfer, noted for his long drives. Titanic offered to let his opponent make three drives on each hole and play the best drive of the three. It sounded like a big margin to spot a strong hitter, and the party of the second part snapped the bet up. Playing his best drive, he piled up a big lead on the first nine holes. By that time, his arms were so tired from three full swings a hole that he

could hardly knock the ball off the tee. Titanic breezed home in the last nine.

3. Titanic once bet $10,000 that Nick (the Greek) Dandolos, another high operator, would not sink a 25-foot putt. Kissed by the goddess Athena, the Greek holed the ball. Thompson, however, was not one to let $10,000 of his money rest long in someone else's jeans. He bet Nick double or nothing that he could hit a silver dollar with a gun eight times out of eight, from ten feet away. After the ceremony, the Greek gave back the ten grand and kept what was left of the dollar for a souvenir.

4. Titanic's mathematics were as sound as Pascal's. In fact, they were based on the reasoning of that great seventeenth-century Frenchman. He once bet a fellow gambler that two of the first thirty persons they met and spoke to would prove to have the same birthday. Strong in the thought that he had 365 days running for him, the second hustler was pleased to accept. Suspecting, not unnaturally, a frame-up, he was careful to approach total strangers and chance passers-by, who could not be known to Titanic. He lost the bet on the twenty-eighth question, when a duplicate birthday turned up.

"To tell you the truth," said Titanic afterward, "on each of the last five guys we spoke to, the odds were better than even money in my favor. I'll explain the mathematics to you some time."

Your correspondent will also be glad to explain the mathematics some time, to any reader. He does not quite understand them, but he knows what they are. Titanic's reasoning on the birthday proposition was founded on the fact that the chance against him at first was 364/365th, which, when multiplied by the succeeding chances —363/365th, 362/365th, and so forth—came fairly soon to represent ½, or one chance in two, or even money.

5. Tony Penna, the golf professional, tells of a bet by Titanic that he could throw a pumpkin over a three-story house. The pumpkin, when he produced it, was the size of an orange— but still a pumpkin. Going perhaps into the realm of pure myth, Penna adds that Titanic once bet he could throw a baseball over the Empire State Building. He won it (says Penna) by taking an elevator to the top platform and throwing from there.

6. Titanic once bet a dice impresario named Nutts Nitti

that he could find a hairpin in each block of a stretch of twenty consecutive New York City blocks. He won. The hairpins had been planted in advance.

7. Titanic once bet he could throw a quarter at a potato, from fifteen feet away, and make it stick in the potato at least once in ten tries. Encountering resistance from his opponent, he agreed to settle for seven tries, and scored on the fourth one.

8. Titanic was motoring into Omaha, his temporary base, with a friend one day. As they passed a signpost on the road, Titanic, without looking at it, offered to bet that they would reach the city limits within ten minutes. The signpost made it ten miles to town. The friend, a noticing sort of man, took the bet. He lost. Titanic had moved the signpost five miles closer that morning.

9. There is a standard prop in Titanic's repertory—a two-headed quarter, which he uses with more than standard speed, skill, and acting talent. His opening line, after dinner, is "Let's toss for the check." His next line, while the coin is in the air, is "You cry." If his opponent cries tails, Titanic lets the quarter fall—heads. If the other fellow cries heads, Titanic swings his hand nonchalantly, catches the coin, puts it back in his pocket, and speaks to this effect: "Oh, to hell with gambling for ham and eggs. Let's go Dutch."

10. Titanic is credited with being the man who introduced Rothstein to the art of betting on automobile license plates, at Rothstein's expense. He bet Rothstein, as they stood on a Broadway corner, that the first New Jersey plate to come along would make a better poker hand than the first New York plate. Thirty seconds later, from his parking spot around the corner (there were parking spots in those days), a colleague of Titanic's drove into view in a New Jersey car. His plate number carried three threes.

11. In a Hot Springs, Arkansas, stud-poker game, a player named Burke became justly incensed one evening because he could not win.

"That deck is ice cold, and so is the other one," he bawled. "I ain't had a pair in an hour."

"You ought to know," said Titanic soothingly, "that the odds are against getting a pair in any five-card hand. Now, if you dealt yourself six cards—"

"With these cards," yelled Burke, "I couldn't pair myself if I dealt all night!"—and the way was paved for a Thompson proposition. Titanic offered to let Burke deal himself ten cold hands of six cards each. Before each hand, he offered to bet that there would be a pair in it. They say that the agony of Burke, as he paired himself in eight of the ten hands and thus lost $300 by the sweat of his own fingers, was something to see. Titanic had known that the addition of a sixth card changes the odds on catching a pair from 13 to 10 against to nearly 2 to 1 in favor. And to bet even money on a 2-to-1 favorite, he would walk quite a distance and stay quite a while.

12. In his early days, Titanic, going through a storeroom in the basement of a sporting club in Ohio on his way to the men's room, spotted a rat and nimbly tipped a barrel over the animal. Later, in the course of the dice game upstairs, he raised the subject of the prevalence of rats in Ohio sporting clubs and made a bet that he could find and shoot one any time. The bet was taken. Titanic returned to the cellar, shot the dead rat, and brought it back to the table with him.

13. Titanic, shooting right-handed, lost a close golf match to an amateur who played in the 90s. Next day, he bet the winner double their first bet that he could beat him playing left-handed. Left-handed, his natural style, Titanic shot an 80. The victim continued to shoot in the 90s.

14. Titanic once bet he could drive a golf ball 500 yards. The bet was popular on all sides, and the interested parties followed Titanic out to the golf course of his choice, on Long Island. He picked a tee on a hill overlooking a lake. It was wintertime. His drive hit the ice and, it seemed to his opponents, never did stop rolling. It went half a mile, if it went a yard.

Titanic, as the district attorney found out in the Rothstein case, does not talk much. All that anyone knows about his origins and early life comes from stray remarks, spaced far apart, that he has let fall to other gamblers on the golf course or at the card table. This writer has seen him only once. It was in the "private" or "upstairs" crap game at the old Chicago Club in Saratoga. Joe Madden, the literary barkeep, pointed him out to me from the sidelines. I saw a slender fellow about six feet tall, his dark hair cut long, wearing a neat gabardine suit and two fair-sized diamond rings. When Titanic left the game a little later, Madden said, "He's going down to the drugstore to get a load of ice cream. That's his dish."

"That's his dish for breakfast," corrected one of the gamblers at the table. "But he don't eat breakfast till he gets up for the races, maybe two o'clock in the afternoon."

A discussion of Titanic's habits ensued. It reminded me of a session of fight men on Jacobs Beach or in the press room at the Garden, discussing some figure of legend like Stanley Ketchel. I asked where the name Titanic had come from. The answer was one I'd heard before, the only one I've ever heard. It may or may not be true.

In a poker game in New York on Thompson's first tour of the East, one player said to another, "What's that guy's name?"

"It ought to be Titanic," said the second player. "He sinks everybody."

The logic here was a little unsound—if I remember the *S.S. Titanic* story, "Iceberg" would have been the right name. But gamblers are seldom good on names. Thompson, for instance, is an easy garbling of Titanic's real name, Thomas. There seems to be no doubt, judging by police files, that he was born Alvin Clarence Thomas, in the state of Arkansas, about 1893. He still talks with a slight Southwestern accent. As a boy, he once said, he acquired the throwing skill that served him handsomely later by killing quail with rocks. He was a good horseshoe pitcher and an expert shot.

Athletic talent is a rare thing in a professional gambler, but what surprised the golf pros of the Pacific Coast and the Southwest, who knew him in his early days and accepted him as an athlete to begin with, was his lightning speed of mind at gambling. He would make twelve to fifteen bets on a single hole, keeping track of them in his head while others took time to make notes. He would lose one bet and make another on the next shot that would bring his stake back doubled. Penna and others noticed that his bets during the match often were bigger than his bet on the match as a whole.

"Yeah, that's right," said Titanic, when someone spoke of this.

"I like to bet 'em when they're out there on the course with me. Especially on the greens. Why? Figure it out for yourself."

It was not hard to figure. When a golfer is out there on the course, any new bet he makes is probably made with his own money, without the help of a backer. When he bets with his own money, he gets nervous. Especially on the greens.

In Titanic's youth, they say, he was impatient with mental slowness of any kind, but it could not have been long before he came to recognize that quality, in the people around him, as so much bread and jam for him. Among the money golfers who knew him at one time and another were Penna, Dick Metz, Len Dodson and Ben Hogan. He always told them, as he often told the cops when they picked him up on the curious charge of shooting golf too well, that he was "a former pro." It may have been so, but the chances are that he was a former caddy who, on discovering his own skill at the game, almost immediately became a professional gambler rather than a professional golfer. It was a nice economic choice. The best professional golfers in the country, even in these days of rich prizes, do well to earn $30,000 in a year from tournaments. Titanic has sometimes made $50,000 in a few weeks of well-timed chipping and putting at golf resorts.

"I've been broke," he told a Coast newspaperman once, "but never for more than six hours at a time. When I tap out, somebody I once helped loans me a stake, and I'm back in action again."

Titanic Thompson broke into the Rothstein game, as a young man, because he was good company and a good player—though the state of New York tried to prove, a little later, that trained fingers had something to do with it. The fateful game that led to Rothstein's death and to Titanic's first appearance in print took place on the night of September 7-8, 1928. It was held at the apartment of Jimmy Meehan, a regular member of the circle, on the West Side of New York. Rothstein, because he was rumored to have a finger in every branch of organized crime in the city, was the best-known player in the game, but all the others were noted figures in the gambling, bookmaking, and horse-playing worlds. They included Martin "Red" Bowe, Nigger Nate Raymond, Sam and Meyer Boston, Abe Silverman, George A. McManus, and Titanic Thompson.

The game was stud poker, but as it went along it took on a pattern familiar in that group—it became a "high-card" game, with the biggest money being bet on the size of the first-up card in the stud hand.

There were rumors along Broadway in the following week that Rothstein had lost a packet. There were also rumors that the winners had not been paid in full. It took a gunshot, however, to make the story public property. On November 4, 1928, someone put a revolver slug into Rothstein's body in Room 349 of the Park Central Hotel. Rothstein staggered from the room and died just outside it. The killer pushed aside a screen and threw the gun into the street below. The New York newspapers went to town. It became the biggest crime story since the murder of Herman Rosenthal by Whitey Lewis, Dago Frank, Lefty Louie, and Gyp the Blood.

The overcoat of George McManus, a smiling gambler, brother of a police lieutenant, had been found in Room 349. Soon afterward McManus was indicted for murder, along with three gunmen who never did show up for trial. On November 26, the D.A., Joab H. Banton, arrested Jimmy Meehan, Red Bowe, Sidney Stajer (Rothstein's secretary), Nigger Nate Raymond, and Titanic as material witnesses. All of them but Bowe were held in $100,000 bail. For some reason it was Titanic, then and later, who caught the public's fancy—maybe because he was said to be a Westerner, a lone wolf, a romantic and single-duke gambler of the old school.

It turned out that Titanic had a wife, Mrs. Alice Thomas, who had been living with him at the Mayflower Hotel. A few days after his arrest, she paid him a tearful visit at the West Side prison on Fifty-fourth Street. Titanic then sent for the D.A.'s men, made "important disclosures" (the papers said), and was released in $10,000 bail. What kind of minstrel show he gave to win his freedom is not known. Unofficially it was reported that he had admitted to being in Room 349 just before the murder, leaving when he saw that there might be trouble. Whatever he said, it was plain that the D.A. thought he had laid hold of a fine, friendly witness. The D.A. was very wrong.

When the McManus murder case came to trial, in November 1929, Titanic was running a night club and gambling spot in Milwaukee. He was also running a fever in a Milwaukee hospital. So important was his evidence considered by the prosecution that the trial was delayed for a week. Titanic, in Milwaukee, showed for the first time that he was in no mood to blow whistles.

"I don't know what they want me as a witness for," he told reporters, whom he received in scarlet pajamas in the hospital. "I wasn't with Rothstein on the night of the murder and hadn't seen him or McManus for two months previously. We played cards at that time, and McManus lost a lot of money. That's all I know about the case."

When he did get to New York to testify, the courtroom was packed. Titanic sat in the rear of the room, twisting his fingers nervously, till he was called. The crowd buzzed as he took the stand. McManus, in the dock, sat up and smiled at Titanic. Titanic nodded to McManus. Ferdinand Pecora, later a famous judge, then an assistant D.A. and a strong trial lawyer, moved in on Titanic confidently. It had been established that McManus had lost $51,000 to Rothstein in the celebrated high-card game while Rothstein was losing about $219,000 to some of the others. Pecora's pitch was obvious. He implied that Rothstein, possibly with Titanic's help, had fleeced McManus of the fifty-one grand. Titanic would have no part of this hypothesis. After identifying himself by saying that he gambled on everything from golf to horse races, and referring to McManus as "a square and honest guy," he began to spar Pecora to a standstill.

"Was the game on the level?" asked the prosecutor.

"It couldn't be any other way on high cards," said Titanic with a deeply scornful gesture. "A man who never dealt in his life was peddling the papers. We had to show him how to shuffle."

To "peddle the papers" is to deal. The crowd was delighted with this local color.

"Now, think," said Pecora angrily, after a while. "Wasn't this game crooked?"

"Anyone ought to know," said Titanic, still scornful, "that that's impossible."

"Couldn't a clever dealer give the high card to any man he chose?"

"Certainly not," said Titanic. "It ain't being done."

On other questions, his memory failed.

"You see," he told Pecora patiently, "I just don't remember things. If I bet on a horse today and won ten grand, I probably would not be able to recall the horse's name tomorrow."

While the public gasped at this spacious statement, the defense took over for cross-examination. At once, Titanic's memory improved, and his attitude got friendlier. He said that McManus had shown no ill will after the game.

"He's a swell loser," said Titanic tenderly. "Win or lose, he always smiles."

In short, he probably gave the state less change for its money than any state's witness in recent memory. And it's a matter of record that George A. McManus was acquitted of the murder of Arnold Rothstein.

It's a matter of record, too, that Titanic was annoyed by his notoriety during the trial. For several months afterward, he complained that he could no longer get a "good" game of golf, by which he meant a game with gravy on the side. He may have misstated the case a little. Recently I asked Oswald Jacoby, the card wizard, about a story in the newspapers that said that John R. Crawford, an ex-G.I. and a spectacular newcomer to card-playing circles, resented the publicity he got in a big Canasta game for charity because no one wanted to play cards with him any more.

"Don't you believe it," said Mr. Jacoby. "People always want to play with a man with a big reputation. The more money they have, the more they like it."

Be that as it may, Titanic, in Tulsa soon after the trial, was bothered by the galleries that followed him—but he did find one man who wanted to play golf with him just to be able to say he'd done it. Titanic fixed up "a little proposition" for him and won $2,000. There must have been other men with the same ambition, or else Ti's celebrity began to fade, for we cross his trail again in Little Rock, Arkansas, soon afterward, playing golf for $2,000 and $3,000 a round.

True, even a roving gambler likes to stop and run a "store" now and then, but since the time of his first fame, Titanic has found it more comfortable to keep on the move. He and a large restaurant operator and racketeer, whom we will call Tony Rizzo, were moving by train not long ago from California to Tony's base at Hot Springs.

"Tony," said Titanic, "do you ever regret being illiterate?"

"Whaddya mean?" said Tony, hurt. "I ain't so dumb."

"I'm going to teach you to spell two ten-letter words," said Titanic. "The words are 'rhinoceros' and 'anthropoid.' If you can still spell them when we get off the train, I'll pick up the checks for this trip. But take a tip from me—keep spelling them or you'll forget them."

For the rest of the trip, Rizzo kept spelling out, in order, the letters r-h-i-n-o-c-e-r-o-s and a-n-t-h-r-o-p-o-i-d. He still knew them at the Hot Springs station. Titanic paid off.

The gambler set the second stage of the proposition for Tony's restaurant. He first brought an unknown partner, a respectable-looking fellow as shills go, into the act. He rehearsed the shill in the spelling of ten ten-letter words, including "rhinoceros" and "anthropoid." The next night he sat down in Rizzo's restaurant, as usual, with Owney Madden and other lovable tourists. Rizzo himself, as usual, was sitting at a table by himself, wolfing his pizza in solitary grandeur.

"Do you know," said Titanic confidentially, "that that Rizzo just pretends to be ignorant? He puts on a dumb front for business. The guy has got diplomas from two colleges."

This speech aroused great skepticism at Titanic's table, which in turn aroused bets. Titanic covered a thousand dollars' worth, his argument being that Tony could spell any ten-letter word, any one at all, that Mr. Madden and the boys chose to mention. As Titanic expected, a pause followed, while the boys tried to think of a ten-letter word to give Tony. They were somewhat embarrassed. At this point, Titanic's partner hove into view, and Titanic hailed him.

"Excuse me, sir," he said, "but you look as though you might be able to help us. May I ask your business? A lawyer? Fine. Would you mind writing down ten ten-letter words on a piece of paper here, for these gentlemen to choose from?"

The stranger obliged. Looking around, he wrote down the word "restaurant," which appeared on Tony's window. He wrote down several others he found on the bill of fare, such as "cacciatore." In and among the rest he inserted the words "rhinoceros" and "anthropoid." He turned the paper over to the boys, who immediately set to work making scratches in the morning line, to protect their bets. They scratched "restaurant"—Tony saw it on the window all day, he might know it. They scratched "cacciatore." "He's Eyetalian," said Mr. Madden, "and he might know all that kind of stuff." This left them, in the end, with "rhinoceros" and "anthropoid." At random, they scratched "rhinoceros." They summoned Mr. Rizzo and desired him to spell the word "anthropoid."

"Sure," said Tony, taking a deep breath. "R-h-i-n-o-c-e-r-o-s."

Titanic paid off the $1,000. The bet belongs to his legend partly because he lost it and partly because he won the money back, with galloping dominoes, the same night. As I said before, he is prosperous just now. A fellow gambler who ran across him in Evansville, Indiana—you are apt to find him anywhere—says that Titanic's pajamas and dressing gowns, always brilliant, are more brilliant than ever. His supply of jewels, rings, and stickpins is at high tide. A man like Ti, my informant explains, buys jewels whenever he is in the money, to sell or hock when times are hard.

The Titanic legend would not be so solidly honored in the gambling world, it would not be complete, if the quiet Mr. Thompson had never used the gun he always carries, in defense of the money he takes from the rich to give to himself. The police of Little Rock, years ago, found a letter in Titanic's room which demanded "2 thousand cash or you will be sorry." The police of St. Louis, more recently, found him ready to draw at the sound of a door being opened.

And in Tyler, Texas, a few years back, it was proved clearly that in matters involving Titanic Thompson and his money there is very little kidding. Titanic had had a good day on the golf course. His caddy noticed it. The caddy was sixteen years old, but he had grown-up ideas. At a late hour the same evening, a shot was fired in Tyler, and the police arrived to find the caddy with a bullet in him, while Titanic stood in attendance.

"I shot him," said the gambler. "It was self-defense. He tried to stick me up for my roll."

The young man died next day. A mask and an unfired gun were found on his person, and the plea of self-defense was allowed. Titanic moved along, with a stronger toehold on history than ever.

The Lindbergh Legends

1949

IN MAY 1927, a slim, comely man of twenty-five years flew an airplane from New York to Paris all by himself, without stopping. His performance was instantly recognized as the climactic stunt of a time of marvelous stunts, of an epoch of noise, hero worship, and the sort of "individualism" which seems to have meant that people were not disposed to look at themselves and their lives, in general, and therefore ran gaping and thirsty to look at anything done by one man or woman that was special and apart from the life they knew. The farther the hero went—whether he went upward, downward, sideways, through air, land, or water, or hand over hand on a flagpole—the better, provided he went alone.

The year 1927, which came about two thirds of the way through this time of escape from mass realities, was the perfect year for the perfect feat. It was the apex of the era, chronologically and emotionally. The young flier, Charles A. Lindbergh, did not know this. He picked his time by chance, as far as any ordinary reader of human instincts can say; though then and later he was so repeatedly and so overwhelmingly famous, and showed such a sense, friendly or not, of the rhythms and uses of notoriety, that many newspapermen of his period refuse to lay any part of it to chance. Newspapermen have always felt superstitious, among other things, about Lindbergh.

At any rate, he rang the bell at the top of the range, in that country fair of a setting. I do not want to belittle the skill and cool efficiency of Lindbergh's Paris flight, or his long-standing talent for flying in general, when I liken his deed of that time to such another as, say, Gertrude Ederle's swim across the English Channel a year earlier. With Lindbergh, it was all more so and better—everything was right. He was young, he was photogenic (as they came to say later), he was apparently modest and unaffected by the first wild sweep of fame, and so simple and understandable in what he said and did that the public turned handsprings in delight and self-congratulation. But basically the reaction was the same as to Ederle and the other heroes and heroines of the era. Its flavor was strong and sweet, and people took their time over it, drawing it out. But a one-day wonder can last weeks or months and still be, at bottom, a one-day wonder. Some men said Lindbergh's nonstop leap to Paris was a vital stimulus to aviation; those closest to aviation thought the growth was inevitable, in view of the more studious flights made before and after Lindbergh's, and will tell you today, looking back, that Lindbergh in 1927 had no noticeable statistical effect on the public's attitude toward flight. In short, he was one for the book; a world-wide love affair; confetti which cost sixteen thousand dollars to clean off the streets of New York.

And that, by every known precedent, should have been that.

But it wasn't. The end of the story was delayed, spectacularly, time and again. Lindbergh lived on in the world's interest in a recurrent series of reactions—Lindbergh's reactions to the public and the public's reactions to Lindbergh—some violent, some cold, some maudlin. One event which came a few years after the flight to Paris, the kidnaping and murder of Lindbergh's son, calls for no psychological explanation of Lindbergh; it was done to Lindbergh and his wife, brutally and as far as we know objectively, from outside. Yet by and large people have attempted to explain the phenomenon of Lindbergh—the phenomenon of the story that refused to die, that may be smoldering now for another burst into print— in terms of the man's character. I know that the temptation to psychoanalyze Lindbergh has been too much for many men and women in the last ten years. Harold Nicolson, the English writer who rented his home to Lindbergh and his family when they first fled America, later wrote about him as follows, reviewing the years after 1927:

"It was almost with ferocity that he struggled to remain himself.

And in the process of that arduous struggle his simplicity became muscle-bound; his virility-ideal became not merely inflexible, but actually rigid; his self-control thickened into arrogance, and his convictions hardened into granite. He became impervious to anything outside his own legend—the legend of the young lad from Minnesota whose head could not be turned."

If that sounds a bit portentous, remember that Nicolson was writing at a time when England was in danger and Lindbergh was openly opposed to saving her. Otherwise it is a fair specimen of the widespread effort to find the answer to the riddle of Lindbergh in Lindbergh himself, and nowhere else. There is as much truth in it, probably, as in many of the other analyses which rolled off angry lips and pens at the time of Lindbergh's isolationism, when he opened a part of his mind to the world by fighting American intervention in the Second World War. Certainly Lindbergh was deliberately responsible to some extent for his continuing fame and notoriety after 1927. Loathing the blatant contactual phases of publicity, he showed nonetheless one of the truest gifts ever seen on this planet for attracting it, seeming sometimes to go out of his way to get it when otherwise it might not have been forthcoming. It almost appeared that he needed fame to subsist, to support his confidence in the role he had won. Here is the paradox that engrosses his analyzers: a man supernormally ingrown and aloof becoming with sure instincts a chronic public figure. Lindbergh once said of "interventionists" and "idealists" before the war that they were "men who were too far separated from fact and life." No man of note was ever further separated from life and fact than Lindbergh. No man could be more reluctant to admit it.

There was a good deal of glibness, in the heyday of the movement called America First a few years ago, about marking the parallel between Charles A. Lindbergh, Jr., and his "isolationist" father. Possibly Lindbergh wanted to believe that such a parallel existed, but it didn't. His father seems to have been quite another sort of man.

Lindbergh's father was Charles Augustus Lindbergh, Sr., and the father of Charles Augustus Lindbergh, Sr., was Ola Mansson, born in Sweden and for twelve years a member of the Swedish Riksdag, or parliament. The present Lindbergh is, in fact, the only man of his line in three generations who has not held public office. Ola Mansson went about Sweden crusading against a number of things, including the whipping post, which he helped in the end to abolish. In the 1850s he changed his name to Lindbergh. In 1860, with his new wife and a new son (his first wife had died), he sailed to America, as a great many other people from a great many other nations were then doing. Eighty years later his grandson was to speak with marked disparagement of the immigrant as opposed to the home-grown American.

The Lindberghs went across the land by boat and train as far as St. Anthony Falls, Minnesota, and then by wagon another hundred miles to a homestead near Melrose, in the neighborhood of the Sinclair Lewis town of Sauk Center. The old man is said to have been a robust character who once axed himself in the forest and refused to leave off work. His son Charles went for a few years to a school conducted by a Roman Catholic priest in Sauk Center. In his free time he worked on the railroad cars as a newsboy and candy butcher, and when he was old enough he entered the law school of the University of Michigan, earning his way through by washing dishes and waiting on tables. He was practicing law in Detroit when he met and married a schoolteacher of chemistry and science, Irish by ancestry, the daughter of a Detroit dentist named Dr. Land. Their son was born in Detroit on February 4, 1902. Before the boy was two months old, his father took the family to Little Falls, Minnesota, and set up a law practice there.

Charles A. Lindbergh, Sr., was known as "C.A." to the people of Little Falls, some of whom are reported to have recognized him early as a soft touch for a loan and to have set in motion maneuvers which forestalled the possibility of his dying wealthy, although he was successful in his work and a rising force in the town, the state, and the region.

"He made money, but he was generous," said his law partner, Walter Eli Quigley. "He seldom refused a farmer a loan."

The farmers liked the elder Lindbergh, and the elder Lindbergh liked the farmers. He lost no time in making them the keystone of his liberal and freethinking—in fact, socialist—economic theories.

C. A. Lindbergh was bookish but gregarious, a thinker and writer but a practicing politician. One of his interests was the creation of an insurance co-operative for farmers, to free them from the big insurance companies of the East. For a time he ran a magazine stumping for co-operatives, which failed, and he became increasingly obsessed by the situation which centered the nation's money in a few hands. He was anti-Morgan, anti-Kuhn, Loeb, anti-National City Bank—the champion of workers in farm or factory. His son never shared in all his life, as far as anyone has been able to detect, this anticapitalist bias. On the other hand, C.A., though an affectionate father, never shared his son's growing interest in mechanics, which passed through bicycles and motorcycles and iceboats to jalopies and eventually to planes. C.A. staked his son to eight hundred dollars for his first plane, but he did not, according to Quigley, care much for the notion.

The father and son looked a good deal alike: lean, handsome faces with deep eyes and firm mouths. C.A.'s face, however, began in time to take on the lines of maturity and suffering which come, not unnaturally, to those who mature and suffer. One of the men who in later years made a hobby of publicly psychoanalyzing his son said that the latter's face never seemed to age or to reflect grief or any other experience, keeping a sort of cherubic aspect through its fortieth year.

In 1906 C.A. ran for Congress and was elected. He ran, it should be noted, on the Republican ticket. He was as yet a socialist in word and precept only, and the Farmer-Labor party, which he helped to found, was still in the future. His son, five years old, went to Washington with him in 1907 and watched the swearing-in ceremony. C.A. remained in Congress eight years. During much of that time his boy Charles stayed in Washington too, helping with such office work as running errands and licking envelopes. For a time he went to the Friends' School there, along with the children of Theodore Roosevelt, and was part of a "drugstore" gang led by Quentin Roosevelt, which used to convene at the store and run up mild tabs in confectionery.

There was a panic in 1907, and C. A. Lindbergh swung into action with a campaign for investigation of his great enemy, the "money trust." The newspapers began to work him over. He stored up thousands of clippings denouncing him as a demagogue, a "dangerous radical and dissenter." He fought, fruitlessly, the Federal Reserve Bill of 1913 and published a book called *Banking and Currency* in support of his views. In 1915 he was in at the birth of the Farmers League, a political group which was launched in Minnesota, scored its first successes in North Dakota in 1916, and then turned and drove a wedge into C.A.'s home state with our entry into war. Lindbergh and the League, till then fundamentally progressive, socialistic, and anti-money, at once acquired an antiwar and anti-Britain following—still and always based, in Lindbergh's view, on the suspicion of collusion between British and Wall Street finance. They lined up a heavy farm and labor vote. C. A. Lindbergh ran for Governor of Minnesota on the Farmers League ticket in 1918, and it was a wild, bitter campaign.

He electioneered in his old car, his son driving. Mobs booed him, eggs and garden stock were thrown. This, mark you, was not a prewar campaign, like the younger Lindbergh's before Pearl Harbor. This was actually in wartime, and the elder Lindbergh, called pro-German by his rivals, worked against big pressures and heavy clubs. Department of Justice agents broke the plates of his old book on banking and his new one, *Why Is Your Country at War?*, in which he denounced the sale of Liberty Bonds as manipulated and forced by bankers and said at one point:

"Our purpose is humane; nevertheless I believe I have proved that a certain 'inner circle,' without official authority and for selfish purposes, adroitly maneuvered things to bring about conditions that would make it practically certain that some of the belligerents would violate our international rights and bring us into war with them."

This theory of "maneuver" was in the mouth of the younger Lindbergh twenty-two years later, but not "Our purpose is humane." Our purpose had become stupid to him, a waste of supermen and white Western civilization. There were no "supermen" or "yellow breeds" in C.A.'s vocabulary. Since we were at war, C.A. favored seizure and state ownership of mines, trains, plants, and resources to stop profiteering. He had no personal opposition to Woodrow Wilson, and Wilson scolded mob tactics against Lindbergh. When

C.A. lost the election he was offered a place on the War Industries Board by Bernard Baruch. Conservative circles in Minnesota killed this appointment, Baruch withdrawing the offer politely and C.A. going his way a little more bitter than before. He was a Farmer-Laborite by 1920, campaigning for Henrik Shipstead, and in 1923 an author again and for the last time—with *The Economic Pinch,* which showed him still obsessed by the evils of big money but brimful, too, of gentle socialist slogans and advice against such things as the exploitation of children.

His own child was a flier by then. In 1923, in a campaign for a special Senatorial primary, the young Lindbergh flew campaign literature and speakers for his father, and once, only once, flew his father too.

Afterward, C.A. said to his partner, Quigley, "I don't like this flying business. See if you can't get the boy to come into our office, study law, and join the firm."

Quigley mentioned it to Charles, and the son smiled, shook his head, and said the law was not for him. C. A. Lindbergh died of a brain tumor in 1924. His son, then in the Army, was able to visit him once during his illness, but his leave was up before his father died. Quigley saw the young man off on his way back to camp in Texas, and he recalls: "I could see he was deeply moved, but outwardly he was stoical."

One day in 1925 Charles A. Lingbergh, Jr., carried out a request his father had made before he died. From a plane he scattered C.A.'s ashes over the old Lindbergh homestead near Little Falls, by the Mississippi.

In a letter to the younger Lindbergh when he was training for his army commission as a flier, an old college classmate asked, among other things, how Lindbergh's love life was coming along. Lindbergh answered: "In this respect, I am situated in about the same position that I was in at Madison—i.e., no prospects, past, present, or future."

He was quiet and in-dwelling from early boyhood on. Some who knew him in those years called his manner "grim," and there is no doubt that there was a feeling of withdrawal in him, a discomfort when he came into the world outside planes and mechanics, that made him awkward socially. He seems to have found relief from this social strain and repression chiefly in practical jokes—and they were the sort of practical jokes, complicated, strenuous, and "virile," about which a monograph might be written in connection with American life. The prank called the "snipe hunt," for instance, is apt to cost the jokers themselves a full night of sleep and miles of walking, running, and crawling. Lindbergh arranged a snipe hunt at least once, at the expense of a fellow pilot. Another time he went to great pains to introduce a cow into the neighborhood of an airplane mechanic who had a mortal fear of bulls, and again, he filled the ice-water pitcher at the bedside of a roommate, one Bud Gurney, with kerosene. His jokes are what his early comrades remember best about him; those, and his eating. The young man known to everyone as "Slim" was a spectacular performer with a knife and fork. Apparently he took a shy pleasure in the sociable kidding which he earned by this gift. He would sometimes put away six eggs plus a steak or a chop for breakfast, and later, at Curtiss Field on Long Island, when he was waiting to fly to Paris, he hung up local records at the hot-dog stand.

If he looked grim, it is pretty certain that Lindbergh was content in his life and work and an amiable enough fellow by his own lights. He lost little time in finding the work, the pleasure, that suited him above everything else. After graduation from high school in Little Falls—where he once wrote an elaborate and not uncomical satire on the finicky methods of his English teacher—he took three semesters in engineering at the University of Wisconsin, where the only thing that seemed to interest him much was shooting (he made the rifle team). Then of his own accord he organized a clean break with the past and enrolled at a flying school in Lincoln, Nebraska. Within four years he was known from Chicago to the West Coast by the narrow but shrewd circle of men in his own profession as one of the country's best fliers. Seldom has any man shown a quicker and more natural aptitude for flying a plane.

Lindbergh barnstormed a little at the age of twenty-one, but he needed to know more. The Army was the great practical school of flying at the time, so Lindbergh enlisted in March 1924 in what was

known as the "War Department's Air Service," and was commissioned a second lieutenant the following spring. After some more
barnstorming he joined the 110th Squadron of the 35th Division,
Missouri National Guard, winning the reserve commission of captain
in December 1925. His flying had already given him associations in
St. Louis. He went to work there early in 1926 for Major William
B. Robertson, whose company had just been licensed to fly the mail
between St. Louis and Chicago.

For this job Lindbergh got $350 a month in salary and another
$100 a month in flying allowances. He also became the outstanding
member of the Caterpillar Club. The Caterpillars were Army or
Army Reserve fliers who had parachuted from their planes—strictly
of necessity, no daredevil stuff. Lindbergh was never an easy leaper.
"He was likely to stick with a plane in trouble longer than the average good flier," said another pilot on the run. Yet Lindbergh made
four jumps in the year 1926. Once, jumping near St. Louis when
his controls jammed, he dislocated a shoulder. Twice he went over
the side when his gas ran out in bad weather and "walked the mail
in"—locating his plane on foot, salvaging the mail, and arranging
to have it trucked the rest of the way to its destination. Lindbergh
broke into print for the first time, as far as I know, through his
Caterpillar Club record. A slightly sob-sisterish story of the time
referred to him as "a supple, young, blond giant just past twenty-
four."

Then Monsieur Raymond Orteig moved into his life, or, rather,
Lindbergh moved into M. Orteig's and the world's.

Writing about the American Middle West recently, an Englishman, Graham Hutton, said that most of the Middle Westerners he
talked with thought, among other things, that Lindbergh was the
first man to fly the Atlantic. Quite possibly people think so all over
the country and all over the world. Actually, the Atlantic had been
flown several times from 1919 through 1926, nonstop or otherwise,
by dirigible and plane. There were various transatlantic flights in
various stages of preparation in late 1926 and early 1927. This was
partly the responsibility of M. Orteig, who had offered $25,000 to
the man or men who would fly from New York to Paris or vice-
versa. Some people spoke unkindly of M. Orteig's offer as homicidal

in effect if not in spirit. I know that this elderly landlord burned with desire for Franco-American good will and was so well disposed toward mankind that he once gave me the freedom of the Hotel Lafayette's kitchen, and the best eating in downtown New York, in return for a very small favor. At any rate, his $25,000 was on the line. Talk of flying the Atlantic was in the air. Toward the end of 1926, Lindbergh set out to hustle himself a stake.

He was not ideally equipped for salesmanship. He could not work up interest among the usually farsighted editors of the St. Louis *Post-Dispatch*. The rival *Globe-Democrat,* however, listened to his plans, and eventually, in early 1927, money was forthcoming, mostly from Mrs. Lora Josephine Knight, widow of a St. Louis stockbroker. At San Diego, California, in the spring of the year, Lindbergh was camped at the Ryan aircraft plant supervising the final touches on a silver monoplane built to his order, which he named "The Spirit of St. Louis." He had for some time been practicing staying awake for thirty to forty hours at a stretch.

He had never had much to do with newspapermen except for his cash-finding campaign in St. Louis. Now he made proposals to the San Diego reporters which they were to think back on a few weeks later with some irritation. He wanted the press to work for him. He asked the reporters to keep quiet about himself and his plans and to keep him posted on what they heard from the East of the moves of his competitors—principally Clarence Chamberlin and Charles A. Levine in their Bellanca, and Richard E. Byrd and his big, distinguished crew in their Fokker.

The reporters said sure. A few days later they said, "So long," and Lindbergh was off. Being the flier he was, he at once made American air history with the longest nonstop American flight recorded up till then, San Diego to St. Louis, and the fastest over-all time from coast to coast. He arrived at Curtiss Field at 5:33 on the afternoon of May 12, 1927.

The public and the papers were aware of him now, but doubtful. Once, during the week that followed, the *Post-Dispatch* of St. Louis rang up a man at the *Times* of New York to ask if he thought Lindbergh, of St. Louis, was going to amount to anything. The *Times* man could not give a definite answer. Lindbergh himself was not certain how he stood in the matter of news value, but he knew he was going to take off; so he subscribed, in the neat, private, foresighted way in which he did everything else for this flight, to a press-clipping service. Then, with no pontoons on the plane to weigh her down, he took off at 7:51 on the morning of May 20 and headed a little north of the sunrise, while his rivals remained on the ground to wait to be sure about weather.

Probably excitement never grew with more terrible momentum, from a puff of curiosity to an earth-shaking tension, than it did through the night of May 20 and the morning of May 21. Probably everyone who knew of the flight remembers today where he was or exactly what he was doing at some moment in the course of it. There was a fight that night in a baseball park in New York between Jack Sharkey and Jim Maloney; I remember that Joe Humphreys, a little announcer with a bow tie and a voice of brass, arose in the pool of light in the center of the darkness and called for silence and prayer, and his words were maudlin, moving, and eloquent.

It was not a flight that can be spoken of in detail. That was the happy thing about it in the end: nothing happened, except that the plane was sighted now and then, true on its course and making good time. What went on in the flier's mind the flier might have said, but the chances are he could not. He wrote a book afterward called *We,* in which he told some things about the flight to Paris. He spoke of the preparations he made, the food and water he took along, sandwiches, Army concentrated rations for five days, an Armbrust Cup, "which," wrote Lindbergh, "is a device for condensing the moisture from human breath into drinking water. The cup is cloth-covered and contains a series of baffle plates through which the breath is blown." In those sentences is the detachment, the cool, scientific preoccupation, the avoidance of bravado or any sense of great adventure, which make *We* the best memento we have of the man who made the flight.

Lindbergh flew 3,610 miles to Paris in 33 hours and 29 minutes, landing cleanly at Le Bourget field on the evening of May 21. A sea of Parisians flowed out to the field, broke down steel fences, swept over the runways. Lindbergh, escaping to some pilots' quarters, "identified" himself—"I am Charles A. Lindbergh"—and showed letters of introduction to Ambassador Herrick and others. He was whisked away from the joyous mob, and the line began to form for more mobs in London, Washington, New York. From that moment, which seemed to be the beginning of the end of the most glorious story of the era of glorious stunts, two forces—circumstances and Lindbergh's character—set to work to prevent such an ending. At the very time he seemed to be trying most desperately to efface himself, Lindbergh unerringly prolonged his fame and shaped himself for new stories to come. At no time in the next fifteen years did circumstance fail to lend a hand in this process when a hand was needed.

Eight months after the Paris flight, a New York editor wired a reporter who was covering Lindbergh on a good-will tour through Latin America: "No more unless he crashes."

It was the first suggestion—and only one man's suggestion—that the point of surfeit had been reached in the first of the great Lindbergh stories. There is no telling how many tons of newsprint were consecrated to the Lone Eagle (to use the sobriquet which pleased the flier best, or offended him least) in those eight months. His effect on the world had been orgiactic and orgastic. He returned to America to find 500,000 letters, 75,000 telegrams, and two freight-car loads of press clippings awaiting him. He was decorated in swift succession by the President of France, the King of England, and the President of the United States, who also commissioned him a colonel. His laundry disappeared every time he sent it out, and he could not write checks because people kept them instead of cashing them. Of the many sentimental songs which were written about him, the most popular, as I recall, was "Lucky Lindy." This was an epithet which Lindbergh hated in each of its parts and *in toto*. He set to work at once to destroy any impression that he was either lucky or "Lindy." It was a sort of battle no other quick celebrity had ever put up, but Lindbergh did not mean to be a quick celebrity. He aimed to perpetuate his fame and what he considered his dignity at one and the same time. His resistance to any other kind of attention was fanatical, skillful, and wholly successful.

Lucky? He promptly flew through all the forty-eight states, through Mexico, Central America, South America, and the West

Indies, always alone, touching on sixteen different countries, covering 7,860 miles, without a slip or a flaw.

Lindy? He had been Slim, a good, hard, technician's name, to his old friends. To his new ones—and they were all new now; his social life broke off cleanly and began along fresh lines in 1927—he was Charles, a hard man to talk to but a man to be respected at the highest levels. No vaudeville junkets, no movie contracts, no testimonials, no clasping of the hands above the head in response to the yells of the crowd. His new friends were ambassadors, statesmen, high-ranking officers, scientists, executives, almost exclusively men of capital. Lindbergh became a scientist, an executive, and a man of capital himself. But his sense of public relations, unconscious or not, did not fail him. Among the premiums spread before him, he chose the cleanest, the most respectable: a Guggenheim charter, a government prize of $25,000 for his Latin American flight (the Orteig prize which spawned his Paris trip and his fame was a little more sensational in nature, but, of course, inescapably his), the Woodrow Wilson Medal, writing payments (his articles were staid and objective) from the New York *Times* and the *Saturday Evening Post,* advisory positions and stock in Pan American and Trancontinental Air Transport, the second of which became "TWA, the Lindbergh Line." He could not keep the masses from calling him Lindy, but he convinced them that he was not the Lindy type. No publicity genius could have charted a campaign better. The public changed its first frank, friendly love for awe and admiration—but Lindbergh stayed in its mind and stayed pre-eminent, instead of dwindling to a line or two of fine type in the World Almanac.

Two years after Paris he married Anne Morrow, whom he met in Mexico while her father was American Ambassador there. She was then twenty-one, a year out of Smith College, a dark, shy, quiet girl with a fine mind and a small but pure and valuable gift for putting her thoughts and fancies about the earth, sky, and sea on paper. Their first son, Charles, was born in June 1930. In the next year Lindbergh and his wife flew together to Canada and Alaska, and then to Siberia, Japan, and China. Lindbergh, in his book *We,* preserved for the future a record of what was best and most honest in his own native character. His wife, writing about their flights and adventures in such books as *North to the Orient* and *Listen, the Wind,* set down with a richer literary talent something of the high romance and exaltation that were implicit in Lindbergh's life in the air.

During the years when he was enforcing his resistance to precedent, to the fate of the skyrocket, a small group of men was developing a resistance to Lindbergh—and doing it all alone, in silence. To many people it may not seem important that Lindbergh was antipathetic to newspapermen, and they to him. Yet it is a curious fact, worth noting; for reporters were the key to the fame that sustained him. Knowing the power of his position, Lindbergh seemed to feel that he could point up his hatred of nonprivacy—which is an entirely different thing from publicity—by taking it out on the working press. The working press tried time and again to show him the way to privacy: Swallow your medicine, the shouts and the fury, at a quick gulp, like a good patient, and then go off and stop being public. But with strange perversity Lindbergh continued to gag at the medicine and invite the disease.

He once, in the early days of his celebrity, flew coast to coast in record time. The flight was advertised as a record attempt, through the channels Lindbergh thought proper; in short, it deliberately invited reporting. Yet Lindbergh flew into a rage at the men who met him to report its consummation firsthand.

It's hard to say when this cycle of frictions began. It was soon. On his first stop in San Francisco after the Paris flight, Lindbergh took to a hotel room and the press gathered in the corridor outside. Lindbergh sent out word that he would not be available for some time. The reporters waited. Presently a dark and genial face peered out from behind a mustache, through another door in the corridor, and its owner, Señor Alvaro Obregón, of Mexico, said, "If you're waiting for Colonel Lindbergh, why not wait in here?"

Inside Señor Obregón's room the press got a lively speech on Señor Obregón's plans to be President of Mexico in 1928, and quantities of liquor to wash it down with. When Lindbergh's emissary finally traced the reporters, with the news that the Colonel was ready to talk, he found them agreed that the story was not Lindbergh but Obregón. That is what the papers showed next day.

There are many such episodes accessible for the record, though few of them ended the same way, for, as I said, Lindbergh's position was powerful, and the press was seldom able or willing to sacrifice the public's curiosity to its own irritation. To the overwhelming bulk of the public, in the words of a writer commenting on Lindbergh in 1930, he "remained Godlike."

It might be borne in mind, however, that from 1930 on Lindbergh's closest friend was Dr. Alexis Carrel. The doctor was, first, a scientist and technician. But he was also a colorful and persuasive writer, with certain "philosophical" ideas. These ideas, not unheard of before 1930 or since, had to do with the natural supremacy of the white race, the rule of the weak by the strong, and the breeding of supermen.

Lindbergh's baby son, Charles, was kidnaped from the flier's home in New Jersey on March 1, 1932. He was found dead seventy-two days later in a patch of woods in the same neighborhood after Lindbergh, with a plea to the police and the newspapers to help him by keeping their hands off the case, had paid ransom money to the unknown and unseen kidnaper. The crime was at once so cold-blooded and so violent that it would have had nationwide publicity no matter who the victims were. Since the victims were the Lindberghs, the impact upon the press and the public was tremendous; the law of the land itself was affected. Within a few months of the murder, long before the arrest of Bruno Richard Hauptmann, Congress enacted the so-called Lindbergh Law," which gave Federal agents national freedom in the pursuit of kidnapers.

This second Lindbergh story was so "big" that it was seldom out of the newspapers for even a day during the next four years. Nor did the papers see any reason, especially after the baby was found dead, to tone it down or to miss such a sterling chance to play cops-and-robbers. Every manner of reporter and cop, official and unofficial, from Walter Winchell down, or up, took a hand. Naturally enough, a score of newspaper "characters" sprouted on the fringe of Lindbergh's fame and tragedy.

Most of them are forgotten, or at least half forgotten, today. There was Dr. John F. Condon, a mild, sententious old Bronx schoolteacher, nicknamed "Jafsie." Young reporters used to see and hear him at an annual schoolboy reunion party that sometimes made the papers on dull days. Now he enjoyed a front-page run for a while as a far from backward negotiator between Lindbergh and the kidnaper, who lived in Jafsie's neighborhood. There was Ellis Parker, a rural New Jersey detective with a nationwide reputation for hawkshawing, who involved himself in the case and wound up in the Federal penitentiary for kidnaping and torturing the wrong suspect. There were Irving Blitz and Salvy Spitale, New York underworld operators, who were called in by the police for the not unsympathetic assignment of trying to find out if someone in the "profession" had done the kidnaping. Every reporter in New York worked on some part of the case at some time. I trailed Mr. Blitz through lower East Side tenements and was one of those eventually summoned to the handsome apartment of Spitale to take a statement. It was plain that the name and prestige of Lindbergh reached far, wide, and deep.

"If it was someone I knew, I'll be god-damned if I wouldn't name him," said Spitale. "I been in touch all around, and I come to the conclusion that this one was pulled by an independent."

Bruno Hauptmann, a Bronx carpenter of German birth, was arrested in 1934. He was convicted of the Lindbergh crime in 1935, after a trial in which the renown of Lindbergh, who was a witness, and the furious public interest in the case had the result of sending those connected with it, lawyers, writers, state executives, and witnesses other than Lindbergh, into a mad spin of histrionics and hysteria.

It has been said by more than one person that the killing of his son and the blatancy of the hunt and the trial which followed not only drove Lindbergh out of his country but formed in his mind the somber ideas which he gave to the world a few years later. That is probably, like so many other easy opinions, the truth but not the whole truth. The details of the crime tell what its effect on the father and mother of the baby must have been, and it is certain that Lindbergh's appearance in court, where his son's clothes were spread before him, brought a shock to his sense of what was private, fitting, and decent. He had another son now, born a month before Charles was found dead. A picture of the second son appeared in a newspaper. There is no doubt that the kidnaping and its sequel, including this last detail, were directly responsible for the fact that the Lindberghs sailed secretly for England on December 22, 1935, three months before the execution of Hauptmann.

But Lindbergh had long since shown dissatisfaction with the state of affairs in America and his own relations with it. He had a problem: He could not enjoy the things he wanted, and these included fame and respect as well as work and privacy, in the way he wanted. Even the kidnaping, in the end, seems to have become fused in his mind with dislike for a "state of affairs," not for one man or for any single evil. In the next several years—the years of the clash between fascism and democracy—he spoke of America more than once in private conversation as "immoral" and "disorderly."

Sir John Ervine wrote a plea for privacy for the Lindberghs in England, when they arrived there. It was not heeded at first by the British press, which put on a pursuit race and a public picnic, but after a few days the English reporters followed the formula which American reporters had so frequently offered for procedure between themselves and Lindbergh, and which Lindbergh himself was so often loath to accept: "Get it over with and the veil is yours." They gave him plenty of privacy—more of it, some who knew him said later, than he wanted. Time appears to have grown heavy on his hands after a few months at Long Barn, the Kentish house rented by him from Harold Nicolson and Victoria Sackville-West.

The villagers answered when he said hello, and the Vicar of Weald came to dinner and described him as "a thorough good fellow"; but not long afterward the Lindberghs were dining with the King (later the Duke of Windsor), in company with the Stanley Baldwins and the Ernest Simpsons. Then Lindbergh dropped over to Ireland, where he flew, as was his custom, with the highest ranks available, De Valera and the Free State Army Chief. Coming home, he gave England a taste of the whimsey that had sometimes jangled the nerves of American newsmen. Instead of flying to the airport where he was expected, he came down at a small coastal field to spend the afternoon and night, asking the army men there not to report his presence. For a day and a night there were scareheads in the press of the world: "Lindbergh Lost." The government sent

word to its ships at sea to be on the lookout, and the ships looked
in vain.

The Lindberghs toured Germany, France, Italy, Egypt, and
India. They dined or flew with Crown Prince Friedrich, Hugo
Eckener, Italo Balbo, the Viceroy of India, and the new King and
Queen of England. Balbo and the Crown Prince aroused Lindbergh's deepest suspicion by trying to take snapshots of him. He
went to Denmark with Dr. Alexis Carrel to demonstrate the "mechanical heart," or Lindbergh perfusion pump, on which the two
had worked together in America—a device to promote life and circulation in an organ divorced from the body. By 1937 Lindbergh
was calling England "stupid," and by 1938 he had added France,
where he lived for a summer and winter, to the now threefold list,
with the adjectives "frivolous" and "corrupt." A pair of visits to
Hermann Goering had brought him criticism from anti-Nazis in
America. Apparently Lindbergh did not realize that such a school
of thought existed, until he heard of the criticism. It angered him
so much that he told friends he would go to Berlin to live the following winter, 1938–39. He was dissuaded by the same friends. The
Jewish purges of 1938 were at their height in Germany.

Obviously the mere catalogue of Lindbergh's voyages and visits
between 1935 and 1939 does not explain what was happening in
his mind, what had led him to reject, at any rate to doubt, the
future and the character of three nations in rapid succession. Two
men influenced him strongly: one, Dr. Carrel, whose association
with Lindbergh, as an intimate friend, was now more than half a
dozen years old; the other, Goering, whose knack of salesmanship
helped turn Lindbergh's notions about power and war and politics
in the same direction as his thoughts about man and society.

"The most highly civilized races, the Scandinavian, for example,
are white," wrote Dr. Carrel in 1935, in a book called *Man the
Unknown*.

"Caesar, Napoleon, Mussolini . . ." mused Dr. Carrel in the same
book. "All great leaders of nations grown beyond human stature."

It seems a fair inference that the doctor's thoughts and private talk were of a piece with his published philosophy. Born in France, he had been a distinguished physician since 1906 in the fields of suturing blood vessels and transplanting organs. He won the Nobel Prize in 1912, and his scientific work, including that with Lindbergh, was undoubtedly valuable. But in the sciences of philosophy and ethnology, which were not his own, the doctor went along with the most superficial, dime-magazine eugenic theories and the racist cant of the Count de Gobineau and Houston Stewart Chamberlain. These men, whose works have been discredited by every objective technical study and all recorded statistics, are important in that they influenced, among others, Kaiser Wilhelm II and Hitler, and inspired *Mein Kampf*. Their views are reflected in Dr. Carrel's book.

Dr. Carrel and Lindbergh summered on adjoining tiny islands off Brittany in 1938, often strolling on the beach and talking together, and in the early part of 1939 Lindbergh wrote (in the *Atlantic Monthly*): "No system of representation can succeed in which the voice of weakness is equal to the voice of strength."

And, speaking of aviation in the *Reader's Digest:* [It is] one of those priceless possessions which permit the White Race to live at all in a sea of Yellow, Black, and Brown."

Lindbergh, with his wife, first went to Germany in July 1936, at Goering's invitation. The German air chief, delighted by the opportunity, dined and feted the Colonel and spread his planes, his plans, and his experiments before Lindbergh's eyes. There was another, more extensive tour in 1938, when Goering escorted Lindbergh through the plants of Messerschmitt, Heinkel, Junkers, and Focke-Wulf and showed him the best of his activated squadrons. At a stag dinner given by Ambassador Hugh Wilson, Lindbergh was assisting in the reception line when Goering, pausing in front of him, deftly and unexpectedly decorated him "in the name of the Führer" with the Service Cross of the Order of the German Eagle, with Star. Lindbergh never returned it to Goering. His attitude was that he did not care to embarrass any of the parties to the gathering crisis.

The Colonel went in the same year to Russia, for an air fete at Tushino Airport. He saw little except gross and hopeless inefficiency (and he knocked down, at one point in his stay, a police agent who was detailed to guard him and whom he mistook for a newspaper-man). Lindbergh still clung at this time to the hope that British stupidity was not so crass as to reject the prudent moral he had drawn from Goering's flashy display of air power. He was every inch the salesman of German strength that Goering thought he might be when he went to Baldwin, then Prime Minister, with the tip that Germany was strong, Russia inept, and England and France far behind in preparations for air war. The course he then urged on Baldwin, and on anyone who would listen, is no secret; he stated it openly in a speech in 1941:

"I said that war in the west [of Europe] would result in German victory or a devastated and prostrate Europe. I therefore advocated that England and France build . . . their military forces . . . but that they permit Germany to expand eastward into Russia without declaring war."

Baldwin gave Lindbergh a courteous brush-off which, according to his acquaintances, annoyed the Colonel profoundly and rein-forced his disgust with British "stupidity." As it happened, he was a better salesman than he knew, for at Munich, France and Eng-land followed his prescription almost to the letter, at Russia's expense. But Lindbergh went away, home to America at last, think-ing only of Baldwin's bullheadedness.

A year later, again in a public speech, Lindbergh dropped neatly into the same bracket to which he consigned Baldwin when he said, arguing that America was safe from attack, "An air invasion across the ocean is, I believe, impossible at this time or in any predictable future."

In fact, in the role he now chose to play, Lindbergh exactly opposed his father's published thought: "The world is in constant change." Behind his position he put all of his personal prestige. That prestige was based on skill and foresight in terms of aircraft, and in this very sphere he made what his warmest admirers could only describe, in the light of the record through 1945, as one wrong guess after another. Each guess or prediction involved a denial that any real change was in store for the world through the channels of the air.

Lindbergh's home-coming to the United States in April 1939 was unobtrusive. Shortly after his arrival he made private reports to the War Department and Congress—the factual substance of these could not have been too important, as an American military attaché had accompanied him throughout his inspections in Germany—and embarked on a four-month tour of Army study. When the war began in Europe in September he suddenly—and surprisingly—accepted a suggestion by a radio commentator that he state his views over the air.

It is a curious thing that never before in the twelve years during which the people of the world had known Lindbergh had they seen him open his mind or speak his thought. When they did, it was on topics no one had associated with him in 1927 or 1932: international politics and the state of civilization. As always, the reaction of press and public to the name of Lindbergh was immense.

He broke his lifelong public silence from Station WOL in Washington, two weeks after the war's start. Three networks carried the speech, which, written painstakingly by his own hand, favored "strong neutrality" for the United States. Lindbergh said we should make defensive rather than offensive weapons. This form of neutrality, applied to the facts of the moment, markedly favored Germany at the expense of England and France. Lindbergh spoke of the folly of involving ourselves in the problems of alien "breeds," "yellow" people, "Moors and Persians."

As one speech followed another—he made five in 1940 and nearly a dozen in 1941—Lindbergh began to attract criticism both literate and violent, and as he did so his own talks became less dry and measured, more bitter, personal, and revealing. Plainly sincere, he was having trouble dissociating himself and his program from crackpots and ax-grinders. Lindbergh's embarrassment over such teammates as Joe McWilliams and Gerald L. K. Smith was intense. He did quite stoutly share the views of Lawrence Dennis, author of *The Coming American Fascism,* who wrote to a known German agent, "I saw Lindbergh last week and will see him often from now on." But Lindbergh offered, on the platform in Madison Square Garden, to go down and eject the curly spellbinder McWilliams from the crowd of twenty thousand, which had shouted, in response to Lindbergh's own remarks, "Hang Roosevelt!" and "Impeach the President!"

He soon satisfied himself with the respectability of America First, a movement which included several U.S. Senators and the president of Sears Roebuck and Company, General Robert Wood. America First, of course, was hugely pleased to have Lindbergh. But there were phases of the partnership which pained and annoyed other prominent isolationists. Membership multiplied, but it was noticeable that the crowds began to leave the hall as soon as Lindbergh's talk was over—and at no mere trickle. How many came to see the dream prince of 1927, and how many to save America?

Lindbergh denounced the Presidential election of 1940 as dishonest: Both sides were interventionist. He spoke of "Jewish financing" of the war. He resigned his Army commission when President Roosevelt, in April 1941, called him a "copperhead"—an allusion to the Northerners in the Civil War who did not think the South could be beaten.

Visibly stung, Lindbergh retorted, "A refugee who steps from the gangplank and advocates war is acclaimed as a defender of freedom. A native-born American who opposes war is called a fifth columnist."

Translations of his speeches were turning up everywhere in the official propaganda of Germany, Italy, and Spain. Japanese planes dropped them over Chungking. Less than four years before Okinawa, Lindbergh said that "modern aviation made it impractical, if not impossible, for an expeditionary force to cross an ocean and land successfully on a hostile coast against strong enemy air power." He was speaking every two or three weeks now, in St. Louis, Minneapolis, New York, Philadelphia, Hollywood, San Francisco. He had planned a speech in Boston for late December 1941. But on December 7, America was attacked, and a thick, damp muffler fell on America First and on Lindbergh.

It is true that ten days after Pearl Harbor, at a private dinner, he made a speech, widely quoted afterward by those present, regretting that the white race was divided in this war instead of banded together against the Mongolian. A little later Henry L.

Stimson, the elderly Secretary of War, watched and listened coolly when Lindbergh, in Washington, expressed his willingness to serve the Army in any way he could. Stimson glanced at one of his aides. The aide said carefully that he thought it might be better if Mr. Lindbergh served the Army, or the country, as a civilian. Stimson nodded. Lindbergh also nodded, and left the meeting. In the early spring of 1942 he went to work as a planner and adviser in the Willow Run plant of Henry Ford.

Most of the news stories that came between the two great wars can be looked back on with pleasure, amusement, or nostalgia, but certainly with detachment. They are over and done with. Lindbergh's story is not, because it is the story of a man's life and character, and he is still living and his character is still at work. I think it is impossible to write with detachment about Lindbergh at this moment. I don't pretend to have done so.

During the war it was only strict Army press censorship that kept Lindbergh off the front page again, when he went along with a P-38 escort on a bombing mission over Borneo and apparently shot down a Japanese plane. General George Kenney, air commander of the area, said later, "I couldn't swear on a stack of Bibles he didn't do it." Probably he did. There is little that much younger men can do in the air today that Lindbergh at forty-six cannot do. Navy fliers in the Pacific, to whom Lindbergh as a civilian gave valuable technical advice in 1944, were cold to Lindbergh at first for his isolationist crusade, but they conceded that no one could untie a mechanical knot more surely. In the summer of 1945 he was in Germany doing technical work again for the Navy and for the United Aircraft Corporation.

For years, however, Lindbergh's aviation talents have gone hand in hand with a strong compulsion to influence people to see the world as he sees it, and his fame and mechanical gift are the tools he uses to make himself heard. He is still at it. Months after the end of the war Lindbergh was shut in a hotel room with a band of Midwest Congressmen, giving them his recipes: Keep the atom bomb completely secret. . . . Put no confidence in the United Nations. . . . The war we fought against the Nazis cut directly across Lindbergh's social and racial views, and his feeling of what constitutes civilization. He was never a man to change his mind, and since the flight to Paris in 1927 he has not been a man to undervalue himself or to overvalue obscurity.

There is still time— and there seems to be a growing opportunity —for a fourth Lindbergh Story.

Down Great Purple Valleys

1954.

STANLEY KETCHEL was twenty-four years old when he was fatally shot in the back by the common-law husband of the lady who was cooking his breakfast.

That was in 1910. Up to 1907 the world at large had never heard of Ketchel. In the three years between his first fame and his murder, he made an impression on the public mind such as few men before or after him have made. When he died, he was already a folk hero and a legend. At once, his friends, followers and biographers began to speak of his squalid end, not as a shooting or a killing, but as an assassination—as though Ketchel were Lincoln. The thought is blasphemous, maybe, but not entirely cockeyed. The crude, brawling, low-living, wild-eyed, sentimental, dissipated, almost illiterate hobo, who broke every Commandment at his disposal, had this in common with a handful of Presidents, generals, athletes and soul-savers, as well as with fabled characters like Paul Bunyan and Johnny Appleseed: he was the stuff of myth. He entered mythology at a younger age than most of the others, and he still holds stoutly to his place there.

There's a story by Ernest Hemingway, "The Light of the World," in which a couple of boys on the road sit listening to a pair of seedy harlots as they trade lies about how they loved the late Steve Ketchel in person. This is the mythology of the hustler—the shiniest lie the girls can manage, the invocation of the top name in the folklore of sporting life. Ketchel is also an article of barroom faith. Francis Albertanti, a boxing press agent, likes to tell about the fight fan who was spitting beer and adulation at Mickey Walker one night in a saloon soon after Mickey had won a big fight.

"Kid," said the fan to Walker, "you're the greatest middleweight that ever came down the road. The greatest. And don't let anybody tell you different."

"What about Ketchel?" said Albertanti in the background, stirring up trouble.

"Ketchel?" screamed the barfly, galvanized by the name. He grabbed Walker's coat. "Listen, bum!" he said to Walker. "You couldn't lick one side of Steve Ketchel on the best day you ever saw!"

Thousands of stories have been told about Ketchel. As befits a figure of myth, they are half truth—at best—and half lies. He was lied about in his lifetime by those who knew him best, including himself. Ketchel had a lurid pulp-fiction writer's mind. He loved the clichés of melodrama. His own story of his life, as he told it to Nat Fleischer, his official biographer, is full of naïve trimmings about bullies twice his size whom he licked as a boy, about people who saved him from certain death in his youth and whom he later visited in a limousine to repay a hundredfold. These tall tales weren't necessary. The truth was strong enough. Ketchel was champion of the world, perhaps the best fist fighter of his weight in history, a genuine wild man in private life, a legitimate all-around meteor, who needed no faking of his passport to legend. But he couldn't resist stringing his saga with tinsel. And it's something more than coincidence that his three closest friends toward the end of his life were three of the greatest Munchausens in America: Willus Britt, a fight manager; Wilson Mizner, a wit and literary con man; and Hype Igoe, a romantic journalist. They are all dead now. In their time, they juiced up Ketchel's imagination, and he juiced up theirs.

Mizner, who managed Ketchel for a short time, would tell of a day when he went looking for the fighter and found him in bed, smoking opium, with a blonde and a brunette. Well, the story is possible. It has often been said that Ketchel smoked hop, and he knew brunettes by the carload, and blondes by the platoon. But it's more likely that Mizner manufactured the tale to hang one of his own lines on: "What did I do?" he would say. "What could I do? I told them to move over."

Ketchel had the same effect on Willus Britt's fictional impulse. When Britt, Mizner's predecessor as manager, brought Ketchel east for the first time from California, where he won his fame, he couldn't help gilding the lily. Willus put him in chaps and spurs and billed him as a cowboy. Ketchel was never a cowboy, though he would have loved to have been one. He was a semi-retired hobo (even after he had money, he sometimes rode the rods from choice) and an ex-bouncer of lushes in a bagnio.

"He had the soul of a bouncer," says Dumb Dan Morgan, one of the few surviving boxing men who knew him well, "but a bouncer who enjoyed the work."

One of Bill Mizner's best bons mots was the one he uttered when he heard of Ketchel's death: "Tell 'em to start counting ten, and he'll get up." Ketchel would have lapped it up. He would have liked even better such things as Igoe used to write after Ketchel's murder—". . . the assassin's bullet that sent Steve down into great purple valley." The great purple valley was to Ketchel's taste. It would have made him weep. He wept when he saw a painting, on a wall of a room in a whorehouse, of little sheep lost in a storm. He wept late at night in Joey Adams' nook on Forty-third Street just off Broadway when song writers and singers like Harry Tierney and Violinsky played ballads on the piano. "Mother" songs tore Ketchel's heart out. He had a voice like a crow's, but he used to dream of building a big house someday in Belmont, Michigan, near his home town of Grand Rapids. In it there would be a music room where he would gather with hundreds of old friends and sing all night.

The record of his life is soaked in fable and sentiment. The bare facts are these:

Ketchel was born Stanislaus Kiecal on September 14, 1886. His father was a native of Russia, of Polish stock. His mother, Polish-American, was fourteen when Ketchel was born. His friends called him Steve. He won the world's middleweight championship in California at the age of twenty-one. He lost it to Billy Papke by a knockout and won it back by a knockout. He was champion when he died by the gun. He stood five feet nine. He had a strong, clean-cut Polish face. His hair was blondish and his eyes were blue-gray.

When you come to the statement made by many who knew him that they were "devil's eyes," you border the land of fancy in which Ketchel and his admirers lived. But there was a true fiendishness in the way he fought. Like Jack Dempsey, he always gave the impression of wanting to kill his man. Philadelphia Jack O'Brien, a rhetoric-lover whom he twice knocked unconscious, called Ketchel "an example of tumultuous ferocity." He could hit powerfully with each hand, and he had the stamina to fight at full speed through twenty- and thirty-round fights. He knocked down Jack Johnson, the finest heavyweight of his time, perhaps of any time, who outweighed him by thirty to forty pounds. He had a savagery of temperament to match his strength. From a combination of ham and hot temper, and to make things tougher on the world around him, he carried a Colt .44—Hype Igoe always spoke of it dramatically as the "blue gun"—which was at his side when he slept and in his lap when he sat down to eat. At his training camp at the Woodlawn Inn near Woodlawn Cemetery in the Bronx, New York, Ketchel once fired the gun through his bedroom door and shot his faithful trainer Pete (Pete the Goat) Stone in the leg when Pete came to wake him up for work. Ketchel then leaped into his big red Lozier car and drove Stone to the hospital for treatment.

"He sobbed all the way," said Igoe, "driving with one hand and propping up Pete's head with the other."

The great moments of Ketchel's life were divided among three cities: San Francisco, New York, and Butte, Montana. Each city was at its romantic best when Ketchel came upon it.

Ketchel was a kid off the road, looking for jobs or handouts, when he hit Butte in 1902 at the age of sixteen. He had run away from Grand Rapids by freight when he was fourteen. In Chicago, as Ketchel used to tell it, a kindly saloonkeeper named Socker Flanagan (whose name and function came straight out of Horatio Alger) saw him lick the usual Algeresque bully twice his size and gave him a job. It was Flanagan, according to Ketchel, who taught him to wear boxing gloves and who gave him the name of Ketchel. After a time the tough Polish boy moved west. He worked as a field hand in North Dakota. He went over the Canadian line to Winnipeg, and from there he described a great westering arc, through mining camps, sawmills, and machine shops, riding the rods of the Canadian National and the Canadian Pacific through rugged north-country settlements like Revelstoke, Kamloops and Arrowhead, in British Columbia, till he fetched up on the West Coast at Victoria. He had a .22 rifle, he used to recall, that he carried like a hunter as he walked the roads. In Victoria, he sold the .22 for boat fare down across the straits and Puget Sound to Seattle. In Seattle he jumped a Northern Pacific freight to Montana. A railway dick threw him off the train in Silver Bow, and he walked the remaining few miles of cinders into Butte.

Butte was a bona fide dime-novel town in 1902. It was made for Ketchel. Built on what they called "the richest hill in the world," it mined half the country's copper. The town looked sooty and grim by day, but it was red and beautiful by night, a patch of fire and light in the Continental Divide. As the biggest city on the northwest line between Minneapolis and Spokane, it had saloons, theaters, hotels, honky-tonks, and fight clubs by the score. Name actors and name boxers played the town. When Ketchel struck the state, artillery was as common as collar buttons.

Ketch caught on as a bellhop at a hotel and place of amusement named the Copper Queen. One day, he licked the bouncer—and became bouncer. As Dan Morgan says, he enjoyed the work; so much so that he expanded it, fighting all comers for twenty dollars a week for the operator of the Casino Theater, when he was not bulldogging drunks at the Copper Queen. If Butte was made for Ketchel, so was the fight game. He used to say that he had 250 fights around this time that do not show in the record book. In 1903 he was already a welterweight, well grown and well muscled.

All hands, including Ketchel, agree that his first fight of record, with Jack (Kid) Tracy, May 2, 1903, was a "gimmick" fight, a sample of a larcenous tradition older than the Marquis of Queensberry. The gimmick was a sandbag. Tracy's manager, Texas Joe Halliday, who offered ten dollars to anyone who could go ten rounds with his boy, would stand behind a thin curtain at the rear of the stages on which Tracy fought. When Tracy maneuvered the victim against the curtain, Texas Joe would sandbag him. Ketchel, tipped off, reversed the maneuver. He backed Tracy against the curtain, and he and the manager hit the Kid at the same time. The book says, KO, 1 round.

The book also says that Ketchel lost a fight to Maurice Thompson in 1904. This calls for an explanation, and, as always, the Ketchel legend has one ready. A true folk hero does not get beat, unless, as sometimes happened to Hercules, Samson, and Ketchel, he is jobbed. At the start of the Thompson fight a section of balcony seats broke down. Ketchel turned, laughing, to watch—and Thompson rabbit-punched him so hard from behind that Ketch never fully recovered. In the main, the young tiger from Michigan needed no excuses. He fought like a demon. He piled one knockout on top of another. He would ride the freights as far as northern California, to towns like Redding and Marysville, carrying his trunks and gloves in a bundle, and win fights there. In 1907, after he knocked out George Brown, a fighter with a good Coast reputation, in Sacramento, he decided to stay in California. It was the right move. In later years, when Ketchel had become mythological, hundreds of storytellers "remembered" his Butte adventures, but in 1907 no one had yet thought to mention them. In California the climate was golden, romantic, and right for fame. And overnight Ketchel became famous.

When minstrels sing of Ketch's fights with Joe Thomas, they like to call Thomas a veteran, a seasoned, wise old hand, a man fighting a boy. The fact is, Thomas was two weeks older than Ketchel. But he had reputation and experience. When Ketchel fought him a twenty-round draw in Marysville—and then on Labor Day, 1907, knocked him out in thirty-two rounds in the San Francisco suburb of Colma—Ketchel burst into glory as suddenly as a rocket.

Now there was nothing left between him and the middleweight title but Jack Twin Sullivan. The Sullivans from Boston, Jack and Mike, were big on the Coast. Jack had as good a claim to the championship (vacated by Tommy Ryan the year before) as any middleweight in the world. But he told Ketchel, "You have to lick my brother Mike first." Ketchel knocked out Mike Twin Sullivan, a welter, in one round, as he had fully expected to do. Before the fight he saw one of Mike's handlers carrying a pail of oranges and asked what they were for. "Mike likes an orange between rounds," said the handler.

"He should have saved the money," said Ketchel.

Mike Twin needed no fruit; Jack Twin was tougher. Jack speared Ketchel with many a good left before Ketchel, after a long body compaign, went up to the head and knocked his man cold in the twentieth round. On that day, May 9, 1908, the Michigan freight-stiff became the recognized world champion.

His two historic fights with Billy Papke came in the same year. Papke, the Illinois Thunderbolt from Spring Valley, Illinois, was a rugged counterpuncher with pale, pompadoured hair and great hitting power. Earlier in 1908 Ketchel had won a decision from him in Milwaukee. The first of their two big ones took place in Vernon, on the fringe of Los Angeles, on September 7. Jim Jeffries, the retired undefeated heavyweight champion—Ketchel's only rival as a national idol—was the referee. The legend-makers do not have to look far to find an excuse for what happened to Ketchel in this one. It happened at the start, and in plain sight. In those days it was customary for fighters to shake hands—not just touch gloves—when the first round began. Ketchel held out his hand. Papke hit him a left on the jaw and a stunning right between the eyes. Ketchel's eyes were shut almost tight from then on; his brain was dazed throughout the twelve rounds it took Papke to beat him down and win the championship.

Friends of Ketchel used to say that to work himself into the murderous mood he wanted for every fight he would tell himself stories about his opponents: "The sonofabitch insulted my mother. I'll kill the sonofabitch!" No self-whipping was needed for the return bout with Papke. The fight took place in San Francisco on November 26, eleven weeks after Papke's treacherous *coup d'état* in Los Angeles. It lasted longer than it might have—eleven rounds; but this, they tell you, was the result of pure sadism on Ketchel's part. Time after time Ketchel battered the Thunderbolt to the edge of coma; time after time he let him go, for the sake of doing it over again. It was wonderful to the crowd that Papke came out of it alive. At that, he survived Ketchel by twenty-six years, though he died just as abruptly. In 1936, Billy killed himself and his wife at Newport Beach, California.

It was around this time that Willus Britt brought his imagination to bear on Ketchel—that is, he moved in. Willus was a man who lived by piecework. An ex-Yukon pirate, he was San Francisco's leading fight manager and sport, wearing the brightest clothes in town and smoking the biggest cigars. He once had a piece of San Francisco itself—a block of flats that was knocked out by the 1906 earthquake. When Willus sued the city for damages, the city said the quake was an act of God. Willus pointed out that churches had been destroyed. Was that an act of God? The city said it didn't know, and would Willus please shut the door on the way out?

Britt won Ketchel over during some tour of San Francisco night life by his shining haberdashery and his easy access to champagne and showgirls. In this parlay, champagne ran second with Ketchel. He did drink, some, and the chances are that he smoked a little opium. But he didn't need either—he was one of those people who are born with half a load on. "His genes were drunk" is the way one barroom biologist puts it. His chief weaknesses were women, bright clothes, sad music, guns, fast cars, and candy.

Once, in 1909, after Britt had taken him in high style (Pullman, not freight) from the Coast to New York, Ketchel was seen driving on Fifth Avenue in an open carriage, wearing a red kimono and eating peanuts and candy, some of which he tossed to bystanders along the way. The kimono, gift of a lady friend, was a historical part of Ketchel's equipment. A present-day manager remembers riding up to Woodlawn Inn, Ketch's New York "training" quarters, with Britt one day, in Willus's big car with locomotive sound effects. As they approached the Inn, the guest saw a figure in red negligee emerge from the cemetery near by.

"What's that?" he asked, startled.

"That's Steve," said Britt, chewing his cigar defiantly.

Britt had looked up Wilson Mizner as soon as he and Ketchel reached New York. Mizner, a fellow Californian and Yukon gold-rusher, was supposed to know "the New York angles"; Britt signed him on as an unsalaried assistant manager. Free of charge, Mizner taught Ketchel the theory of evolution one evening (or so the legend developed by Mizner runs). Much later the same night Mizner and Britt found Ketchel at home, studying a bowl of goldfish and cursing softly.

"What's the matter?" said Mizner.

"I've been watching these ———— fish for nine hours," snarled Ketchel, "and they haven't changed a bit."

Mizner, a part-time playwright at this time and a full-time deadbeat and Broadway nightwatchman, was a focus of New York life in 1909–10, the gay, brash, sentimental life of sad ballads and corny melodrama, of late hours and high spending, in which Ketchel passed the last years of his life. Living at the old Bartholdi Hotel at Broadway and 23rd Street, playing the cabarets, brothels and gambling joints, Ketchel was gayer and wilder than ever before. He still fought. He had to, for he, Britt, and Mizner (unsalaried or not) were a costly team to support. Physically the champion was going downhill in a handcar, but he had the old savagery in the ring. His 1909 fight with Philadelphia Jack O'Brien ended in a riddle. O'Brien, a master, stabbed Ketchel foolish for seven rounds. In the eighth, O'Brien began to tire. In the ninth, Ketchel knocked him down for nine. In the tenth and last round, with seven seconds to go, Ketchel knocked O'Brien unconscious. Jack's head landed in a square flat box of sawdust just outside the ropes near his own corner, which he and his handlers used for a spittoon.

"Get up, old man!" yelled Major A. J. Drexel Biddle, Jack's society rooter from Philadelphia. "Get up, and the fight is yours!"

But Jack, in the sawdust, was dead to the world. The bout ended before he could be counted out. By New York boxing law at the time, it was a no-decision fight. O'Brien had clearly won it on points; just as clearly, Ketchel had knocked him out. Connoisseurs are still arguing the issue today. Win or lose, it was a big one for Ketchel, for O'Brien was a man with a great record, who had fought and beaten heavyweights. The next goal was obvious. Jack Johnson, the colored genius, held the heavyweight championship which Jim Jeffries had resigned. To hear the managers, promoters, and race patriots of the time tell it, the white race was in jeopardy—Johnson had to be beaten. Ketchel had no more than a normal share of the race patriotism of that era; but he was hungry, as always, for blood and cash, and he thought he could beat the big fellow. Britt signed him for the heavyweight title match late in the summer of 1909, the place to be Sunny Jim Coffroth's arena in Colma, California, the date, October 16.

"At the pace he's living, I can whip him," Ketch told a newspaperman one day. He himself had crawled in, pale and shaky, at 5 A.M. the previous morning. Johnson—on whom, at thirty-one, years of devotion to booze and women had had no noticeable effect whatever—called around to visit Ketchel in New York one afternoon in his own big car. He was wearing his twenty-pound driving coat, and he offered to split a bottle of grape with the challenger.

"I wish I'd asked him to bet that coat on the fight," said Ketchel afterward. "I could use it to scare the crows on my farm."

Ketchel was still dreaming of the farm, the big house in Belmont, Michigan, where he would live with his family and friends when he retired. He had a little less than one year of dreams left to him. One of these almost came true—or so the legend-makers tell you—in the bright sunshine of Colma on October 16. Actually, legends about the Ketchel-Johnson fight must compete with facts, for the motion pictures of the fight—very good ones they are, too—are still accessible to anyone who wants to see them. But tales of all kinds continue to flourish. It's said that there was a two-way agreement to go easy for ten rounds, to make the films more saleable. It's also said, by Johnson (in print) and his friends, that the whole bout was meant to be in the nature of an exhibition, with no damage done, and that Ketchel tried a double cross. It's also said, by the Ketchel faction, that it was a shooting match all the way and that Steve almost beat the big man fairly and squarely. Ketchel fans say Ketchel weighed 160; neutrals say 170; the official announcement said 180¼. Officially, Johnson weighed 205½; Ketchel's fans say 210 or 220.

There's no way of checking the tonnage today. About the fight, the films show this: Johnson, almost never using his right hand, carried his man for eleven rounds. "Carried" is almost literally the right word, for Johnson several times propped up the smaller fighter to keep him from falling. Once or twice he wrestled or threw him across the ring. Jack did not go "easy"; he did ruthless, if restrained, work with his left. One side of Ketchel's face looked as dark as hamburger after a few rounds. But in the twelfth round all parties threw the book away, and what followed was pure melodrama.

Ketchel walked out for the twelfth looking frail and desperate, his long hair horse-tailed by sweat, his long, dark trunks clinging to his legs. Pitiful or not to look at, he had murder in his mind. He feinted with his left, and drove a short right to Johnson's head. No one had ever hit Li'l Artha squarely with a right before, though the best artists had tried. Ketchel had the power of a heavyweight; and Johnson went down. Then, pivoting on his left arm on the canvas, he rolled himself across the ring and onto his knees. In the film you can almost see thoughts racing through his brain—and they are not going any faster than referee Jack Welch's count. Perhaps it was the speed of this toll that made up his mind. Johnson, a cocky fellow, always figured he had the whole world, not just one boxer, to beat, and he was always prepared to take care of himself. He scrambled to his feet at what Welch said was eight seconds. Ketchel, savage and dedicated, came at him. The big guy drove his right to Steve's mouth, and it was over.

No fighter has ever looked more wholly out than Ketchel did, flat on his back in the middle of the ring—though once, just before the count reached ten, he gave a lunge, like a troubled dreamer, that brought his shoulders off the floor. This spasmodic effort to rise while unconscious is enough to make the Ketchel legend real, without trimmings. It was an hour before Ketchel recovered his senses. Two of his teeth impaled his lip, and a couple more, knocked off at the gum, were caught in Johnson's glove.

Ketchel recuperated from the Johnson fight at Hot Springs, Arkansas. Sightseers saw him leading the grand ball there one night, dressed like the aurora borealis, with a queen of the spa on his arm. A few months later he was back in New York, touching matches to what was left of the candle. He kept on fighting, for his blonde-champagne-and-candy fund. They tell you that Mizner (Britt had died soon after the Johnson bout) once or twice paid money to see that Steve got home free in a fight—like the one with the mighty

Sam Langford in April 1910, which came out "No decision—6."
Dan Morgan says a "safety-first" deal was cooked up for Ketchel's
second-to-last fight, a New York bout with a tough old hand named
Willie Lewis. Dan's partner, and Willie's manager, was Dan Mc-
Ketrick. On the night before the fight the two Daniels went to mass;
and Morgan heard McKetrick breathe a prayer for victory (which
startled him) and saw him drop a quarter in the contribution box.
In the fight, Willie threw a dangerous punch at Ketchel, and
Ketchel, alerted to treachery, stiffened Willie.

"You're the first man," said Morgan to McKetrick afterward,
"that ever tried to buy a title with a two-bit piece."

"Tut, tut," said McKetrick. "Let us go see Ketchel, and maybe
adopt him. If you can't beat 'em, join 'em."

McKetrick's hijacker's eye had been caught the night before by
the sight of Mizner, nonchalant and dapper, sitting in a ringside
seat drawing up plans for a new apartment for himself and Ketchel,
instead of working in his fighter's corner. Maybe Ketch could be
pried loose from that kind of management. Morgan and McKetrick
called on Ketchel at the Bartholdi Hotel. They offered to take him
off Mizner's hands. Ketchel, who respected Mizner's culture but not
his ring wisdom, was receptive. The two flesh-shoppers went to see
Mizner, to break the news to him.

"Why, boys, you can have the thug with pleasure," said Mizner.
"But did he remember to tell you that I owe him three thousand
dollars? How can I pay him unless I manage him?"

They saw his point. Mizner would need money from Ketchel to
settle with Ketchel. Ketchel saw it, too, when they reported back to
him. He turned white and paced the floor like a panther at the
thought of being caged in this left-handed way. But he stayed under
Mizner management.

Hype Igoe was Ketchel's closest crony in the final months that
followed. To Hype, the supreme myth-maker, whatever Steve did
was bigger than life. He used to tell and write of Ketchel's hand
being swollen after a fight "to FIVE TIMES normal size!" He wrote
of a visit Ketchel made, incognito, to a boxing booth at a carnival
one time, when he called himself Kid Glutz and "knocked out SIX
HEAVYWEIGHTS IN A ROW!" He told a story about a palooka who

sobbed in Ketchel's arms in the clinches in a fight one night. "What's the matter, kid?" asked Ketchel. Between sobs and short jolts to the body, his opponent explained that he was being paid ten dollars a round, and feared he would not last long enough to make the sixty dollars he needed to buy a pawnshop violin for his musical child. Ketchel carried him six rounds, and they went to the pawnshop together, in tears, with the money. The next time Hype wrote it, the fiddle cost two hundred dollars, Ketchel made up the difference out of his pocket, and he and the musician's father bailed out the Stradivarius, got drunk on champagne, and went home singing together.

There was a grimmer, wilder side of Ketchel's mind that affected the faithful little sports writer deeply. Ketchel used to tell Hype— he told many people—that he was sure he would die young. The prediction made a special impression on Igoe on nights when the two went driving together in the Lozier, with Ketchel at the wheel. As the car whipped around curves on two tires and Igoe yelped with fear, Ketchel would say, "It's got to happen, Hype. I'll die before I'm thirty. And I'll die in a fast car." Luckily for Hype and other friends, it happened in a different way when it happened, and Ketchel took nobody with him. The world was shocked by the Michigan Tiger's death, but on second thought found it natural that he should pass into the great purple valley by violence. To Igoe's mind it was the "blue gun" that Steve romantically took with him everywhere that was responsible.

Ketchel had knocked out a heavyweight, Jim Smith, in what proved to be the last fight of his life, in June 1910. Though he could fight, he was in bad shape, like a fine engine abused and over-driven. To get back his health he went to live on a ranch in Con-way, Missouri, in the Ozarks, not far from Springfield. His host, Colonel R. P. Dickerson, was an old friend who had taken a fatherly interest in Ketchel for two or three years. Ketchel ate some of his meals at the ranch's cookhouse—he took an unfatherly interest in Goldie, the cook. Goldie was not much to look at. She was plain and dumpy. But because she was the only woman on the premises, Ketchel ignored this, as well as the fact that Walter Dipley, a new hand on the ranch, was thought to be her husband.

On the morning of October 16, as Ketchel sat at the breakfast table, Dipley shot him in the back with a .38 revolver. Ketchel was hit in the lung. He lived for only a few hours afterward.

Igoe used to say that it was because Ketchel had his own .44 in his lap, as always at meals, that he was shot from behind, and that he was shot at all. There was evidence later, after Dipley had been found by a posse with Ketchel's wallet in his possession, that husband and wife had played a badger game with money as the motive. Goldie, it turned out, was a wife in name only. Dipley, whose right name was Hurtz, had a police record. They were both sent to jail; Dipley, sentenced to life, did not get out on parole till twenty-four years later.

Ketchel's grave is in the Polish Cemetery in Grand Rapids. Visitors will find a monument over it, built by Colonel Dickerson—a slab of marble twelve and a half feet high, topped by a cross and showing these words:

STANLEY KETCHEL
BORN SEPT. 14, 1886
DIED OCT. 16, 1910
A Good Son and Faithful Friend

Legend has built an even more durable monument to Ketchel. Of the one in stone, a neighbor with a few drinks in him once said, "Steve could have put his hand through that slab with one punch."

Lieutenant Lemick-Emden

1946

THERE WAS a German war criminal in Italy in the fall of 1943 whom three or four newspapermen, including myself, came to know quite well without ever seeing him. His name was Lemick-Emden, and he was a lieutenant in the third company of the 29th

Panzer Grenadier Regiment. He was a slight, dark little man with horn-rimmed spectacles. We crossed his trail during the northward fighting between the Volturno River and Cassino, and we had something, though not a lot, to do with the fact that he confessed his crime to our army soon after he committed it. This confession made him a rare bird at the time. The Americans did not capture a great many German officers in the first two years of the war, apart from the bag in Tunisia, and those among them who were self-confessed atrocity committers you could count on your thumbs. Almost as soon as they had him and knew for sure what they had, the Army leaders in Italy became darkly secret about Lemick-Emden and forbade us to make his story public. He was an embarrassing case in those early days. For one thing there was no agreement among the Allies on what to do with war criminals or when to do it. The Russians were reported to have hanged a few not long before, but the Americans couldn't be certain they had and, whether they had or not, didn't seem to be in the same legal position. Lemick-Emden's victims were Italian civilians, not Americans. Most of all the Army feared that any publicity about Lemick-Emden's affair which even suggested he was liable to punishment would make trouble for American prisoners in the enemy's hands.

I've wondered lately if the wide but somewhat staggered wave of official postwar justice has got around to Lemick-Emden yet. He was alive the last I heard, and apparently it had been decided to postpone an accounting till after the war. He may have been a hard man to keep waiting for two years. Once, some months after he was captured, he walked out of the gate of a prison camp in Algeria and had almost reached the safety of the Spanish Morocco border before they picked him up again. I learned this one evening in the spring of 1944 from an officer connected with prisoner administration. Knowing Army policy, he was furtive in his mention of Lemick-Emden. "What are they going to do with him?" I asked. "Far as I know," the officer muttered, "they'll wait till after the war and return him to the scene of the crime for a civilian trial. That is, if they've still got him by then and somebody remembers what he did." At that time, especially in the Mediterranean area, it was hard to think of the end of the war as a near, or even a likely, prospect.

The scene of Lemick-Emden's crime was Caiazzo, a village a few miles north of the Volturno, in the general region of Capua. It's impossible to suppose that the people there do not remember Lemick-Emden or that they will have forgotten him fifty years from now, for the effect of his stay in Caiazzo was the annihilation of some half-dozen families in a not very large population and the burning of one in every three of the town's buildings. In Caiazzo the question would be not of memory but only of Lemick-Emden's availability for trial. However, what occurred there in 1943 was not in itself highly unusual or spectacular, even for that neighborhood; a little later, in the nearby village of Bellona, fifty-four men, including five priests and the town's doctor, were shot in shifts of about ten by the Germans and buried informally by a dynamite charge in a quarry at the edge of town. What was singular about Lemick-Emden was that he, an obscure lieutenant in a line company, was a known criminal before his capture, like Ley and Himmler, and that he was—uniquely, as far as I know—picked up, questioned, and convicted by his own words within a month of his crime. Lemick-Emden had no notion, when American troops by sheer chance rounded him up with others of his company in a skirmish some distance from Caiazzo, that our Army Intelligence knew him from Adam. Neither did the troops who took him. The truth was sprung on the lieutenant later, with melodramatic trimmings, by the author Hans Habe, then an Army interrogator working with the Psychological Warfare Branch in Italy.

It's not only easier but more correct to speak of Lemick-Emden as Lemick rather than as Lemick-Emden. His father had served aboard the German cruiser Emden, famous in the First World War, and had reinforced the family name of Lemick in honor of his ship not long before his son was born. The boy was about eighteen when the second great war began, and therefore in the neighborhood of twenty-two when his fortunes brought him to Caiazzo. Since nobody who encountered him seems to have thought of him as a mental case in any plain, downright sense of the term, it may be that he was simply a superpatriot who followed the hints of the Nazi party and the Army High Command more seriously and enthusiastically than most and, when these were a bit too ogreish for the taste of his companions, was ready and willing to do their share along with his own. Habe, discussing him, said he found him on the surface neither antisocial nor unsociable, but it is a fact that the men in his company referred to him as "the horn-rimmed bastard," or German words to that effect, and that his loyalty or inclination or whatever it was led him to order and to join in the killing of twenty-two unarmed civilians, largely women and children—this on the testimony of a good many eyewitnesses and, finally, his own as well.

Lemick's unit had been in and around Caiazzo for a week or more on October 13, 1943. Some of its members were well known in the village. A general German withdrawal was in progress throughout that month, from the Volturno River line, not far above Naples, to the strong mountain line through Monte Cassino and Veanfro, but the Germans had time here and there to linger and stock up on supplies and labor troops. In every town where they paused they tried to draft civilians for work duty in their army. Four Fascist party agents from Rome had been to Caiazzo in early October to urge the village's able-bodied men to join the German labor crews, but by the time the Americans were getting near the place and the Germans were preparing to pull out, only one man in town had signed up with them of his own free will, and he was stone-blind. Lemick regarded Caiazzo as both stubborn and subversive. On the thirteenth of October he told an *Oberleutnant* of the company, the only man there who was superior to him in rank, that he suspected some of the Italian farm people of blinking signals to American planes or ground troops by opening and closing their window shutters at night. (Actually, no planes had bombed or strafed anywhere in the area, and the advancing American ground forces were still forty-eight hours away, with a good many hills ahead of them.) The *Oberleutnant* appeared to feel—according to a sergeant of the company, who described the events later—that Lemick was working himself up to some very unpleasant gesture. At any rate, the *Oberleutnant* withdrew from Caiazzo with most of the company, telling Lemick to suit himself but pointing out to the men that he, the *Oberleutnant*, was having no part of it. The sergeant witness said he saw nothing strange in this. The *Oberleutnant*, he said, naturally wanted to stay popular with the troops and keep his conscience fairly clear. On the other hand, he would never interfere with his subordinate in the execution of an act which might be construed by someone even higher up as useful and patriotic. "You got to be careful with bastards like that," the sergeant explained, "or they get to be martyrs."

Caiazzo, a gray, dingy cluster of stone along two streets, is perched on a slope of ground, with an ancient abbey sitting on a hill just above it and farms spread out all around for a distance of a mile or two. Beside the abbey is a graveyard. The men of the American 34th Infantry Division, when they reached Caiazzo on October 15, did not go immediately to the hill, which seemed deserted, or into the town itself. Their leaders bivouacked them outside the village and sent advance units north and west to see where the Germans had got to. To the soldiers who spoke no more than the normal handy dozen words of Italian, the people of Caiazzo looked and sounded pretty much as was usual in newly liberated towns. They were excited and curious and grateful, and anxious for food and tobacco. Our interrogators, however, though their interest at the moment was exclusively in German movements, began to sense that something had happened to the town. Two German prisoners, left unguarded for a few minutes, were beaten up by townspeople. A civilian being questioned about the German departure said he would like as soon as possible to get some coffins for his dead. Then a couple of privates of the 168th Regiment of the 34th who had been wandering about came in to say they had found the bodies of a man, a woman, and a child lying half buried in loose dirt in a farmyard to the east of the village, and, not far away, the bodies of other children; they were not sure whether there were two children or three in the second heap.

By the time the small group of war correspondents in which I was traveling came to Caiazzo, on the morning of the sixteenth, a young interrogator, Lieutenant Arthur Gutenberg, had formed a rough idea of what went on just before the last Germans left. A few of these had been taken prisoner by our patrols beyond the village. The villagers told their stories, and these Germans supplemented them. Gutenberg's first job was to get tactical information from the Germans, and the townspeople were still too stunned or incoherent to state their own case in full, so what we found out in the next few hours came piecemeal from several sources. The first and most obvious fact was that every third building in Caiazzo had been gutted by fire. The second was that a good many civilians were dead, though no bombs or shells had fallen near there.

The first correspondent to reach the village was William Stoneman, of the Chicago *Daily News,* who spoke Italian. He was taken by natives to a farmhouse where women and children and a couple of men lay dead in their blood on a terrace before the front door. The need of burying them was very plain by then, but they had been discovered only about twenty-four hours earlier, the farm being somewhat set off, and the people who found them were too shocked and confused to know what to do. Stoneman organized a search for informal coffins and turned up several old boxes and chests. He got a few of the bodies loaded on a wagon and told the driver to take him to a graveyard. They were stopped by military traffic at a crossroads on the way, and Stoneman pleaded desperately with the M.P.s to let him through. They did so as soon as they came close to the wagon.

Meanwhile, the rest of us drove with a guide to the abbey on the hill. The dead from another farm had just been brought to the burying ground in boxes like Stoneman's. One of these, with a child in it, was a clothes chest about four and a half feet long. Some of the men of the town were digging graves, while other villagers stood around pressing handkerchiefs or field flowers to their noses, and watched and talked. They told us very willingly and quite calmly what had happened, as far as they knew it. What with the excitement of the burning of the buildings in town, the Germans' retreat, and our arrival, they had not yet felt the full impact of the killings. One of the diggers, who stopped work when the others called him over, was a stout, gray-haired man of sixty-five, Antonio di Sorbo, whose daughter, son-in-law, and four grandchildren, all the near relatives he had, had been shot by the Germans on the thirteenth and now lay in the boxes at the edge of the graveyard. Holding a big blue handkerchief to his face, Di Sorbo talked, not cheerfully but with a certain solemn zest, as though it were some neighbor's story he was telling. Raffaele Perrone, the brother of Di Sorbo's son-in-law Nicola, the murdered husband, was subdued and listless, but

he offered to take us to his brother's farm and show us what had
happened. Di Sorbo resumed his digging.

The farmhouse of Nicola Perrone was on a small hill about a
mile and a quarter from the town. Down the path that led from its
door was a trail of dried blood thirty feet long. It came from a
shallow pit near the house, where Perrone had found his brother,
his brother's wife, and one of the children the day before, when he
had gone to visit them. Perrone had thought the blood must be
some animal's when he saw it. Then he went up the path and at
once identified the victims through the thin layer of dirt that was
scattered over the pit. He found the three other children together
about a hundred feet away, lightly covered with straw. He also saw,
as we did when we went there, the casings of a number of machine-
gun and Luger-pistol shells outside the front door of the farmhouse.
A child's polka-dot headdress lay among the casings.

We walked with Perrone to the farmhouse, a quarter of a mile
away, where sixteen bodies had been found covered with straw.
There was more blood here and more empty shells, and a gathering
of neighbors who described the radius of the shooting party's operations. The sixteen dead people were from three farms including the
one at which they were killed—one of them half a mile south of
there and the third some distance beyond that, a full two miles from
the house of Nicola Perrone, where the killings, according to the
later evidence of German prisoners, had begun. It had taken good,
purposeful hiking over rough fields to touch at all three points and
round up the victims for the second shooting. It seemed clear from
the start that it had not been done by drunken men in a random
lynching spirit. Drunk, the Germans might have killed the first available subjects and got it out of their systems. Miles of legwork on a
cold night calls for organization and sustained purpose.

Back at the command post of the 168th Regiment, we heard
Lemick-Emden's name for the first time, and that of a German
sergeant, Arthur Schuster. The interrogator, young Gutenberg, had
been told by prisoners that these were the men chiefly responsible
for the shooting of the farm people and the burning of the houses
in town, and their descriptions of the murderers tallied with those
given by civilians of a pair who arranged and directed the firing of
the buildings, at the head of a squad of troops with gasoline and

torches. Two or three villagers, among them the former owner of a restaurant in New Haven, Connecticut, also said that the lieutenant —Lemick—had been threatening violence and "example" for some days before the Germans left. "Short fellow with horn-rimmed glasses," said Gutenberg. "He made quite an impression around here. One of the fellows that beat up our prisoners told me that Lemick-Emden—only he didn't know his name—was the one he was looking for. We didn't have him, so he settled for what he could find."

"He'd be nice to have, the German lieutenant," said a reporter.

"Yeah," said Gutenberg, "but you know how many German officers we take."

The Caiazzo man from New Haven, John J. Pannone, was violent, but a little nonconsecutive, on the subject of Lemick. "A son of a bitch like that, you couldn't believe what makes him do it," he told me. "The Yale college boys used to come into my place sometime. You a Yale college boy?"

"No," I said.

"I used to sell 'em beer," said Pannone. He returned to the shootings, saying that twelve of the victims were children under fourteen. He asked me if I could spare a cigarette, lit it, cursed Lemick some more, and finally gave an opinion which I thought was influenced more by motion-picture plots than by a knowledge of the facts and probabilities of the war we were in. "Anyway, your army will get him," said Pannone.

This was the first certified atrocity of the Italian campaign, except the burning of the University of Naples library and the shooting of one man who protested it, a month before, and, for most of the Americans who saw its traces, it finally made the stories we had heard of pogroms and "examples" in Poland, Czechoslovakia, and Russia come alive for the first time. I know that a good many American soldiers at Caiazzo had been candidly skeptical about such stories till then. There was nothing in their experience to make them real, and they thought of them, with the stout sales resistance so widely shared at home, as propaganda. The war was still quite young then for us. We had uncovered nothing of Europe but the toe of one peninsula. In the last half of 1945, people could sit in American movie theaters watching newsreel pictures from Central

Europe that left practically nothing to the imagination, but just two years earlier the same people lived in a state of dogged innocence, from which a few hundred of them were first promoted at the village of Caiazzo by the sight of Lemick's handiwork.

It was something out of the ordinary, the newspapermen there thought, to know the name, description, company, and regiment of a man apparently responsible for such crimes as these so soon after they had been committed. Gutenberg and the local American commander, a colonel, had their hands full with their respective jobs. At their suggestion we went back to Naples with the information that had been collected, and two of us turned it over to an officer we knew in the Psychological Warfare Branch. The P.W.B., generally associated by the troops with leaflets fired out of big guns or dropped from planes on a very unsusceptible enemy, was performing a variety of other odd tasks at the moment and even running its own intelligence service concurrently with the Fifth Army's. "We will bear this boy in mind," said the man in the P.W.B. office.

A week later he telephoned H. R. Knickerbocker, one of the correspondents of the Caiazzo expedition, who was still in Naples, and said, "They have captured that friend of yours. We are going to question him."

"Question who?" said Knickerbocker.

"That German lieutenant you told us about. At least, I guess it's the same one. His name's on the list of prisoners."

Knickerbocker and I went down to the P.W.B. office in a state of considerable excitement not unmixed with disbelief. Nothing happened that fast—not in Italy. The name of Lemick-Emden, however, was there on a list of prisoners of war, most of them belonging to the 29th Panzer Grenadiers, who had just been taken, to the northwest of Caiazzo, after a fight with American troops. The P.W.B. men said they had got permission from the Fifth Army for Hans Habe to question Lemick and others of his company. We went with Habe to a restaurant to tell him what we had seen and heard in Caiazzo.

Habe, a Hungarian, the stepson-in-law of Joseph E. Davies, our former Ambassador to Moscow, is a lean, ruddy, intense fellow for whom the war had few dull moments. He fought with the French Army against the Germans, was captured, escaped, came to America, wrote a book, joined the American Army, and, at the time we saw him, was interrogating Germans in Italy with unconcealed relish. It was clear that he saw the dramatic possibilities of a séance with Lemick if Lemick was all that the evidence suggested he was, and particularly if Lemick did not know that we knew what we did. He could hardly wait to question him. As it turned out, the interview, or interviews, lasted a week. In that time, Habe spent a total of twenty-four solid hours in Lemick's company, and while some of these hours were difficult and brought both parties to a physical and mental sweat, Habe told us later that he enjoyed every minute of them. The detective-story unities of the case, he said, appealed to him strongly. He was a hard character as well as a literary one, but there was nothing soft about Lemick either. I would have liked very much to attend their conferences.

Some of us did, as a matter of fact, petition the Army to let us sit in, having reached a point in our acquaintance with Lemick at which it seemed a little silly never to have seen the man. The Army returned us a firm, polite "No" through the medium of a two-star general and two full colonels. What I know about Lemick's examination I learned off the record from Habe, from three other men who had a direct hand in the case, and from patches of a report which I had no business seeing, and which, since I'm not sure whether the enlisted man who showed it to me is still in the Army or not, I won't identify further.

Habe and the other interrogators first talked to the prisoners from Lemick's company who had been with him in Caiazzo at the time of the killings. They were free and comprehensive in their information, as was usual with enlisted-men prisoners from the German Army. Sergeant Arthur Schuster, still at large, was said to have helped Lemick in the shooting of the civilians. Lemick had been quartered at the farm of Nicola Perrone. After the departure of the rest of the third company from Caiazzo and the systematic gutting of every third house in the village, Lemick walked out to Perrone's with Schuster and three or four other enlisted men. He began to browbeat Perrone on a matter he had brought up with him before and had mentioned to his men on the way to the farm—signaling to the Americans with lights. The young farmer denied it violently. Darkness had begun to come on by then, and Lemick suddenly

walked to the front door of the house and called to the others that
he saw a light flickering in the next farmhouse to the south. One
of the men later taken prisoner went out and looked in the direction
Lemick was pointing, but saw nothing.

Lemick, according to the Germans of his unit whom I talked with
myself, was not a man who flew into stage rages or gestured with
his hands. He seemed always to be acting the part of a cold, efficient servant of his country, and when he got excited or emotional
he showed it only by walking around very rapidly and speaking
more quickly than usual. He went back and shot Perrone with his
Luger. Then he told Schuster and the others to take Perrone's wife
and four small children, three girls and a boy, out in front of the
house. He mounted a machine gun and with Schuster's help shot
them all, adding a few more shots from his pistol to finish them. The
party, carrying the machine gun, then went to the next farmhouse,
the one where Lemick had said he saw a light. A guard was put
over the half-dozen people there while other men, including Schuster,
were sent out to find the inmates of the two nearest farms in the
neighborhood and bring them back. All the sixteen Italians they
collected were shot with the machine gun and Lemick's Luger, some
inside the house against the walls, some on the terrace outside. The
Germans scattered straw over the bodies. Before midnight that same
night, the thirteenth, Lemick and his men went back to the village
for their vehicles, joined the rest of the German troops left in
Caiazzo, and pulled out to the north to catch up with their outfit.

That was the substance of the story of the prisoners from Lemick's
company who had seen the shootings. It was not volunteered, naturally, but brought out through questions. When it was on record,
Lemick was sent for. He had been kept apart from the other prisoners till then, but he seems, since he was the only officer in the group,
to have expected this and found nothing suspicious about it.

Habe saw him alone at first, in a small room. He asked the
questions that the German Army permitted its officers and men to
answer when taken prisoner—name, rank, army unit, place of residence—and then chatted with him easily and in fluent German
about Germany, Austria, the places they had both known and
seen, the course of the war and the campaign. All German soldiers
were taught to anticipate efforts to get tactical information out of

them when they were captured, and the officers the Americans took commonly made a game out of this process and matched wits with their interrogators with irony and self-satisfaction. Habe and Lemick went through all the standard motions in a friendly enough spirit. Lemick appeared to find everything correct and as it should be, even when Habe began to take him over his movements in recent weeks in the country between the Volturno and Caiazzo. At length, lighting cigarettes for himself and his guest and undoubtedly tasting the sensation of an actor about to deliver the punch line of the performance to a totally unprepared house, Habe said, "What about the evening of the thirteenth of this month? That was a Wednesday. What happened then?"

"The thirteenth?" said Lemick. "I don't remember."

"You don't remember the evening of the thirteenth?" said Habe, raising his eyebrows.

"Not especially. There was nothing unusual," said Lemick, setting up Habe's line.

"Nothing unusual? I think you had better change that answer, *Herr Leutnant*," said Habe, getting to his feet. "I advise you to change it. Because if the murder of women and children is nothing unusual for the German Army in Italy, then God help every one of you we catch. For the sake of your fellow officers, I advise you to change that answer."

It cannot be said that Lemick went white at this point or made an instinctive movement toward the door. Habe, who was looking for flattering signs of reaction to his bombshell, told me he detected only a flutter of the eyelids and then a freezing of Lemick's countenance. Being a realist, the examiner settled for that. He knew he had a job ahead of him and went to work on it forthwith.

In the next week, he spent long stretches with Lemick—once four hours, once six hours. Other interrogators worked with him now and then. The statements of Lemick's fellow prisoners were read to him. The men themselves were brought in and questioned in front of him. They went over the tale of their last evening in Caiazzo, staring curiously at Lemick, who sometimes stared back at them and sometimes gazed at the ceiling. After a few days he began to argue with the witnesses, seemingly trying to catch them in contradictions of their own statements. Toward the end of the week's examination, he called one of them a spy. The soldier called Lemick a liar. Not long after this, looking very tired, Lemick told Habe he would give the facts in his own way—a correct account. He gave them in great detail, subtracting almost nothing from the story of the witnesses but pointing out that his men did not appreciate the military danger of the situation to which the treachery of the Italian farmers had brought them. He signed the confession in a state of growing excitement and immediately afterward, Habe said, broke down in nervous terror and asked repeatedly what would happen to him.

What happened to Lemick in the next few months—and this is the last I know of him—may have done something to restore his coolness. He was shipped with other prisoners to a camp in North Africa and remained there passively accepting the routine life for some time. On the day he made the break that nearly got him to Spanish territory, there had been an inspection of the camp. When the members of the inspection party left by the stockade gate, Lemick simply walked out with them. I asked the officer who told me about it, a colonel, how this could be accounted for.

"Why," the colonel said, "he was in a pretty good position to take liberties. He was the leader of the camp—the head trusty, you might say."

I asked him if Lemick went on being head man once they had him back.

"I don't know," said he colonel. "He would if they stuck to procedure. The only officer in the bunch, you know."

Battling Siki

1949

HELL'S KITCHEN, the region west of Eighth Avenue around the Forties, won its name many years ago and continued to deserve it until about the time the Eighteenth Amendment was repealed. Things are different there now. So its residents will tell you, and so you can see for yourself if, having known the neighborhood a little during Prohibition, you visit it even briefly today. Once it was carpeted, for nearly all its length and breadth, with low, swarthy brick tenement houses containing a warren of flats, speak-easies, six-table cellar "cabarets," hole-in-the-wall stores and restaurants, back-room stills, and "social clubs," where a portion of the manhood of the district stored guns and ammunition and planned stick-ups and highjackings. Right along the equator of Hell's Kitchen ran the Ninth Avenue "L" tracks, throwing a grim, significant shadow by day and night. Other parts of town had clip joints, or "buckets of blood," scattered through them, but the Kitchen, as a detective friend of mine used to say, was one big bucket of blood. Nowadays the Kitchen is a bit more shiny and much more respectable. Neon lights and modern shops and garages have pushed their way into it. The McGraw-Hill Building has gouged out half of what was considered one of the hottest blocks in Hell's Kitchen in the nineteen twenties—the block bounded by Eighth and Ninth Avenues and Forty-first and Forty-second streets. The Lincoln Tunnel approaches have formed an asphalt plaza west of Ninth Avenue. The sleek New Jersey buses and automobiles bound for and away from the West Side Highway plow across the old badlands in steady procession. The retail liquor traffic thereabouts has become negligible; the city's center of gravity of crime has shifted elsewhere, perhaps to Brooklyn. Broadly speaking, Hell's Kitchen is not a frontier community any more but a sort of vehicular gateway to the heart of Manhattan. However, if you want to conjure up the atmosphere of earlier times, you can still find islands of squat tenement houses here and there to help you, many of them boarded up and condemned, and the empty shells of many basement grogshops. In the unlikely event that you want to visit the scene of the murder, twenty-four years ago, of a man called Battling Siki, which is what I did one day recently for no useful reason, you will come across a few surviving landmarks. You can pace off distances in the same gutter and seamy street—Forty-first—down which Siki crawled forty feet west toward Ninth Avenue, with two bullets in his body, before he collapsed and died. He crawled in the direction of the "L," the cave of shadows that no longer is there. His killer threw away the gun in front of a grimy old house that is now gone; the McGraw-Hill Building is there instead. These changes make the setting less sinister than it used to be, but even now there's plenty to show that it was a drab and lonesome place to die.

Siki, who held the light-heavyweight boxing championship of the world for six months in 1922 and 1923, was born in Senegal, in French West Africa, in 1897 and was killed in Hell's Kitchen twenty-eight years later, in 1925. He was the Kitchen's most turbulent citizen in the short time he lived there. He was thought by neighbors who knew him to have an honest heart and a generous soul, but when he drank the newly cooked liquor of the parish, as he often did, the cab drivers, cops, bartenders, and hoodlums whom he chose, with impeccable lack of judgment, to knock around, found it hard to take him philosophically. Rear-line observers, on the other hand, were usually able to be philosophical about Siki. During the three years of his life in which he received international publicity—the last three—he was referred to repeatedly as a "child of nature," a "natural man," and a "jungle child," and at least once as "the black Candide." After his murder, the New York *World* said editorially, "What is all this [Siki's physical strength, his brawling and dissipation] but the sulks and tempers of Achilles, the prank of Siegfried and the boars, the strutting of Beowulf, the armours of Lemminkaïnen? We have had a walking image of our beginnings among us and did not know it. . . . He had, it is true, the mentality of a backward toad. . . . But he had the soul of a god."

It strikes me that tributes paid by civilized people to a "natural man," especially one who has walked among us, are apt to sound either patronizing, like the *World*'s, or uneasy, like some delivered by American correspondents when Siki won his boxing championship in Paris in 1922 and was first interviewed. After praising Siki's strength and simplicity, one reporter wrote apprehensively, "He is very black and very ugly." Siki's manager at the time, a M. Hellers, was quoted as saying that Siki was a fine lad but "just a little bit crazy." I can discover no support among those who were acquainted with Siki in America later on for the idea that he was crazy, except when he drank, or the idea that he was mentally toadlike. He was illiterate, never having been to school, but he could make himself understood in several languages including English, French, Spanish, Dutch, and German. As far as Candide is concerned, Siki resembled Voltaire's hero in that he had a sheltered boyhood, was thrown suddenly into the thick of the best of all possible worlds, and found society both violent and larcenous. At seventeen, he was involved in a civilized world war. At twenty-five, he was permitted to box a champion on the condition that he lose the match. Having ignored the condition and won the championship, he insured his loss of that title, in all innocence, by fighting an Irishman in Dublin on St. Patrick's Day. He entered American life in the heyday of the Volstead act. He could not master the strong waters or the social customs of the West Side of New York City. He was killed by gunfire, after surviving a stabbing earlier in the same year. It may seem, offhand, that Hell's Kitchen was a curious place for the curtain to fall on a twenty-eight-year-old Mohammedan born in St. Louis de Senegal on the fringe of the Sahara Desert, but Voltaire has shown that when civilization gets its hands on one of these natural men, it pushes him about at random from curious place to curious place. Candide was lucky to wind up safely cultivating his garden. He came close to meeting his end in an auto-da-fé in Portugal and, another time, on a roasting spit in Paraguay. Siki's story is perhaps more realistic. He failed to last out the course.

The newspaper writers of the 1920s were merely being wishful when they called Siki a jungle child. St. Louis, his African home, is a seaport ten miles above the mouth of the Senegal River, on a bare plain that marks the Sahara's southwesternmost edge. It's doubtful whether anyone in Europe or America today knows what Siki's real name was. Legend has it that when he was ten or twelve years old, a French actress touring the colonies saw him in St. Louis, was impressed by his appearance, and took him into her personal service, giving him, for reasons based on classical Greek, the name of Louis Phal. Whatever its origin, this, Anglicized as Louis Fall, was his legal name when he was married, and when he was murdered, in America. He did not become known as Battling Siki until he began to box professionally, in 1913; apparently the word "Siki" was coined or borrowed by French fight promoters, to whom it had vague "native" or colonial connotations. The tale about the actress was told widely in Paris in the days of Siki's first fame, when he knocked out the celebrated Georges Carpentier, but it was never, so far as I know, closely checked up on. It accounts, plausibly enough, for the abrupt shift of Siki from dusty African streets to the perils of Western civilization. The lady is said to have taken him to her villa on the French Riviera and dressed him in a page boy's uniform of bottle green. Subsequently, he worked in one town and another as a bus boy. He was fifteen when he started boxing.

Siki had just time for a handful of fights, most of which he won, before the war of 1914–18 broke out and he was conscripted into the 8th Colonial Infantry Regiment of the French Army. His war record was distinguished; in fact, he is reported to have been the bravest soldier in his outfit, which saw action on several fronts and gave a strong performance generally. For heroism under fire, Siki won not only the Croix de Guerre but the Médaille Militaire. After demobilization, he could have had his choice of a variety of ordinary civilian jobs; his record guaranteed him that. However, he went back to the prize ring, where the rewards were intermittent but came in good-sized pieces when they came. He barnstormed in France, North Africa, Spain, Belgium, and Holland. From a tour of Holland in 1921 he returned to Paris, where he lived with a Dutch girl who was thought to be his wife and by whom he later had a child. Siki did not work especially hard at his trade. He fought once or twice a month, which is not often for a "club," or journeyman, fighter, and, while he usually won, he beat nobody of major importance. Between bouts he drank more absinthe than is normal in the profession. American critics were to speak of him three or four years later as a fighter of considerable natural ability who might have been much better than he was. Weighing about a hundred and seventy-five pounds, the maximum for light heavyweights, and standing five feet eleven inches tall, he was a well-muscled young man with a leaping, bounding, lunging style from which he got slapstick effects that amused the galleries, and himself as well. In the early months of 1922, he happened to defeat a couple of men of some slight reputation and thus came to the notice of François

Descamps, then the most influential and artful character in French boxing. Descamps offered him a bout for the world's light-heavyweight championship with Carpentier, whom Descamps managed.

The prizefight business in Continental Europe in those days was an odd blend of laissez faire and team play—laissez faire being understood to mean "Let Descamps do it his way," and "team play" to mean that all hands share in the spoils. Descamps owned a large stable of fighters and also, it was commonly believed in Paris, a large stable of sports writers. Some of the latter were growing restive in 1922, possibly because of a failure in the team-play system as administered by Descamps. When the Carpentier-Siki match was announced, certain journalists expressed a distrust of it. They suggested that, in Siki, Descamps had laid hold of a small-time, happy-go-lucky trouper with no ambitions beyond getting all the absinthe he could consume, who would be glad to bolster Carpentier's fortunes—Carpentier had not fought for really big money since his knockout by Jack Dempsey in New Jersey, fourteen months before —without making too much trouble for the champion in the ring. Their hints were undoubtedly read by the public. Carpentier was a war hero, the toast of the boulevards, a boxer still regarded, in spite of his defeat by Dempsey, as peerless in Europe, but though the crowd of 55,000 that came to the new Buffalo Velodrome in Paris on the afternoon of September 24, 1922, to see him fight Siki was the largest in European boxing history, it showed before the day was over that it was on the alert for signs of skulduggery. Its suspicions were inflamed during the preliminary bouts by the work of Harry Bernstein, a referee charged by sports writers with occupying a special compartment in the hip pocket of M. Descamps. In one preliminary, the opponent of a Descamps featherweight named Fritsch was disqualified by Bernstein for hitting too low; in another, the opponent of a Descamps heavyweight named Ledoux was disqualified by Bernstein for not fighting hard enough. Bernstein's rulings brought a volley of *coups de sifflet* from the customers, particularly those in the seven-franc seats, who had mustered their sous at a sacrifice and wished for their money's worth of equality and justice.

The main bout was scheduled for twenty rounds. Carpentier, pale and blond, weighed 173½ pounds, Siki 174. In the first round, Siki fought cautiously and less acrobatically than usual; Carpentier jabbed at him with his left hand. Once, hit lightly, Siki dropped to one knee; Bernstein, who was refereeing this bout, too, did not bother to count. "Get up, Siki, you're not hurt," he said. After the round, ringside spectators saw Carpentier smile broadly and heard him say, "I'll get him whenever I want to." The champion, boxing easily, won the first two rounds. In the third, Carpentier sent a right-hand blow to Siki's jaw, and Siki dropped to his knee again, this time taking a count of seven. When he got up, he rushed at Carpentier and hit him violently in the body with a left and a right. Carpentier, looking startled as well as hurt, went down for four seconds. The rest of the fight was all Siki's. Siki battered Carpentier about the ring in the fourth round while Carpentier hung on to Siki's arms whenever he could and tried to pinion them with his own. In the fifth, Carpentier fell against the ropes. Siki leaned over him ("I whispered to him to quit," Siki said later), and Carpentier, pushing himself up, butted angrily at Siki's belly. Carpentier could hardly stand when the sixth round began. Siki hit him at will. A right uppercut followed by a shower of right and left swings sent Carpentier to the floor unconscious one minute and ten seconds after the start of the round. As he fell, one of his feet became tangled between Siki's, assisting the fall.

It was plain that Carpentier was completely knocked out, but at that point Bernstein ruled that Siki had lost the fight by tripping his opponent illegally. The third disqualification of the day was more than the crowd was prepared to stomach. It pushed its way to the ring from all quarters of the stadium and stormed around it, yelling furiously. Police were called up to protect Bernstein. Descamps, meanwhile, for whose blood the demonstrators were also shouting, slipped out of the arena behind a couple of gendarmes. Three judges—Victor Breyer, Jean Pujol, and an Englishman, Tom Bannison—who, before the fight, had been appointed by the French Boxing Federation to make a decision in case there was no knockout, were now appealed to. After conferring briefly with Federation officials, they announced that they would give a final and formal verdict either supporting or overruling Bernstein's. They deliberated for three quarters of an hour while Bernstein stood in one corner of the ring among his police guards and practically no one in the audience went home, or even stopped talking unkindly to the referee. The judges, willingly or not, at last did what the crowd wanted: they declared Siki the winner by a knockout and, in the name of the Federation, awarded him the light-heavyweight championship of the world, plus a subsidiary title of Carpentier's— the heavyweight championship of Europe. Siki said to Hellers, his manager, "Tell America I am ready for Dempsey," and repaired in triumph to his dressing room. The crowd disbanded. The police saw Bernstein safely to the door of his dressing room.

Siki never got a match with Dempsey, but some offers of lesser opportunities did come to him from America. He was lavishly feted in Paris during the first two days after his victory, and after public enthusiasm subsided, his own continued to run high, especially in the Montmartre neighborhood. "No more absinthe. I will train and fight hard as champion," Siki had told a gathering outside the office of the newspaper *Echo des Sports* on the twenty-fifth, the day following the fight. Later that evening, he took a few glasses of champagne, and on touring Montmartre in a rented car with a chauffeur, he reverted to absinthe wholeheartedly at every stop he made. After another week or so he acquired, probably as gifts from fellow colonials, a monkey, which he carried everywhere on his shoulder, and a lion cub, which he led about on a leash. Carpentier was still lying in bed suffering from a sprained ankle, two broken hands, and an unsightly swelling of his nose and lips. Most of the Parisian sporting press was sympathetic toward him but nastily jubilant about Descamps, who, it was implied, had over-reached himself and been double-crossed. Rumors to the same effect circulated through Paris for the next several weeks. In early December, the French Boxing Federation precipitated the publication of what was very likely the true story of the fight by suspending Siki—it was charged that while seconding another fighter in the ring, he had struck the manager of his man's opponent. Siki, deprived of a chance to make a living in France, went for help to M. Diagne, the representative for Senegal in the French Chamber of Deputies. Diagne asserted before the Chamber that the Boxing

Federation was discriminating against colonials in favor of Parisian city slickers who wanted Siki out of the way, and in support of this theory he gave the deputies the account of the Carpentier bout that Siki had given him. When the Chamber appeared unwilling to take any action, Diagne called a press conference and had Siki repeat his story to reporters. It ran as follows:

A fix had been arranged fifteen days before the bout took place, with Descamps dictating procedure to Siki's manager. As a sign of good faith, Siki was to take a short count in the first round and another count in the third. He was to get himself knocked out early in the fourth. Siki followed the scenario through the third-round knockdown—"I stayed down for seven the first time Carpentier hit me hard enough to give me an excuse," he said—but as he knelt on the floor at that point, he decided not to go through with the frameup. It was his pride, he said, and his loyalty to the public that made him change his mind. When he got up, he began to fight in earnest. He ignored a sharp reminder from his manager, between the third and fourth rounds, that his end was expected momentarily. (This detail in Siki's narrative gave Hellers a clean bill of health, in a left-handed way; Descamps had been so suspicious of treachery by Hellers that he quarreled with him in public after the bout.) Siki surprised Carpentier with his counterattack and soon demolished him.

When Siki's story was done, M. Diagne explained to the press what it meant: A simple, uneducated man had defended himself and all underprivileged peoples against exploitation by a predatory society. Siki, who was always emotional, wept freely at these words. His tears and his deputy's arguments got him nowhere. Neither did a court of inquiry appointed by the Boxing Federation to investigate Siki's statement. The court, with a flashy display of ingenuity, hired two deaf-mutes to watch the motion pictures of the fight and see if they could lip-read certain remarks delivered excitedly by Descamps to Hellers in Siki's corner during "a critical phase of the battle," after Siki had begun to knock Carpentier around. The experiment (unique, I think, in boxing history) was later described by the court as "successful," but Siki remained suspended. He never fought in France again until after he had lost his championships elsewhere.

My own opinion is that being champion constituted Siki's chief sin in the eyes of the Federation. Also, I believe his story of the Carpentier match was substantially correct. A "sign of good faith"— a preliminary fall, or lapse of some other kind, by the loser—is a standard device in the plotting of sports frameups. Eddie Cicotte, a Chicago baseball player, hit the first batter he faced with a pitched ball in the crooked World Series of 1919, as a signal to gamblers that the fix was in. Siki's tale confirmed the rumors that were current before and after the fight; it was in keeping with the character of Descamps and of Continental boxing methods in 1922, and it is believed by every European and American I know who was familiar in any degree with the time, the place, and the actors.

As it turned out, the Carpentier bout was the only one of importance in Siki's professional career, except for the next one. The next one was weak and anticlimactic as a show, but it did involve a world's championship, and it demonstrated in a special way how complicated the civilization of the West can be for an unlettered Moslem with no grounding in our rituals and customs. A fairly good light heavyweight from County Clare in Ireland named Michael Francis McTigue happened to pass through Paris with his staff during Siki's suspension. Finding Siki idle and nearly broke, the visitors proposed a match between him and McTigue for the title. (The world's light-heavyweight championship was the one that interested them; the heavyweight championship of Europe had no value in the world market, and has been recognized only sporadically since the day Carpentier lost it.) They spoke of Dublin as a pleasant spot for the Siki-McTigue bout. They mentioned March 17, 1923, as an open date in their engagement book. Siki fell in with these suggestions and met McTigue in the ring in the Irish capital on Saint Patrick's Day. The operation for the removal of his crown was painless. The decision went to McTigue on points. There was nothing particularly wrong with this verdict, I am told by a neutral eyewitness, except that McTigue did not make the efforts or take the risks that are commonly expected of a challenger for a world's championship. There was no need to. In the circumstances, nothing less than a knockout could have beaten him, and he avoided that possibility by boxing at long range throughout.

One device by which a civilized man can avoid a predicament like Siki's in Dublin was illustrated by McTigue himself later in the same year. He went to Columbus, Georgia, to fight a Georgian named Young Stribling before a crowd that was strongly and ostentatiously in favor of his opponent. There was almost no way McTigue could avoid losing within the Georgia state limits, so, to protect his planetary interests, he took along a referee from the North. The referee called the bout a draw. Then, yielding to the howls of protest, he announced that he would deputize the local promoter to give the decision. The promoter called Stribling the winner. The referee, on his way back North by train with McTigue and McTigue's manager, signed an affidavit that his own true and considered verdict was for a draw. That is how the result has been listed in the record books ever since.

Siki had only two more European fights, both in Paris, after he lost his titles. The last two years of his life he spent in America, disintegrating with headlong speed on bootleg gin and whiskey but nearly always able to make money in the ring when he needed it. When he first arrived in New York, in September 1923, his name had a certain value here, based on curiosity, which it no longer had abroad. He signed on with the stable of a veteran New York manager, Robert (Pa) Levy (Hellers appears to have discarded Siki at the time of his suspension in France), and his first fight in this country was a serious one with a respectable opponent, Kid Norfolk, who beat him in fifteen rounds at Madison Square Garden. From then on, American fight fans were not disposed to think of Siki as a boxer of the top rank, but they liked to watch him. His style was eccentric and funny. He was strong and fast enough to knock out most of the palookas he met, when he felt like it. He was booked as far west as California and as far south as New Orleans, and he earned, according to a fairly reliable estimate I have heard, nearly a hundred thousand dollars between November 1923 and November 1925. He was one of the best spenders, in proportion to income, that the United States has ever seen. In restaurants and speakeasies he sometimes tipped five or ten times the amount of the check. Once, having made five thousand dollars from a fight in New York on a Friday, he was turned out of his rooming house the following

Monday for nonpayment of rent. Another time he gave away all the money in his pockets to passengers on a Lackawanna Railroad ferryboat on which he was returning from a fight in New Jersey. Scolded for this by his manager, Siki wept. Most of his cash, however, continued to be spent on gifts, liquor, and clothes. In clothes, Siki's taste was unusual but rich. In the first part of his New York residence, when he lived and roamed mainly in the Times Square area, he almost always wore full dress when he went out at night. By day, ordinarily, he appeared in a high hat, a frock coat, red ascot tie, striped trousers, spatted shoes, and a monocle, and he carried a gold-headed cane. From time to time he gave away all the stylish clothes he had on and went home by cab in his underwear. He was particularly open-handed with his high hats. One of these, Siki's gift to the management, hung on a peg in a West Side saloon I used to visit until a few years ago, when the place closed up.

Siki's New York life was divided into two roughly equal periods, the second of which he passed largely in Hell's Kitchen. He had been married in the summer of 1924, at the Municipal Building, to a woman from Memphis named Lillian Werner. The event attracted just enough attention to stimulate newspaper inquiries in Paris, where neighbors of the Dutch girl with whom he had lived in the suburb of Lanves said she was still there and was still thought to be his wife. She herself was not interviewed or quoted to that effect then or afterward, so far as I know. Siki and his American bride moved into a flat at 361 West Forty-second Street early in 1925. Siki had begun to go downhill physically and professionally by then. His bookings for fights were fewer than they had been, and he did not fulfill all those he made. He got into trouble, almost simultaneously, with the United States Immigration Service and the boxing commissioners of New York State. Siki had come to America on a short-term permit. In July 1925 he was arrested for felonious assault after slashing at a policeman with a knife, at which the Government began deportation proceedings. In August the Boxing Commission, annoyed by a facetious exhibition Siki had given at a small New York City fight club, summoned him and Levy to its office, suspended Siki, and told Levy to make sure that the fighter was somewhere beyond the three-mile limit within thirty days. The order may seem to have been a usurpation of Federal powers, but it coincided with the Government's view. At this point, France told the United States that it would refuse to receive Siki if he were deported. Siki, who had wept in the Boxing Commission office when he heard the order to his manager, now took advantage of the stalemate and, in November, filed application for his first citizenship papers. Government decision on his deportation case was still pending when he died.

Siki had the reputation in Hell's Kitchen in 1925 of being dangerous when drunk, mild and affable when sober. As he drank more heavily and fought less in the ring, he fought more in the street, and his opponents were a rough and active group of men. He was known for his favorite joke of hailing a cab, taking a ride, and then challenging the driver to fight for the fare. Occasionally, too, he would invade the Times Square station of the I.R.T. in the early morning in search of amateur boxing engagements. It is characteristic of many boxers that as they lose their ability in the ring they swing their fists more frequently outside it, as a sort of blurred insistence on the claim that they are as good as ever. That, along with the drinks Siki bought or charged up in the bars of the West Side, may account for his pugnacity in his last months. The only instance of Siki's using a knife that I have found was the time he was arrested for drawing one on a policeman. His wife went to night court to plead for him on that occasion. She made a good impression and got him off with a five-dollar fine. Though he was stabbed in the back himself in August, not long after he had smashed up a speak-easy in the West Forties and spent a few days in the French Hospital on West Thirtieth Street as a consequence, Siki went on using his fists—and now and then a piece of furniture—in nearly all his brawls. He was fined another five dollars on December 6 for slapping a patrolman at the corner of Seventh Avenue and Thirty-fourth Street.

At about seven o'clock in the evening on Monday, December 14, Siki's wife met him on the stairs to their flat on West Forty-second Street. The house they lived in still stands, a house of dingy brick with ten walk-up apartments, two on each of its five floors. Siki told Mrs. Siki he was going "out with the boys" and would be back in time to help her pack for a trip they were making next day to Washington, where Siki was to appear in a theater. Shortly after midnight on the morning of the fifteenth, Patrolman John J. Meehan, of the West Thirtieth Street station, walking his beat along Ninth Avenue, had a brief encounter with Siki, whom he knew by sight. Siki, wobbling a little as he turned under the "L" tracks from Forty-first Street, called to Meehan that he was on his way home. The patrolman told him to keep going that way. At 4:15 A.M., Meehan walked past the intersection of Forty-first Street and Ninth Avenue again and saw a body lying about a hundred feet east of the corner in the gutter in front of 350 West Forty-first. Approaching it, he recognized Siki. The body was taken to Meehan's station house, where a doctor pronounced the fighter recently dead from internal hemorrhage caused by two bullet wounds. Detectives examined the deserted block of Forty-first between Eighth and Ninth avenues. In front of No. 346, some forty feet east of where Siki had died, they found a pool of blood on the sidewalk. It seemed to them that Siki might have been trying to crawl home after he was shot. They could not tell just where the shooting had taken place. The gun, a vest-pocket .32-caliber pistol, was lying in front of No. 333, on the other side of the street. Only two bullets had been fired from it. An autopsy showed that these had entered Siki from behind, one penetrating his left lung and the other his kidneys. The autopsy showed something else which surprised Siki's neighbors a good deal when they heard of it: he had suffered from an anemic condition.

At his wife's request, Siki was given a Christian funeral service at the Harlem funeral parlors of Effie A. Miller. The Reverend Adam Clayton Powell delivered a eulogy. However, seven Mohammedan pallbearers in turbans carried his body to the hearse, chanting prayers as they did so, while a crowd of three thousand people looked on. The body was clothed in evening dress, as Siki would undoubtedly have wished. His estate, estimated at six hundred dollars, was awarded to his wife in Surrogate's Court after Levy made out an affidavit in her favor. The words of the affidavit, while perhaps not strictly accurate in point of fact, told the broad truth about Siki's place in the world better, I think, than the editorial that spoke of Achilles, Siegfried, and "natural man." To the best of his knowledge, Levy said, Siki left surviving "no child or children, no father, mother, brother, or sister, or child or children of a deceased brother or sister." He lived as a man without kin or country, roots or guides, and that, it seems to me, is a hard way to do it.

Siki's murder was never solved. There was an abundance of suspects, but none of them suited the police at all until one day in March 1926 a young man of eighteen who lived a block or two from Siki's house was arrested and booked on a homicide charge in connection with the killing. Detectives disguised as truck drivers had heard him making incriminating remarks, they said, over a telephone in a bootleggers' hangout at Tenth Avenue and Fortieth Street. On being arrested, he allegedly signed two statements which gave two different accounts of the crime. One said that Siki had staggered into a coffee pot at Eighth Avenue and Fortieth Street in the early morning of December 15 and had thrown a chair at the eight men, including the deponent, who were gathered there. Deponent ran out of the place in alarm and heard shots fired in the restaurant behind him. The other statement, which fitted the physical facts of the killing a little better, said that a short while after the throwing of the chair, he, the young man under arrest, lured Siki to Eighth Avenue and Forty-first Street on the promise of buying him a drink. At the corner they were joined by two other men, one of whom, as the party walked west on Forty-first, shot Siki in the back. The young man was held in the Tombs for eight months, until the fall of 1926, and then was released by the court without trial, presumably because the state was not satisfied with its case. I might add that in May 1927 this same young man got five to ten years for second-degree robbery, committed in April in the vicinity of Ninth Avenue and Forty-second Street against a tourist from another state. That was clearly the wrong part of town for a tourist to go to.

TV
AND OTHER
PHENOMENA

What They Did to Jack

1959

I'M NOT Jack Paar, but I'm not a dog either. They can't kick me around. I'm modest, for a plain little writer that makes $20,000 a day, but I'm sensitive to my fingertips (I think I've got nice fingertips), and I'm game. (I've got a kind of thing about gameness.) Last month *Newsweek* printed a long, objective piece about Jack Paar (why should they do a brutal thing like that?), and Jack answered them right back for a week. (It seemed like a week.) If Paar can defend himself, so can Jack Larkin. (I'm Jack Larkin— a humble but gallant kind of guy.)

I'm not the monster they say I am, dear hearts. They said, "Jack has talent and clean teeth." Wasn't that a cruel thing to say? It was given to them by somebody I fired; and you know I've never fired anybody except Joe, Sam, Lavinia, Toodles, Al, Fingers, Sheila, that kid from Philadelphia and the Three Songbirds. The Three Songbirds lied to me. They told me they'd never been on the cover of *Sports Illustrated* and it turned out they were on the cover of *Sports Illustrated* (front and back) for two years.

(So now they're back in Duluth and you never hear about them any more. I'm gentle, but I want loyalty. I've got a thing about loyalty.)

You see, they write about me for circulation. It's a circulation-war kind of thing. The *Saturday Evening Post* is catching up on them, and so is the Brooklyn telephone book. (You want to know a trade secret, dear hearts? That telephone book is the fastest-growing thing in the country. Except me.) They put me on the cover, but I've had that cover thing. They wanted to use me for circulation, like the *Police Gazette* used Lincoln.

What's wrong with having clean teeth? Wasn't that a wicked, slanted thing to say? George Washington had clean teeth. That great man and I had three big things in common, and I say this with a little catch in my throat because I'm basically emotional—honor, integrity, and clean teeth. But they put it out of context.

It's not important that an entertainer was attacked. I say amusingly, it happened to Barrymore. It happened to Booth, the man who shot Jim Bishop. They thought they could do it to me because I'm so easily hurt. That's an important thing about me. I'm easily hurt. But when they attack my honor, I get excited. That's an interesting thing about me—I get excited, and I hit some pretty big targets. Look at that girl soprano. She's back in Philadelphia. Look at Winchell. He's back in New York.

Mr. Kintner said to me, "Jack, you've discovered more talent than any three shows." Amusingly he said, "Where are we going to put all the money you bring us—in the gents' room?" That's an interesting thing about me, I bring them a lot of money and I have a very clean mind, like Joan of Arc's. There's no bigger man in the industry than Mr. Kintner. He has clean teeth. And every night I go straight home, I'm so tired.

That's another thing they said about me. They said I live in Bronxville. Wasn't that a vicious, twisted thing to say? What's wrong with living in Bronxville? That's where I live. But they don't care what they say. It's for circulation. And they said it out of context. I deserve a lot of things, but not that. Ask anyone who knows me —ask Billy Graham—and they'll tell you I'm never out of context. And when I'm home, I'm never out of the house, I'm so domestic. I mean, I'm not imported. That's an interesting thing about me. I'm just about the least imported entertainer this country has had since Mark Twain. I'm a shy person, essentially; quiet, shy, and lovely. But I'll say this for myself—nobody had to bring me here. I came from Ohio, and I bought my own ticket. Ask Mr. Sarnoff.

They went around and they talked to about twenty-five of the people who know and like me best. President Eisenhower, Casey Stengel, Dr. Schweitzer, Pat Suzuki, De Gaulle, Floyd Patterson. And my little girls and my little boy, who just touch my heart so when I look at them. But they didn't want to hear good things. They said, "What do you know that's bad about Jack?"

They don't care what they do.

Thoughts on
Radio-Televese

1959

INTERVIEWING GOVERNOR ROCKEFELLER recently on Station WMCA, Barry Gray, the discless jockey, felt the need to ask his guest a certain question. He also felt a clear obligation to put the inquiry in radio-televese, the semi-official language of men who promote conversation on the air. Though it is more or less required, this language is a flexible one, leaving a good deal to the user's imagination. "Governor," Mr. Gray said, after pausing to review the possibilities of the patois, "how do you see your future in a Pennsylvania Avenue sense?" I thought it was a splendid gambit. Another broadcaster might have said "How do you see yourself in the electoral-college picture?" or "How do you project yourself Chief Executivewise?" The Gray formula had the special flavor, the colorful two-rings-from-the-bull's-eye quality, that I have associated with the work of this interviewer ever since I began to follow it, several years ago. For the record, Governor Rockefeller replied, "I *could* be happier where I am." He might have meant Albany, he might have meant the WMCA studio. As you see, radio-televese is not only a limber language, it is contagious.

The salient characteristic of remarks made in radio-televese is that they never coincide exactly with primary meanings or accepted forms. For instance, Mr. Gray, a leader in the postwar development of the lingo, has a way of taking a trenchant thought or a strong locution and placing it somewhere to the right or left of where it would seem to belong. "Is this your first trip to the mainland? How do you feel about statehood?" I heard him ask a guest from the Philippines on one of his shows (the program runs, at present, from 11:05 P.M. to 1 A.M.). On the topic of Puerto Ricans in New York, he said, "How can we make these people welcome and not upset the décor of the city?" On a show a few years ago he described an incident that had taken place in a night club "that might be called a bawd." A drunk at a ringside table, Mr. Gray said, "interrupted the floor show to deliver a soliloquy." "When did the chink begin to pierce the armor?" he once asked, in connection with a decline in the prestige of former Mayor O'Dwyer. "The fault, then," he said on another occasion, "is not with Caesar or with his stars but with certain Congressmen." Speaking of the real-life source of a character in a Broadway play, he observed, "He was the clay pigeon on whom the character was modeled." When Mr. Gray called Brussels "the Paris of Belgium," I was reminded of an editorial I had read in a Long Island newspaper long ago in which Great Neck was called "the Constantinople of the North Shore." There is an eloquence and an easy confidence in Mr. Gray's talk that stimulates even his guests to heights of radio-televese. Artie Shaw, a musician, in describing the art of another performer to Mr. Gray, said, "He has a certain thing known as 'presence'—when he's onstage, you can see him." Another guest declared that the success of a mutual friend was "owing to a combination of luck and a combination of skill." "You can say that again," Mr. Gray agreed, and I believe that the guest did so, a little later. The same eloquence and the same off-centerism can be found today in the speech of a wide variety of radio and television regulars. "Parallels are odious," Marty Glickman, a sports announcer, has stated. "The matter has reached a semi-head," a Senator—I couldn't be sure which one— said at a recent televised Congressional hearing. "I hear you were shot down over the Netherlands while flying," a video reporter said to Senator Howard Cannon, a war veteran, on a Channel 2 program last winter. "Where in the next year are we going to find the writers to fill the cry and the need?" David Susskind demanded not long ago of a forum of TV directors. "Do you have an emotional umbilical cord with Hollywood?" Mr. Susskind asked a director on the same show.

Mr. Susskind's second question raises the point that metaphor is indispensable in radio-televese. "Wherein water always finds its own level, they should start hitting soon," a baseball announcer said about the Yankees the other day. In an earlier year, Red Barber, analyzing a situation in which a dangerous batter had been purposely walked, with the effect of bringing an even more dangerous batter to the plate, remarked that it was a case of "carrying coals to Newcastle, to make use of an old expression." I suspect that Mr. Barber meant that it was a case of the frying pan and the fire, and I also suspect that if he had thought of the right metaphor afterward, he would have corrected himself publicly. He is a conscientious man, and therefore by no means a typical user of radio-televese. The true exponent never retraces his steps but moves from bold figure to bold figure without apology. There have been few bolder sequences (or "seg-ways," as they are sometimes called on the air) than the one that Mr. Gray achieved in 1957 during a discussion of the perils faced by Jack Paar in launching a new program. I think I have quoted this passage here once before; it still fills me with admiration. "It's like starting off with a noose around your neck," Mr. Gray said. "You've got twenty-six weeks to make good, or they'll shoot you. That sword of Damocles can be a rough proposition." As most of you know by now, Mr. Paar eventually made good before the sword could explode and throttle him.

Perhaps the most startling aspect of radio-televese is its power to move freely in time, space, and syntax, transposing past and future, beginnings and endings, subjects and objects. This phase of the language has sometimes been called backward English, and sometimes, with a bow to the game of billiards, reverse English. Dorothy Kilgallen, a television panelist, was wallowing in the freedom of the language on the night she said, "It strikes me as funny, don't you?" So was Dizzy Dean when he said, "Don't fail to miss tomorrow's double header." Tommy Loughran, a boxing announcer, was exploring the area of the displaced ego when he told his audience, "It won't take him [the referee] long before I think he should stop it."

Ted Husing was on the threshold of outright mysticism when he reported, about a boxer who was cuffing his adversary smartly around, "There's a lot more authority in Joe's punches than perhaps he would like his opponent to suspect!" It is in the time dimension, however, that radio-televese scores its most remarkable effects. Dizzy Dean's "The Yankees, as I told you later . . ." gives the idea. The insecurity of man is demonstrated regularly on the air by phrases like "Texas, the former birthplace of President Eisenhower" and "Mickey Mantle, a former native of Spavinaw, Oklahoma." I'm indebted to Dan Parker, sports writer and philologist, for a particularly strong example of time adjustment from the sayings of Vic Marsillo, a boxing manager who occasionally speaks on radio and television: "Now, Jack, whaddya say we reminisce a little about tomorrow's fight?" These quotations show what can be done in the way of outguessing man's greatest enemy, but I think that all of them are excelled by a line of Mr. Gray's spoken four or five years ago: "What will our future forefathers say?"

It is occasionally argued in defense of broadcasters (though they need and ask for no defense) that they speak unorthodoxly because they must speak under pressure, hastily, spontaneously—that their eccentricities are unintentional. Nothing could be farther from the truth. Their language is proud and deliberate. The spirit that has created it is the spirit of ambition. Posterity would have liked it. In times to come, our forebears will be grateful.

Dixie Deposit

1957

A MAN who keeps driving through the South with Yankee license plates on his motorcar is bound, in the course of the years, to be stopped often enough to learn something about the Dixie deposit system. The more often he is stopped, the more he gets to know. Your correspondent, however, is anything but a mad dog of the highway. I roll along in a prudent way—and after twenty years of research, my information is confined to three well-spaced spots: Fayetteville (N.C.), Liberty County (Ga.), and Prince George County (Va.).

I will give you the general breakdown first:

In Fayetteville they trade by radar. The bond to be posted against court appearance at a later date is $30. The words which go with this music are: "We won't look for you then if we don't see you."

In Liberty County they use human labor, the old hunt-and-peck or naked-eye-and-chase system—a sleuth in a patrol car. The bond is $25. The lyrics are: "You are not necessarily expected to appear."

In Prince George County, the opening move is also human, or nonelectronic. The bond is $22 (including justice's fee for taking recognizance). The curtain line is: "You don't need to be there."

As between radar and the human naked eye, I think the average tourist prefers to be nailed by the second method. But that is just one man's opinion. To me, there is something cold and evil in being shot from behind a bush with a beam of light. The human method has a warmer, more personal quality—except, of course, for the overture, where the law surges up from the rear with a burst of woodwinds and sirens. It's a moment that makes the hair of the driver's neck stand on end, and I can see why nervous types would rather go down by robot, in silence.

As for the crime, I will state frankly that in Fayetteville and Liberty County I would have defended myself had the law been disposed to listen (which is a comical hypothesis). I was driving old D-8286 on those occasions, and one glance at that faithful heap should have made it clear to man and beast that she was incapable of exceeding anyone's speed limit.

In Prince George County the other day, however, I concede that I was going through Virginia slightly faster than the late General Grant did, because of a slightly newer vehicle, name of 5C8592. If Grant was stopped—as he was, more than once—it was only fair that Chief of Police West Lowe should stop me. Which he did, with a short burst from Wagner's *Walküre* on his alto siren.

"How are you?" were his first words to me.

"Beg pardon?" said your correspondent, being distraught.

"I said, 'How are you?' " repeated the chief civilly.

"Not as well as I was a minute ago," I told him.

The reaction to this remark was calm but not enthusiastic. It seemed obvious that Chief Lowe was not a vaudeville fan, so I suspended the Marx-Benny gambit and let the chief handle the script alone, which led to a short excursion to the cottagelike office off the highway shared by the police of Prince George County and Justice of the Peace W. D. Williams. The justice told me that the date of trial would be a couple of weeks hence and, as is usual in these cases, added with barely a pause that the county was willing to take my recognizance and $22 and never see me again.

I am always struck by the fundamental friendliness of this formula. What struck me even more, as I stood there amid walls lined with fishing rods and counted out the forfeit, was a conversation between Chief West Lowe and another member of the force. It seemed to have to do with the comparative advantages of radar and the naked-eye-and-chase system, and the boys seemed to think that radar is overrated and that the naked eye is here to stay.

I hope they will pass this hunch along to the law of North Carolina, at the next interstate convention. It's time that North-South relations were put on a human basis everywhere.

Small World

1959

The Edward R. Murrow of "Small World," whom I think of as the Higher Murrow, concluded a season of top-level planetary conversations the other day. He'll be back, I'm glad to say, in October. The Lower Murrow, the Murrow of "Person to Person," will carry on till July, by way of filling certain obligations —including, I'm told, the obligation to keep the Whole Murrow clothed and fed during his coming holiday. "Person to Person" has, of course, been something more than just a Murrovian meal ticket. From time to time the Columbia Broadcasting System has sent me sets of statistics and other facts from its "Person to Person" file, among which was a list of guests (meaning people interviewed in their homes by the host) who went more or less straight from Murrow to marriage: to name a few of them, Joanne Woodward, Marilyn Monroe, Bing Crosby, Jayne Meadows, Eydie Gorme, Gisele MacKenzie, and Patti Page. "Somehow or other," the statistician wrote, " 'Person to Person' has had a kind of love-and-marriage effect on guests . . . [they] walked to the altar soon after being visited by Edward R. Murrow." The program has stimulated other trends as well, but this is probably the one that illustrates most clearly the difference between "Person to Person" guests and "Small World" guests—and the difference between the Higher and Lower Murrows.

As far as I know, no guest has been married after appearing on "Small World." Undoubtedly this is partly because most "Small World" guests have been married to begin with and in any case have usually been older and less impulsive people than "Person to Person" guests. But Mr. Murrow's own attitudes, his professional dualism, must have had a contributing influence. On "Small World," he has never been the friend of love and marriage. He has, on the contrary, done what he could to emphasize the danger to mankind of incipient overpopulation. To the best of my recollection, there has not been a word of warning on this point to "Person to Person" guests, who have accordingly gone off in high spirits and compounded the problem. On "Small World," Mr. Murrow has been every inch the responsible thinker—or, to put it more exactly, the organizer of responsible thought. He has arranged, with obvious care, certain intellectual groupings and has tried to project certain ideas into the conversation of each group. In other words, he has been a planner and shaper of discussions rather than a participant in them. I can't say that his plans have always worked out. But there *have* been a few excellent shows, and it's a tribute to Mr. Murrow's judgment that the best of these have been shows in which he was able to set a group to grappling with an idea of his own choosing. There was no "Small World" installment that I enjoyed more, for instance, than the one in which Senator Dirksen, of Illinois, resisted desperately the suggestion—planted in the talk by Mr. Murrow—that Abraham Lincoln might be something other than a Republican if he were alive today.

On that show, which took place in February, the picked conversationalists were the Senator; Carl Sandburg, the poet and Lincoln biographer; and C. Northcote Parkinson, former professor of political science at the University of Malaya and author of the book called *Parkinson's Law*. Senator Dirksen spoke from Washington, Mr. Sandburg from Chicago, and Professor Parkinson from the island of Alderney. (As you probably know, "Small World" specializes in bringing widely scattered thinkers into contact by means of the marvels of modern science. Pandit Nehru, Aldous Huxley, and Thomas E. Dewey have exchanged views while perched in New Dehli, Turin, and Portland, Maine, respectively. "Small World's" ingenuity has sometimes struck me as superfluous; in many cases—if not in the two I've mentioned—I've felt that the results might have been better if Mr. Murrow had assembled three appropriate brains in a single room in Paris, London, New York, Beverly Hills, or East St. Louis.) The thought that Mr. Murrow threw out to the Dirksen-Sandburg-Parkinson group, soon after he had called it to order, was this: Could Lincoln be nominated and elected today, and would he, if he ran at all, run on the Republican ticket? It's hard to say which branch of this complicated heresy disturbed Senator Dirksen more. The Senator is a performer of the old Shakespearean school, who bats his eyes during emotional passages, but there was no doubt of the reality of his emotion. "I do sincerely believe that he [Lincoln] would eschew the liberal stance!" he cried on one of the few occasions when the other speakers gave him a chance to state a view as roundly as he likes. For the most part, Mr. Sandburg and Professor Parkinson shocked and outtalked the Senator steadily, in a fluent, cynical kind of way.

Professor Parkinson's Law is said to deal with aspects of modern bureaucracy, and he seemed to be trying to oblige Mr. Murrow by stretching some of its points to cover the Lincoln argument.

"Today," he remarked vaguely, "the eccentric is suspect as he was not in Lincoln's time."

"Doctor, may I intrude?" said Senator Dirksen, distressed. But Mr. Sandburg took over instead to observe that although Lincoln might enjoy some success today on television as a comedian of the Will Rogers school, he would be doomed as a politician. "To succeed in politics now," the poet said, "one must be a solemn ass."

"Carl, may I intrude?" begged Senator Dirksen. "Look how solemn he was on that misty morning when . . ." The Senator had not gone far with this memory before someone turned the talk to Lincoln's putative politics. Lincoln, Mr. Sandburg said unkindly, would probably not be a Republican. "But," Senator Dirksen protested, "that fact that he was a conservative would make him a Republican in this somewhat accelerated age." Mr. Sandburg refused to allow that Lincoln was a conservative. He quoted from a speech in which Lincoln had aligned himself with "the liberals of the world."

"Carl, may I intrude at that point?" the Senator said plaintively. "May I intrude? His embrasure of Republican principles . . ." Mr. Sandburg, still being troublesome, said that in 1864 Lincoln had run on the National Union ticket. He went on, almost genially, to speak of the Lincoln administration's "expropriation" of slaves in the border states. He used the expression "Marxian seizure of property." And while Senator Dirksen gathered himself to repel these implications, Professor Parkinson came at the Senator with data about the problems of eccentric genius in our era. Lord Nelson, the Professor said, would be an outcast.

"I'd like to intrude at this point," said Senator Dirksen gamely.

"An individualist like Lincoln, an eccentric, simply wouldn't fit in," Professor Parkinson said.

"Doctor, may I intrude?" the Senator implored. "In this accelerated age, there is a great need for Lincoln's kind. There was a profound determinism about Lincoln. . . . In some busy mart of commerce, he would be equally as profound as he was in his day and generation. . . . I could never think of Lincoln as being eccentric," the Senator added, in broken tones.

When Professor Parkinson insisted that the Rail Splitter would be a failure in today's conformist world, Senator Dirksen said, "But Doctor, wouldn't he have adjusted, and in so doing, in this accelerated age, let a fecund mind and a profound spirit do the rest?"

Mr. Sandburg, unmoved, said that Lincoln's loneliness would be a problem. "Today," the Professor chimed in, "the lonely man would be taken over by psychoanalysts."

The Senator, his back to the wall, made a last effort. "One need not be lonely in solitude," he said, lowering his eyelids eloquently. "In daylight or in darkness, there is the opportunity for . . ." The hounds of psychology were on him again at once. But I admired the rich duplexity of his rhetoric and the gallantry of his fight to save Lincoln for the conservative stance.

I also thought that the Senator made a sound criticism when, after one of Professor Parkinson's glib excursions into contemporary cant, he said, "This is a little facetious, of course—unless, Doctor, there is something in your law, something obscure, that I do not see." The fact is that the Professor and his law (the joke of naming a law for oneself has grown threadbare over the years) were somewhat irrelevant in the circumstances; they struck a forced note. "Small World" groupings have suffered more than once on this score.

They have misfired on other occasions because of overresponsiveness by a guest, as in the case of lawyer Joseph Welch, of Boston, or because of a sort of arrogant exhibitionism, as in the cases of Sir Thomas Beecham, the conductor, and Maria Callas, the singer, The last two speakers were grouped with Victor Borge, the comedian, against whom they formed a snobbish coalition.

Not understanding, or perhaps not wanting to understand, the rules of Mr. Murrow's dignified parlor game, Sir Thomas and Mme Callas twitched and roared or snarled like animals in their first exposure to love or gunfire, and consistently snubbed Mr. Borge. "Then you're not a musician, sir!" Sir Thomas shouted at the comedian, the only time he spoke to him. Mme Callas called him "Mr. Borg" when she noticed him at all. Mr. Borge was the only one of the three who tried to talk sense instead of presenting violent or artistic poses. Unfortunately, his serious style of speech is the same as his comic style—he does not communicate well. In time, being an actor at heart, he became irritated by the ranting and mutual backslapping of the others and by their policy of ignoring him.

"Have I put my point, then?" Mme Callas said once, at the end of a monologue that had no bearing on a previous argument of Mr. Borge's.

"Yes, but not mine," said Mr. Borge with an arch but angry giggle.

On a much more civilized level, there was a hint of coalition and of standoffishness in the group that opened and closed Mr. Murrow's season—the Nehru-Huxley-Dewey party. Here, since each man is a calm, thoughtful speaker by habit, the general tone was courteous and serene. Still, Mr. Huxley and Mr. Nehru, the two Old World liberal seers, seemed ever so delicately and diplomatically to dissociate themselves from Mr. Dewey, the pragmatic spokesman for the busy, wealthy American *status quo*. Once or twice I thought Mr. Dewey was on the point of embarrassing himself and the others with a chamber-of-commerce note or an oversimplification. When he cited Japan as an example of postwar recovery in terms of industry and capital, Mr. Huxley reminded him, a little austerely, that the example was not well chosen, Japan having had certain advantages in the way of American Occupation trade and prewar training. Mr. Dewey's concern with "Communist world aggression" seemed to strike Mr. Nehru—though the Prime Minister was infinitely polite —as narrow. Toward the end of the closing show (both Nehru-Huxley-Dewey shows were arranged from film made last October), Mr. Murrow steered the conversation to the subject of "how to educate man to his best potential." The two seers went quickly to work on a high and visionary plane. Mr. Huxley proposed a planetary system of yoga. Mr. Nehru was dubious. Mr. Huxley said that there would have to be some form of "control" technique, and Mr. Nehru agreed. Mr. Dewey broke in eagerly to mention the fact that a great American corporation—"the Telephone Company, as a matter of fact"— has been sending its junior executives to take special courses in the liberal arts in Philadelphia. For a moment, the air seemed electric with stern silence. Then, happily, Mr. Dewey passed off his industrial news item with a joke, at which Mr. Nehru managed to laugh. At the finish, everything came out even, with a sensible, if high-minded, summary by each guest. It was, on the whole, one of the best and wisest "Small World" shows so far.

Docker the Knocker

1956

As EVERY STUDENT of newspapers knows, there are certain traditions of sex, or gender, in the filling of newspaper space.

Sports stories, theater reviews, and comic strips are written, traditionally, by men. (Women are barred from the press box in all major-league baseball parks, and from many a football press box as well. Only one major comic strip, as far as I know, is the work of a woman. It's a very bad strip, but that, I think, is pure coincidence. Two or three equally bad ones are done by men.)

On the other hand, weddings, new movies, and Presidents' wives are usually covered by women reporters.

It often happens to your correspondent that in reading the newspaper reports of a World Series, or of a heavyweight championship prizefight, or of a Broadway opening night, his taste becomes cloyed by the orgy of male writing and longs for an orgy of female writing. Such a revel, as you folks well know, was staged for us last week, when this royal personality got married to this girl from Philadelphia, over in this little locality by the Mediterranean Sea, there.

Weddings are women's work. And, boy, what a constellation of girls went to work on this one! Falkenburg . . . Swanson . . . Paddleford . . . Chase . . . Robb . . . Kilgallen . . . Not a weak spot in the batting order, unless you count Louisa May Alcott, who wasn't there. True, a certain number of male reporters slipped into the coverage, too. But they had the good taste to write just like the women, so it didn't make any difference.

It is hard to pick a favorite in such a line-up, but the wedding writer who won my heart and vote was Lady Norah Docker, the crowd-pleasing British girl who carried the blue-and-canary silks of the International News Service. Docker the Knocker, the railbirds called her. She wrote only one story about the royal couple. At least, I saw only one in print. Then she retired, and the rest of the women began to write about her, which is the mark of true class.

It is a rule among women wedding writers never to knock the bride or groom or anyone else except, perhaps, one another. Lady Docker broke this shibboleth from scratch. But then, she's unique among wedding writers, with the rugged charm of a Pegler, the fast, crisp style of a Bugs Baer. She knocked the bride. She knocked the groom. She knocked their yacht. All, as I say, in one round.

As the bell rang, Lady Docker advanced to the rail of her husband's yacht, which is three or four times bigger than the Prince's yacht. In her familiar role of Clocker Docker, she studied the field through her binoculars. Then she sprang to her typewriter.

"She [the bride] doesn't understand yachting," wrote Lady Docker, "or she would never wear any hat she has to hold on to."

The writer mused a moment, then added, "I suppose one would have to wear flat heels if one is Miss Kelly meeting Prince Rainier."

Ripping one sheet of chinchilla out of the machine and inserting a fresh one, she went on, "Now I'd have worn my ermine greatcoat with matching beret and handbag." Warming to her work, she continued, "The girl probably didn't know the size of Rainier's yacht. I'd call it a bit snug."

Gaining speed and sweetness in the stretch, Lady Docker wound up: "Of course, Rainier doesn't have to worry about the fact that the ceilings on his yacht aren't very high. Neither is he. But Miss Kelly is rather a tall girl." With these words, Lady Docker retired from the wedding-writing grift, as far as the American press was concerned, and went ashore to look for other kinds of trouble.

So strong was her impact that a few days later we find Miss Kilgallen, also of International, denouncing Docker the Knocker in print—a most unusual procedure among INS stablemates, but a blow in defense of wholesome wedding coverage. Miss Kilgallen's stuff was wholesome throughout. In the late rounds at Monaco, Lady Docker was walking up to wholesome wedding reporters, saying to them, "Why don't you go home?"

A Happy Sullivan Day

1959

SUNDAY, JUNE 22, was the tenth anniversary of "The Ed Sullivan Show" (originally "Toast of the Town"), by proclamation of the Columbia Broadcasting System. It was also Ed Sullivan Day in twelve states, by proclamation of twelve governors. A quick count indicates that thirty-six states, as well as several territories and networks, remained out of step. In some of these, June 22 was just Sunday. In others it was, as usual, Re-entry into the Union Day, or Bull Moose Day, or Organic Act Day (Virgin Islands). In New Hampshire it was merely the day after New Hampshire Day; in Massachusetts it was five days after Bunker Hill Day; in Montana it was three days before Little Bighorn Day; and in New York it was three days before Harry K. Thaw Day. On the National, American, and Dumont networks, it was, at best, Steve Allen Day, Maverick Day, and Uncommon Valor (a rerun) Day, respectively. On the whole this represents a pretty disorganized showing, but there's reason to think that by the time the next decennial arrives, Ed Sullivan Day will be recognized nationally and internationally, and even the dissident networks will feel an obligation to run the Sullivan show and nothing else between the hours of 8 and 9 P.M. on the appropriate Sunday. The thought is based on Mr. Sullivan's past form as an influence. In his first ten years in television, for instance, he was able to bring the world of show business so sharply into line that his anniversary hour the other day—devoted to a review, in kinescope, of the "personalities" who have appeared on the program—literally teemed with famous people (some of whom have since passed to their rewards, with a sense of duty fulfilled). A "host of stars" was what C.B.S. called the collection. By my reckoning, there were fifty-five personalities, not counting water skiers and ventriloquists' dummies.

Mr. Sullivan himself is a full-sized personality by now, as the *News,* the paper in which he mounted to glory, pointed out in a sort of memorial issue on Ed Sullivan Day. The *News* added several lines of almost pure poetry on the subject, including the following: "His 20-year contract with C.B.S.-T.V. gives Sullivan $50,000 a week to put together the Sunday night 'Ed Sullivan Show.' By the terms of the contract, his weekly cut is over $8,000 for a period of seven years, after which he will get $100,000 a year for not working for another network. (Half of the seven-year salary is held back by C.B.S.-TV, to be paid to him during the 13-year period. His present take-home pay after taxes is $37,500 a year.)" A point the paper failed to make is that Mr. Sullivan has become, through television, not only an outstanding showman and a seven-year withholdee but also, and perhaps most notably, a graduate student of the races of mankind. C.B.S. emphasized this fact in its own holiday proclamation. Mr. Sullivan, the network said, travels more than two hundred thousand miles a year nowadays in the interest of his program; like John Foster Dulles or a Harlem Globetrotter, he is here today and gone tomorrow. A week before the anniversary he was in Brussels, putting the Fair on the screen. From there he sped home to observe Ed Sullivan Day and to fire an American musical conductor from his next project—the Moiseyev dancers, June 29—for invoking Constitutional amendments at a Congressional hearing. He replaced the American conductor with a Russian conductor, who, presumably, could take the Constitution or leave it alone. The Brussels show and the Moiseyev show, like Ed Sullivan Day in between them, were marked by a guidebook flavor and by a strong awareness of national characteristics and national distinctions. All three events were carried off without regard to race, creed, or color, in keeping with a policy that has long been familiar to admirers of Mr. Sullivan's newspaper column, and that might be stated, in part, as follows: " . . . regardless of race, so long as the audience is told which race it's regardless of." To veteran Sullivan readers, the chief virtue of

"The Ed Sullivan Show" is that it has given a natural-born ethnologist the time and money to study first-hand, in their native habitats, the races he has written about for so many years, and even to bring back certain specimens alive. Mr. Sullivan was the first American to televise a Piaf, a Patachou, and a Señor Wences. As a scout and importer of foreign talent, he is the peer of Barnum, of the Ringlings, and of Walter (Good-Time Charlie) Friedman, the famous collector of exotic boxers who trapped Primo Carnera and shipped him to the American market.

Mr. Sullivan's mind, as his readers and listeners know, is a store-house of exact genealogies and clear-cut racial nuances. It's said that Good-Time Charlie Friedman once went scouting in China for a "white hope" to whip Jack Johnson, a Negro heavyweight champion. Mr. Sullivan's thinking has always been free of that kind of confusion. The mere mention of the word "race" will stimulate him to single out the essential fact of any matter. I remember that a race for horses, the Kentucky Derby, led him to write, a few years ago: "Americans of Italian blood [are] getting a great wallop out of Nashua, Kentucky Derby favorite, as his granddaddy was the Italian horse, Nearco, sire of Nasrullah. The Derby will be an all-paisan affair, with Arcaro aboard Nashua." You'll probably recall that Americans of Italian blood expressed the wallop they got from this state of affairs in scenes of wild excitement from coast to coast as soon as they had it straight in their minds whether it was Arcaro who was Nashua's granddaddy, with Nearco aboard, or vice versa. There were supplementary orgies among the Iroquois and the Creeks, in honor of Nasrullah, before a government directive could be issued to explain that Nasrullah was the wrong type of Indian and to urge the revelers to disband.

The Sullivan show's visit to Brussels, June 15, was a high point in Mr. Sullivan's new career as a field racist. Belgium itself, of course, as a hotbed of ethnic stocks (Flemings, Walloons, Belgae), can provide material for a number of *News* columns. At the Fair, Mr. Sullivan and his staff ran riot as they photographed—with excellent results, in the main, I should add—the symptomatic products of Russia and the Philippines and the tribal diversions of the French (a race compounded of Frankish, Gallic, Aquitanian, and Breton strains, among others) and the British (Picts, Celts, Jutes, Angles, Saxons, Normans, etc.). The program that day included a graveyard sequence—a tribute, couched in muted music, dramatic rhetoric, and artistic camera rhythms, to American soldiers who have died in Belgium. This passage had no visible connection whatever with the Fair. It can probably be accounted for by Mr. Sullivan's scientific emotion at finding himself in a hive of nationalities, and by his grateful thought that America is a melting pot in which races have not yet melted as thoroughly as they have elsewhere. Our graves, the announcer said (as so many writers of screenplays and poems have said before him), contain Caseys, Cohens, Garcias, Joneses, Lombardis, and Swansons alike.

As previously noted, Mr. Sullivan came home from his researches to find that he'd been betrayed, as he considered it, by an American who wouldn't answer certain questions in Congress. The firing of the conductor, Arthur Lief, required more skill and purpose, perhaps, than the average impresario can manage. Mr. Lief's agent made things difficult by revealing that Mr. Lief had not been scheduled to appear on the Sullivan show to begin with. Mr. Sullivan dismissed this argument as a quibble and fired Mr. Lief anyway. "I don't want him in the theater," he said. His statesmanly gesture was made three days before Ed Sullivan Day. The holiday itself was bright and fair. It was cooler, especially after the sun went down, than June 22 can be expected to be in future years. Still, the country has come to accept heat and discomfort as a natural part of some national holidays, like the Fourth of July. The traffic-death toll on Sullivan Day was about what the police had anticipated.

A
VARIETY
OF SPORTS

The Roller Derby

1949

IT DEVELOPS that there are certain parts of this country in which the thing called the Roller Derby is still unknown. The people in such places live in the same state of uneasy innocence as the Indians did before the white man came along, bringing them civilization, uncut whiskey, glass beads for all hands, and two or three new variations of hoof-and-mouth disease.

It's a matter of record that the Indians could not get this kind of civilization fast enough, once they had a look at it, and the same thing is true of the Roller Derby. Those in America who have not yet seen the Derby are sending out loud, clear calls to know what it is all about. The more advanced tribes who have tasted the Derby by television or been exposed to it in person are clamoring and stampeding for more—or so we are told by Mr. Leo A. Seltzer, who sells the stuff to the natives.

Of course, Mr. Seltzer's definition of a stampede is flexible. Back in 1935 B.T. (Before Television), when he tried his first Roller Derby on the public for size, Mr. Seltzer was satisfied with a stampede of three hundred or four hundred people, at any wide place in the road. He did not care how many of them wore shoes. Today, in the age of so-called video, he measures his clients by the million. The incidence of shoes among them is getting higher. Some even wear neckties. In short, Mr. Seltzer feels he has finally got hold of the *bon ton,* and got them where it hurts.

The Roller Derby, mark you, is a sport. Its backers will stand up and raise their right hands and swear it is. And they are right. Defenestration is also a sport, for those who like it (defenestration is pushing people out of windows). So is extravasation (extravasation is blood-letting, with a license). So is lapidation (lapidation is stoning people to death, or near there). So is the grand old game of suttee, which consists of barbecuing live widows over a charcoal fire.

So, for that matter, is wrestling—and here we are getting close to the meat of the matter. For wrestling is the thing that the Roller Derby threatens to replace, in certain ways. When the television business started to warm up, after the war, it was found that many set owners took a morbid interest in the actions of wrestlers like Primo Carnera and Gorgeous George. The more grotesque, the better. Then televised wrestling began to seem a little cold and stately. That was the spot into which the Roller Derby stepped.

Mr. Seltzer and his staff of calculators estimate that of the more than a million new addicts who paid to see his skaters in the last year, 91 per cent were won and brought over by the telecasts of noted television broadcasters like Joe Hasel of WJZ-TV, in New York City, where the Roller Derby broke into Madison Square Garden this year and took its place in Garden history with the Democratic Convention of 1924 (also a sport). That is a pretty solid estimate, that 91 per cent, for Mr. Seltzer did not just pull it out of the air, like a butterfly. He went around to the customers in person, feeling their pulses, and asked them, "What in the world brings you to my place, friend?" Most of them said television, which is good enough for Mr. Seltzer. He now feels that, after thirteen lean years or so, the tide has turned, that the nation is his oyster, that America is about to break out with Roller Derby teams and leagues at every pore.

Your correspondent set out the other day to learn the details of the sport, in behalf of those tribes which have not yet put their wampum on the line to see it. It was a most interesting visit. As I knocked at the door, they were just pulling six inches of light, seasoned timber out of the flank of Miss Marjorie Clair Brashun, daughter of a plumber from St. Paul, Minnesota. Miss Brashun, known to the trade for what seem to be satisfactory reasons as Toughie, is one of the leading female skaters of the Roller Derby troupe. Since she likes to wear wood next to her skin, she had gone on skating for some time before the house doctors learned that she had bumped into the guard rail of the track and acquired a piece of it internally.

The sight of Miss Brashun being defrosted caused a slight argument among the Roller Derby people as to whether she is four feet eleven or four feet ten in height. Personally, I think it might be one or the other. I have never gone close enough to a live rattlesnake to put a tape measure on it, and in the same way I am willing to be an inch or two wrong about Miss Brashun.

"The girls in this sport are tougher than the boys," said Mr. Seltzer.

"That's right," snarled Miss Brashun.

"If the girls have a fight on the track," said Mr. Seltzer, "they go right on fighting after the match, maybe for two or three years. In their spare time they spit in each other's teacups. But the girls have a weakness. They are tender in the coccyx."

The coccyx, it should be said, is a vestigial bone at the southern end of the spine. Women skaters wear a special strip of sponge rubber over this area, since they are always falling upon it and making it ring like a bell. In fact, their uniforms are padded all over, and so are the men's—with hip pads, shoulder pads, and thigh pads, topped off by a helmet borrowed partly from football and partly from Marshal Rommel's Afrika Korps. There is lots of padding, but not enough.

A Mr. Billy Reynolds went to the hospital recently with six breaks in one leg. A Miss Margie Anderson (out of Miami) had twenty-four stitches taken in her shapely Gothic torso. A Miss Virginia Rushing broke her pelvic bone in a warm debate, but went on skating for several weeks before she noticed it. Your correspondent would estimate that the number of stitches embroidered in Mr. Seltzer's troupe each week is about the same as Betsy Ross took in making the first flag.

Before establishing the fact that the Roller Derby is, like cutting throats, a sport, let us glance at its history for a moment. Mr. Seltzer, who operates out of Chicago, is an old dance-marathon man. You can tell by the way he stands erect and looks at the world through clear eyes that he got out of that business long ago. At the peak of the Depression he rounded up a few roller skaters and went on the road with the first Derby. For a while, like Virginia Rushing with her pelvic bone, nobody noticed. Things were tough and slow. Once, among the Southern hills, twenty-two of the skaters were killed in a bus accident. It may be, in view of the way they made their living, that this was an easy and merciful death, but probably not, for the skaters seem to enjoy the work.

Today, old-timers come up to the Derby's doors in each town it plays and introduce themselves as former members of the troupe. Recently a deaf-mute pants presser approached the Seltzer staff and opened conversation with the following written message: "I'm an old Roller Derby ace." He was, at that, and the sight of him reminded Mr. Seltzer that the man was probably responsible for the fact that the Derby today enjoys a strong deaf-mute following wherever it plays.

Now that the show—beg pardon, sport—has struck gold, it plays mostly the big towns in the television belt. It carries a squad of anywhere from thirty skaters up (there were sixty-five at Madison Square Garden), half of them men, half women, and a portable Masonite track which is eighteen laps, or two quarts of blood, to the mile. It also packs a staff of referees, medical men, and penalty boxes. The referees put the skaters into the penalty boxes if the medical men have not previously put them into local hospitals.

There are certain laws of God and man the violation of which, I am told, will get a skater thrown out of the match for the night, but I hesitate to imagine what those could be. The penalty boxes take care of the rest, as in hockey. As in football, blocking is encouraged. As in six-day bike racing, you can jam and sprint at will. As in osteopathy, you can probe for new bones in your fellow man. As in wrestling—well, I was especially interested in the work of a Mr. Silver Rich, who has developed a two-handed kidney punch from behind which puts me strongly in mind of the technique of the five wrestling Duseks from Omaha. It is extremely legal by Roller Derby rules.

The squad is divided into separate teams of boys and girls, the boys playing the boys for fifteen minutes, then the girls playing the girls for fifteen minutes, and so on alternately, while Mr. Seltzer counts the house. In a wholesome, high-spirited way, Mr. Seltzer calls the teams by the names of towns, such as Brooklyn, New York, Philadelphia, and Cleveland. A player like Miss Toughie Brashun (but there are, I am glad to say, no other players like Miss Brashun) will represent Brooklyn in the same way that Mr. Luis Olmo, the Dodger from South America, represents Brooklyn—that is, she wears a Brooklyn shirt.

There is a further similarity, and Happy Chandler can sue me if he likes, between baseball and the skating dodge. The skaters do not like new equipment. They hone, grind, cut, gouge, and chew on their skates and shoes as ballplayers hone their bats, break in their gloves, and cut their shirtsleeves. They sometimes get friends to break in their shoes, and they file down their wooden skate wheels so close that Mr. Seltzer has to supply them with three or four new sets of wheels apiece per evening. The wheels are wooden because metal wheels set up such a vibration that Miss Brashun, for instance, could not hear herself thinking up a plan to murder Miss Gerry Murray, her deadliest rival, in cold blood, if she wore them.

As in bike racing, the fastest skaters on each team sprint for points—one point for passing one rival within two minutes, two points for three, and five points for passing the whole enemy team of five. The other skaters form packs to deter hostile sprinters from passing. At the end of the match, the winning and losing teams split a percentage of the gate on a 60-40 basis and walk, or are carried, home to supper. In their spare time, roller skaters often get married to each other. Miss Brashun is the bride of a skater named Ken Monte, while Miss Murray is Mrs. Gene Gammon in private life. Like other people, skaters have children, and these, Mr. Seltzer hopes, will grow up to be skaters too. The supply is short, and he cannot afford to miss a bet.

That raises the question of where Roller Derby skaters come from. Some of them used to be bike-riders, some of them used to be ice-skaters, some of them used to be ballplayers, and some of them used to be home girls. A Miss Peggy Smalley was a home girl on a high hill in Tennessee when the Roller Derby suddenly surrounded her. The skate shoes they gave her were the first shoes she had ever seen. If it weren't for the skates, she would throw them away. It is claimed that one of the boys in the troupe deserted the St. Louis Cardinal chain for the Derby because he could make more money that way. That may be a gratuitous sneer at baseball, but on the other hand, thinking about the Cardinals, it may be true. Mr. Billy Bogash, recognized as the Ty Cobb of roller skating, makes consistently better than $10,000 a year, and when a good girl skater and a good boy skater have the presence of mind to marry each other, the pair can knock down from $15,000 to $20,000 per annum, as well as everything that gets in their way.

Pending the arrival of the next generation, Mr. Seltzer has got to dig up and train new skaters to keep the market supplied. Toward this end he runs a skating school in Chicago, where prospects are polished at the house's expense. It takes about a year of training to get a skater ready for the "pack," and three years to make a top point-sprinting performer. Like piano teachers who dislike to take on pupils who have learned to play "Yankee Doodle" with one finger, Mr. Seltzer prefers absolutely fresh recruits with no fixed skating tricks and no bad habits. A bad habit in a roller skater, for instance, would be kindness. Those things have got to be pruned out of the subject while he is young.

The new Roller Derby helmets, which were put on view for the first time at Madison Square Garden, are not entirely popular with skaters, especially the ladies (I use the word in a general sense) among them. Neither are all the pads. There is a certain vanity among girl skaters, when they are not too busy tattooing their initials on the shins of the next girl, and they point out that Mr. Seltzer's scheme of padding, while technically useful on the track, does not coincide with nature's scheme. They prefer nature's. As for the helmets, there are two things against them. The ladies like to have their hair float behind them in the breeze when they skate. It looks better. Also, the helmet protects the hair of their victims. A lady skater who cannot sink her hands wrist-deep into the coiffure of an enemy, take a good hold, and pull of the scalp at the roots feels frustrated. She feels that her individual liberties have been violated. She wonders what to do with herself.

"Have a heart," said Miss Toughie Brashun to Mr. Seltzer the other day. "I have my eye on a hair-do that I want to rip open from here to Texas."

"Nothing doing," said the chief sternly. "Helmets will be worn. Safety first. Players desiring concussions must obtain them on their own time. Security and dignity are the rule of the sport."

"That's what you think," muttered Miss Brashun, baring her fangs. The final issue remains in doubt. As we go to press, history awaits the outcome.

No Scar, No Memory

1957

CHICAGO—An oddly shocking and confusing thing— neither good nor very bad, neither just nor very cruel—happened to Gene Fullmer, the young Mormon prizefighter, in the boxing hall here the other night. When he went into the ring, his life was at its peak. He was famous, newly rich, powerful, confident, rising. A few minutes later, he fell from power and glory to frustration and relative nothingness. And he cannot tell you of his own knowledge what happened. Not only power and glory are gone—the facts are missing too. Thirty seconds of time, at a climax of his existence, are lost to him.

To know what went on he has to be told. To believe it he has to look at a set of pictures. And this will be true for the rest of his life. It will be a strange, unsettling way to live.

Fullmer missed seeing the punch that jarred his brain off the track of memory. He missed hearing the sudden yell of rapture that filled the hall at the count of ten. He missed the sight—and maybe he can spare it—of Ray Robinson riding five feet in the air on the shoulders of his henchmen.

After he had been levered to his feet, Fullmer walked to his corner with his gray, bumpy face thirsty for information. A baby looks like that sometimes, when he is trying to catch up with the world all at once. "Why did they stop it?" he asked Marv Jensen, his friend and manager. "Well," said Jensen dryly, with a kind of noncommittal tenderness, "mostly because you were counted out."

A minute or two after that, Fullmer stood side by side in the middle of the ring with Robinson, and they talked a little together as they posed for the cameramen. Fullmer spoke earnestly. The same anxious look was on his face. "I don't know anything about it," I heard him say. "I couldn't tell you what happened." Robinson looked down at him, gave a smile, said something, and patted Fullmer gaily on the top of the head. It was the first time in an hour that anything had distracted Ray's attention from the thought of his own work and his own triumph. Perhaps he was struck suddenly by the curious emptiness of the other man's situation—not a scar, but not a memory either, to show for his night's work and his downfall.

Before that, Robinson's mind had been entirely dedicated to the job in hand, as a great artist's should be. They had been telling him in his corner what he'd already figured out: "Hit him coming in, hit him coming in." It's hard to gauge the speed of a strong, lunging man at close quarters, and harder to check him, without a crowbar. But at the start of the fourth round Robinson smacked Fullmer with a quick right lead, as they came together, and slowed him down, and after that he could time his moves. In the fifth he hit Fullmer with a long right to the body. It was a disconcerting blow. Fullmer took a backward step—and when he came on again he was slower, and he was watching the right. It was the last thing that Gene Fullmer saw, or remembered.

Today, every left-hand punch except a jab (and sometimes even that) is called a "hook." It's one of those language trends, a majority rule of speech which I won't try to resist. But a hook, as the word was conceived for boxing, is a short, intimate punch, thrown laterally, inside, with the left side already forward. It was no left hook that stripped Fullmer of his consciousness and turned his life upside down. It was a full left swing, or larrup, if you like, perfectly pivoted, perfectly timed, thrown from two feet outside, moving up and forward straight to the seat of concussion in the point of the jawbone.

"He got the message," Robinson said afterward, abandoning the use of French for his curtain lines, and stealing one from Archie Moore.

He then spoke well of God, his wife, his son, Joe Louis, the Bureau of Internal Revenue, and his future in the theater. "I may never fight again," he said at dawn next day. At ten o'clock he began to dicker for 35 per cent of the gate with Carmen Basilio. Fullmer will never know how it happened—but he was licked last week by the perfect artist and the perfect dealer in gibberish. In short, the perfect schizophrene.

They Walked by Night

1950

ONE DAY in 1922 a large, convivial fellow from the South, Shufflin' Phil Douglas by name, was thrown out of baseball on a quick double play by John J. McGraw and Judge Kenesaw Mountain Landis. The event took place in Pittsburgh. Mournfully borrowing a hundred dollars from McGraw, the outlaw climbed on a train for New York to collect his wife and children and take them off into exile with him. Sharing the ride with him was his very own personal watchdog. It was their last ride together.

A dog is said to be man's best friend, and there were tears in the eyes of both parties as the train rolled East.

"Let's have a beer at the next stop, Jess," said Mr. Douglas to the watchdog, whose name was Jess Burkett. "I'm gonna miss you."

"I'm gonna miss you too, Phil," said Mr. Burkett with a manly catch in his throat. "Why, hell, I'm so used to following you from saloon to saloon, making notes, that I won't know what to do with myself."

It's a matter of record that the New York Giants didn't know exactly what to do with Burkett, either, once Douglas was kicked out of baseball. They finally sent him on the road as a scout. For many months before that, Jess's only task with the Giants had been to watch Douglas—watch him and report. He always had something to report, too, for in the company of Shufflin' Phil there was seldom a dull moment, or a dry one.

It may well be that the Shuffler was the only man in baseball history ever to have a detective all to himself for the whole season. The great Rube Waddell, one of the game's foremost night-walkers, could not make such a boast. Rube's boss, Connie Mack, was too frugal to waste a whole detective on one man. Casey Stengel, when he played for the Giants, had to share a detective with a teammate, Irish Meusel. When Casey stopped going out with Meusel at night, McGraw sold him to Boston rather than sign the check for an extra shadow at union rates. "If you think I'm going to pay to have you followed all alone, you're mistaken, my friend," said McGraw to Stengel. And he proved it.

But Shufflin' Phil Douglas was something else again. He had to be followed in a big, exclusive way.

The era of the night-walking ballplayer—the man with a single-minded thirst and feet that point away from home—is just about over and gone. So is the era of the detective in baseball. True, Bucky Harris, when he managed the New York Yankees in 1948, is said to have hired gumshoes to stalk a few of his players. The Yankees should have been easy to stalk because, belonging to a high-class ball club, they drank martinis and left a trail of olives. Groping from olive to olive, however, the cops were sidetracked by the onion in a Gibson-type martini one day and lost the scent. Nothing much came of the Harris hunt.

The last outstanding night-walkers in baseball were Rollicking Rollie Hemsley, until he joined Alcoholics Anonymous, and Baron Boots Poffenberger, until he joined the Marines. I rate them close behind Phil Douglas, though a case can be made out for Charles Flint Rhem of Rhems, South Carolina, as the most ingenious of all the night-walkers. It was Rhem, in 1930, after he had been missing from the sight of man for forty-eight hours, who reported back to his team, the St. Louis Cardinals, pale and shaken, with the story that he had been kidnaped by gangsters, locked in a hotel room, and forced to drink great quantities of liquor at the point of a gun.

With Poffenberger and Hemsley, the leading rebels of our own generation, detectives were seldom used. The owners of these two wandering pieces of merchandise resorted to the method of the straight cash fine, or plaster. Life was a race between owner and player to see which would come out ahead financially at the end of the season. There were times when Rollie and the Baron, fighting off drought in the desert sands of Chicago, Philadelphia, or Cincinnati, were fined to a point where their pay checks touched bottom, but they rallied strongly toward the end of each year and almost never failed to break even.

Phil Douglas, who will always be king of the AWOLs in your correspondent's book, was the largest man in baseball in his day, and thus had the most trouble keeping his tanks full, though he worked very hard at the job. The Shuffler, standing six feet four and weighing better than two hundred pounds, was a pitcher—and a great one. He had a spitball, a rubber arm, and a world of shrewdness, which he always left in the ball park after a day's work so as not to be bothered with excess baggage when he went out to the water holes at night.

Philip broke in with the Rome, Georgia, team, and in 1915 worked his way rapidly through the Cincinnati, Brooklyn, and Chicago clubs of the National League, where he attempted to introduce a labor routine that was far ahead of anything the CIO or the AFL has yet proposed. Mr. Douglas liked to consider his absences from duty as vacations, and he argued that he was entitled to a vacation after each pitching turn.

"So long as I win some ball games for the club, which is what I am paid to do," he used to say, "what difference does it make what I do between times? A fella like me has got to relax."

This sounds reasonable to the outside observer but it wore out the nerves of the patient Uncle Wilbert Robinson in Brooklyn, and several other managers. Relaxing in a subway car in Brooklyn one day in 1917, when he worked for the Cubs, Mr. Douglas put his pitching hand in an electric fan suspended from the ceiling. Both the hand and the fan were somewhat damaged, but since Phil could lift beer with his left hand in emergencies, he bore the subway company no ill will and took a pleasant, unscheduled vacation. What with one thing and another, the Cubs decided to sell him to the Giants in the summer of 1919.

The date of the sale coincided with a Douglas vacation, so that the Giants did not see the Shuffler for several days after they had bought him. A little later, on the eve of an important series with Cincinnati, he disappeared again. This absence cost the Giants $40,000, which was the sum they sent to Boston to get Artie Nehf, the southpaw, to fill the hole in their pitching staff. It was a fine investment in the long run, since Nehf became a Giant hero, but at the moment McGraw felt that $40,000 apiece was too much to pay for Douglas vacations.

"You are through for life," he told Phil when the latter reappeared still vibrating slightly from the effects of his holiday. "I can't use you."

"There'll come a day when you'll be sorry, Mac," said Mr. Douglas reproachfully, borrowing an expression from seven hundred and forty-six popular songs.

The day came in 1920, and Shufflin' Phil was reinstated. In a game with the Phillies in June of that year, Mr. Douglas began a vacation a little earlier than usual—while he was still pitching. The Phils got nineteen hits off him. Taking the pitcher aside after the game, McGraw called him four new names for each of the nineteen hits. Phil's feelings were hurt, and he disappeared. This time he was gone four days.

McGraw came to the conclusion that what Philip needed was someone to watch him twenty-four hours a day. The appointment of Jess Burkett as chief inspector in charge of Douglas followed soon afterward. Burkett found that Douglas, because of his size, was hard to lose in a crowd, but that the crowd was always standing around a bar. However, he kept the Shuffler out of important trouble throughout the season of 1921, which turned out to be Douglas' best and driest. Two one-hit games were pitched in the National League that year, both by Douglas. In the World Series against the Yankees he started three games, all against Carl Mays, and won two of them. He began the season of 1922 in high gear, with Burkett closer to him than his own undershirt.

That was, however, the year of the Shuffler's final binge—a beauty—and his final tragedy. On July 31, he won his eleventh game of the season. He felt an overpowering need for a vacation. He could move fast when he had to, and a few hours later Burkett lost him. Before they could get Douglas back in line again, he had washed himself out of baseball for good.

There are two stories of what went on in the first week of August 1922—the Douglas story and the Burkett-McGraw story—and they check pretty closely. Douglas, stopping here and there to take on the high octane fuel of the Volstead age, came to a party at a friend's apartment in New York, where he passed out. Before he did so, however, there was a friendly argument, conducted two octaves above middle C, and the neighbors complained. Two detectives from the nearest police station came to investigate the complaint. When they returned to the station, they took the Shuffler with them in an ambulance. He was a large package to keep around the house, so the law telephoned Judge Francis X. McQuade, a Giant executive, to ask what should be done with him. The Judge got in touch with a snake pit, or sanitarium, on Central Park West, and booked Philip in.

Douglas could not get out of the sanitarium for several days. That, of course, was part of the rules of the treatment—unsolicited—that they were giving him. When he did get out, the Shuffler had several hypodermic holes in his arm and a wild idea in his head. On August 7 he went to the Giant clubhouse at the Polo Grounds, got some Giant stationery from the attendant, and wrote a letter to Leslie Mann, an outfielder then working for the St. Louis Cardinals, who were playing in Boston. It was a letter that led to front-page stories a few days later. It ran:

DEAR LESLIE

I want to leave here. I don't want this guy [meaning McGraw] to win the pennant and I feel if I stay here I will win it for him. You know I can pitch and win. So you see the fellows, and if you want to send a man over here with the goods, and I will leave for home on the next train, send him to my house so nobody will know, and send him at night. I am living at 145 Wadsworth Avenue, Apartment 1R. Nobody will ever know. I will go down to fishing camp and stay there. I am asking you this way so there can't be any trouble for anyone. Call me up if you all are sending a man. Wadsworth 3210. Do this right away. Let me know. Regards to all.

PHIL DOUGLAS.

It was McGraw whom Shufflin' Phil considered responsible for his troubles, and it was McGraw—before he knew about the letter—who bawled Douglas out for taking his last vacation but, to the Shuffler's surprise, did not fire him. According to Douglas, the pitcher then telephoned Mann in Boston and asked him to destroy the letter. It was too late. Mann had turned the hot potato over to his manager, Branch Rickey, fifteen minutes after he received it. Rickey sent the letter to McGraw.

On August 18, after a meeting with Judge Landis in a Pittsburgh hotel, McGraw announced that Douglas had been put on the permanently retired list. Douglas, who had just rejoined the club to go to work, was shuffling through the lobby that afternoon, when he met Landis.

"Is this true, Judge," he asked, "that I'm through with baseball?"

"Yes, Douglas, it is," said the Judge.

It was. The Shuffler and Jess Burkett made their last tearful trip back to New York together, and a few hours later Phil Douglas disappeared from the game forever. In 1934 a reporter found him raising hogs, dogs and grandchildren, fairly happily, in a small town in Tennessee, where he also sang in the church choir. Some years afterward, however, he was found again, this time in Alabama, living in a shack on relief. No night-walker ever paid for his pleasure quite so stiffly as Douglas. On the other hand, the rest of them did not write the kind of letters Phil did. Most of them didn't write letters at all. They were too busy.

Of Rollicking Ralston Hemsley, the Brown, Indian, Cub, Pirate, Red, and Yankee catcher, it can be said that no one ever worked harder to make his pay check come out ahead of his fines for the month. It was an uphill fight, for Rollie had a motion he used for throwing the ball down to second base which he often used in the soda fountains at night, with no ball in his hand. He could clean up a Pullman car, including the inmates, faster than any porter in the trade. Rollie was a serious fellow as well as a good catcher, so that when he decided to quit the sauce he did it in a thorough way, with the help of Alcoholics Anonymous. His gain was history's loss.

For a time, Cletus Elwood Poffenberger of Williamsport, Maryland, carried on the struggle for self-expression alone. Mr. Poffenberger, known to a narrow circle of admirers, which included himself, as Baron Boots, was perhaps the greatest night-walker of modern times. Disappearing was so strong an impulse in the Baron that it became a habit. Once, when fired by the Brooklyn Dodgers, he applied for unemployment compensation in Michigan. On the day his papers and cash were ready in Michigan, Mr. Poffenberger had disappeared. He hated to stand still long enough even to take free money.

The Baron was a man of culture, who had broad views about curfews. The curfew—the deadline for getting to bed at night for ballplayers—was midnight among the Dodgers. Poffenberger was almost always in at midnight—by San Francisco time when the team was in Cincinnati, by Honolulu time when the team was in St. Louis.

Leo Durocher, who managed the Baron for Brooklyn, tells of sitting in the lobby of the Bellevue-Stratford Hotel in Philadelphia for three nights running, watching Boots come home. On the morning after the third night, he grabbed Mr. Poffenberger's buttonhole and charged him with kicking the curfew to pieces.

"You've come in after midnight for three nights," he snarled.

"Not by my calculations," said the Baron suavely. "You've noticed those clocks in the hotel lobby. I go by the second one from the top on the left-hand side, and I'm home by midnight every night."

The clocks in the hotel showed the time of day in all the great cities of the world. The clock the Baron went by showed standard time in Denver.

It may be that Mr. Durocher's stories about Poffenberger are not strictly reliable, for after Boots was fired, Leo denied he had ever wanted to hire him and laid the blame on Larry MacPhail. Other witnesses say it was Leo's idea, that he was sure beforehand that he could reform Mr. Poffenberger. He couldn't, so why should he dwell on his failures?

The Baron was a young right-handed pitcher with a great deal of stuff. "He drank a great deal of stuff, so why shouldn't he have it?" said a teammate one day.

Boots' first big-league club was Detroit, which he joined a few days late, saying that he had taken the wrong train in Chicago. There was no curfew rule on the Tigers when Poffenberger arrived, but there was soon afterward. In 1937 he was good enough to beat Bob Feller one day. In 1938 he was enterprising enough to leave the team in Washington and tour the world by himself. The next that manager Mickey Cochrane saw of Boots was in the Tiger clubhouse in Philadelphia, where the wanderer suddenly turned up in a card game.

On this occasion the Baron was fined one hundred dollars and suspended for seven weeks. Del Baker, the next Detroit manager, complained of Poffenberger's tendency toward fat, especially around the head. "We take two pounds off him every day and he puts on three every night," said Mr. Baker.

Brooklyn paid about $20,000 for Boots in 1939, and a few months later his big-league career came to an end. He missed the train out of New York to Boston one night, though he was thoughtful enough to leave a dummy in his berth for Durocher to talk to when he checked up. The Dodgers recovered two hundred dollars of Poffenberger's purchase price the next day, out of Poffenberger's pocket. In Cincinnati, soon afterward, they got back four hundred dollars more. Touring the hotel at midnight, Mr. Durocher found

Boots absent from his bed. He was also absent from a clubhouse meeting at the ball park next day.

"I saw Poffenberger at the hotel," said Dolph Camilli, the first baseman, to Durocher, "and he asked me to give you a message. He said it was too hot to work today. He also said he didn't like the way you are treating him."

This cost Boots two fines of two hundred dollars each, but before the Baron could be reduced to bankruptcy he was sold to Montreal. He did not appear in Montreal. He appeared in Nashville in 1940. He behaved with great circumspection there until 1941, when he threw a ball at an umpire's head and was sold to San Diego. In the wartime year of 1943 the Baron joined the Marines. The Marines, at last report, have survived the impact.

One day, in the ripe wisdom of his advanced years, Mr. Dizzy Dean, commenting on night-walkers like Poffenberger, remarked that they were foolish men. "You stay in your room like I used to do," said Diz, "and you can't get in trouble."

Yet Mr. Dean, after a night in his room a few years ago, showed up in the morning with a black eye which he attributed to the telephone on his night table. "I was trying to use the phone," he explained, "and it slipped in my hand and hit me."

That never happened to Baron Boots Poffenberger or to Shufflin' Phil Douglas. Maybe a man is safer in the streets, at that.

Death of a Simian and Scholar

1949

As FINE AN APE as I knew was Gargantua, the circus star, who passed from this footstool a couple of weeks ago. He is gone but not forgotten. I have postponed my private obituary of this congenial gorilla until I was absolutely sure he was dead. An airplane transporting his remains lost 1,000 feet of altitude when the pilot heard a thumping noise amidships. It turned out to be a loose crate or a gremlin or something, not Gargy come to life.

Although we were acquainted socially, it was my business relationship with the noted entertainer that I valued most highly. In association with Mr. Gene Tunney, a gifted performer in his own right in a lower weight division, I once tried to promote a match of skill and strength between Gargantua and Tony Galento, the spheroid barkeep of Orange, New Jersey. Had Galento not declined the test, we would all have cleaned up.

As it was, the thing fell through, and the four of us went our separate ways. Tunney became a uranium miner. Gargantua has gone to his reward. Galento is a wrestler, and your correspondent changes ribbons on typewriters. It is useless to sit around and speculate on what might have been.

Gargantua was an up-and-coming young ape of about five years, beginning to make his presence felt in show business, when he caught the eye of Mr. Tunney. Tunney was then sports editor of a paper called the *Connecticut Nutmeg*. As an editor, he thought he had to take a stand. So he took a stand against Gargantua. "Gorillas are overrated" was the editorial policy of Mr. Tunney.

That, of course, was directly opposed to the policy of another editor, the late Arthur Brisbane, who thought a gorilla could lick any five human beings. Reaching for his Encyclopaedia Britannica, Mr. Tunney made some rapid notes and announced that any third-rate heavyweight fighter could lick Gargantua. When your correspondent proposed Galento, a third-rate heavyweight second to none, as a worthy contender, Mr. Tunney leaped at the idea. So I went around to contact the rival camps.

Now it happened that Mr. Tunney had misread his Britannica or got hold of an early edition with incomplete returns. He thought it said that a gorilla has thirteen ribs, as against twenty-four for a human being or an Orange, New Jersey, barkeeper. What a gorilla really has is thirteen pairs of ribs, making twenty-six in all.

"Tunney is being ridiculous," said Gargantua's manager, a Mr. Dick Kroener, whom I found moodily biting his fingernails while Gargantua did roadwork around the inside of his cage. "It never

pays to knock gorillas. My principal, here, can make shredded wheat
out of the likes of Galento."

Galento's manager, Mr. Joe (Yussel the Muscle) Jacobs, seemed
to share that suspicion, though he put it in another way.

"Let Tunney fight the ape. I will carry the bucket for him," said
Mr. Jacobs coldly. "My tiger fights nobody but humans and such.
Besides, our engagement book is full up. Ain't it, Anthony?"

"Right to the ears," agreed Mr. Galento. "I would like to belt
over this circus bum, but I got no time."

Soon afterward a rumor began to circulate in the prizefight business that Mr. Tunney had deliberately misrepresented the number
of Gargantua's ribs in order to lure Galento into the ring with the
crowd-pleasing African. Now, since I know that Mr. Tunney was
prepared to bet handsomely on Galento, that he is the soul of honor,
and that he still thinks gorillas are overrated, I am certain that no
such stratagem was in his thoughts. If ever a chap believed in the
cause of man over monkey, it is this same Tunney.

However, I am forced to disagree with him. I saw a good deal
of Gargantua between that time and the time of his death. We had
little to say to each other, both being of a reserved, introspective
turn of mind, but whenever I watched him tear an automobile tire
in two, I mused on the folly of man and his vaulting ambitions. So,
no doubt, did Gargantua. May he walk in green pastures.

The Great
Spring Training Nonsense

1953

ONE DAY in the late winter of 1951-52, Joe DiMaggio,
who had just quit the artistic branch of baseball for the promotional
branch, led a camera crew to Miller Huggins Field, on the outskirts

of St. Petersburg, Florida, to make pictures of the New York Yankees for future use on television screens. St. Petersburg is a bright, lovely town on which, by arrangement with the chamber of commerce, the sun shines as it shines nowhere else in the world, except in other towns with equally powerful chambers of commerce. The Yankees go there every winter and spring to train for the coming season. Calling to a young friend and ex-teammate of his, a lean, long-necked second baseman named Billy Martin, DiMaggio asked for an action shot—a slide into base.

"Sure," said Martin, and slid.

A few days later Martin hobbled on crutches up to the desk of the Yankees' hotel in St. Petersburg to check out. He was bound North for extensive rest and repairs. A couple of baseball reporters waved to him from their pews in the lobby.

"That's the beauty of spring training, Billy," said one of them. "Without it you couldn't have broken your ankle till late April, at the earliest."

"That's right," said Mr. Martin. He might have added that without it the newspapermen would not have been so sunburned and gay at that time of the year as they were. Diplomatically, however, he left the subject where it was. Ballplayers are too deeply committed, by contract and precedent, to the institution of spring training to speak their full minds about it to reporters unless—as is rarely the case these days—they have been mellowed by a few extracurricular beers or unless they are old and successful enough at their trade to feel they can get away with free speech.

Being young and resilient, Martin was able to go back to work in midsummer and to help his team win the pennant and the World Series. If he had spoken freely at the time he broke his leg sliding, he would not have blamed his old friend DiMaggio. Joe and his cameras merely represented one of the common, though newer, hazards of spring training. Nor would Martin have argued that he could have broken his leg only in training camp. Sliding into bases is always a tricky business; accidents can happen anywhere, at any time.

But he could have pointed out that there are special perils connected with ill-timed activity by ball players in February and March.

The joints and muscles, stiffened by a winter of idleness, make trouble if they are asked for too much response too soon—whether by cameramen or by employers who schedule full-dress exhibition games instead of easy, unlimbering exercise. No one who was there will ever forget the shock at the moment when the brilliant but aging little Rabbit Maranville's leg snapped in two, just below the knee, as the Rabbit tried to score a run in a training game one spring. Arms are not loose; Clem Labine, a gifted young Brooklyn pitcher, got himself what may be a permanent sore arm last year trying to break off sharp curve balls in Florida. Eyes and reflexes are faulty; the career of Hank Leiber, a fine hitter, was shortened when Bob Feller's fast ball hit him on the head in a springtime exhibition game. There is also the fact that a player's state of mind tends to be sulky and nervous in the throes of spring training. Because of this, Babe Ruth, one day in early April, ate two dozen defiant hot dogs at a time, instead of his usual ration of half a dozen, and had to be rushed from the South to a New York hospital with what was described as the stomach-ache heard round the world.

The player's state of mind is sulky and nervous in spring training for many reasons, and especially for one. What irritates him above all else, and plucks at his ganglia like banjo strings, is this: No matter what happens to him—whether it is a broken leg, or overexposure to Pullman cars, eating on the move, and run-down, bush-country ball parks, or merely homesickness or dislike of toil in the dust and heat—he is not being paid for it. The ballplayer is paid for games he plays in the regular season, between late April and the first week of October. What precedes the season is a rat race on the cuff, a "gesture of co-operation," enforced by contract between the player and his owner, with the idea of producing a smoother grade of baseball. And most ballplayers will tell you privately that the gesture is grossly mismanaged and overdone.

"As far as the grade of baseball goes," Edd Roush, one of the best hitters in National League history, said, "it'd be as good after two weeks of regular play as after two months of training."

Mr. Roush had his own way of meeting the problem. Almost invariably he spent the spring training season sitting at home negotiating for a higher salary.

"Three weeks in a good college batting cage in the North, and maybe one week of exhibition games, is all any club needs," an outfielder on a first-division team told me last summer. "If you don't think that's enough work, try paying the players a hundred dollars a week for the four-week period, and see how sharp they'd get."

What makes the pageantry of spring training especially droll, from an outsider's point of view, is the fact that the club owners and managers, the lineal descendants of the founders of spring training, are inclined to agree, privately, with the players. They too, though for different reasons, have their doubts about spring training. They wonder—at least, some of those I've talked with do—if this vast complex of publicity, travel, calisthenics and barnstorming is worth the time, trouble, and money it costs. Today's training season lasts from late February till the opening of the playing season, a matter of roughly two months.

"Call it eight weeks," says a baseball executive who has now worked for three different clubs in the major leagues. (Perhaps his mobility is due in part to the fact that he is easily stimulated to frank speech.) "Three of those weeks are real training. You need the other five to get off the hook for the expense of going South in the first place."

To be fair, spring training is fun for a lot of people. It is fun for sports writers like myself, who travel the sunshine trails, working lightly and relaxing strongly. Obviously the readers of sports pages, who are hungry for baseball news after three or four months of winter blight, get a certain amount of nourishment, and even pleasure, out of it. But the truth is that baseball has wandered into an odd predicament. In this matter of spring training, modern baseball clubs are in the position of a fellow who, getting up earlier and earlier every morning to keep ahead of his neighbor, finally meets himself coming home to bed.

It all began very modestly. In the 1880s, ballplayers spent most of the winter taking on fuel and food. Their appetites were as wide as their mustaches. By April, beer trickled out of their ears. They huffed and puffed as they reported to begin the season's business. The huffing and puffing were agony to the ears of the strong-minded

Adrian C. (Pop) Anson, who managed the White Stockings, or Colts, of Chicago. If only to soothe his own aesthetic sense, Anson decided that his athletes must bulge less and wheeze less. It occurred to him at the same time, however, that a little preliminary conditioning would give the team a jump on the field when the time came to start playing ball. So he gathered up most of the Chicago players —squads were small in those days; only twelve or fifteen men, compared with the fifty or sixty who may turn up for the beginning of spring training today—and took them to Hot Springs, Arkansas, a short while before opening day. There, what with the local waters and his own Simon-Legreevian principles in regard to road work, Pop boiled and churned the beer out of their systems.

The results were good. The White Stockings dominated the National League in the '8os. It's true that they had the best players to begin with, and a question was asked at the time which is still being asked in other forms: How much of Chicago's success lay in training, and how much in native talent? From time immemorial—or, to be exact, from 1876, when baseball magnates came into being— baseball magnates have been reluctant to part with a dollar. But a special pressure existed in baseball in the old days, as it does now. If your club doesn't win, you have no dollars to part with or keep. Follow the leader is as much a rule of the game as thrift. It seemed likely that spring training gave Anson's team a head start, even if, in the long run, he didn't need one. The other clubs felt that they could not afford to spot Pop, or anyone else, that sort of advantage.

Within a few years every big-league team had set up some kind of spring-training program. In 1888, as Connie Mack, the sage, recalls it, the team he played for, Washington, took up quarters in two wooden shacks in Jacksonville, Florida, at a dollar a day per man; at mealtime, the club owner herded his players into the cheapest restaurant he could find in the neighborhood. Each year, cautiously but competitively, the teams edged a little farther into the sunshine zones to the south and southwest. Spring training, as the magnates saw it, might or might not be a physical necessity, but, like keeping up with the Joneses, it had become a public-relations necessity. As squads, distances, and physical plants increased in size, it grew into a painfully expensive necessity, to which the magnates reacted at first with natural squeals of pain but eventually with the anesthetized docility of cattle following the Judas steer to slaughter.

Today the yearly cost of spring training for the sixteen major-league clubs alone—minor-league clubs in the upper brackets also go well afield for the training—is upward of $8,000,000. The larger part of the training period is spent in desperate efforts to get the cost back. Yet it is only in very occasional spells of clarity and brooding, and almost always strictly off the record, that the baseball operators say, "Is it worth it?" or "Whither are we drifting?" or "What hit me?"

It is generally suspected, as it was in Anson's time, that a ball team with an edge in physical training has an edge on the field when the time comes to play for keeps. But a pennant race is like a horse race in many ways, one of which is that the most important running is done in the stretch. Rogers Hornsby, now with Cincinnati, is a manager famous for, among other things, his vigorous, rigorous methods of training players. Last year he managed the St. Louis Browns. The squad was assembled at the Browns' California camp at the earliest possible moment in February. Hornsby had his players gasping for breath in no time—but they made a good record in exhibition games with other big-league teams, and by opening day they were as lean and ready as so many whippets. It was a green team, but, partly because it had so many new players, it put its fans into a state of high excitement in advance.

The excitement continued for more than a month after opening day. The critics said, and rightly, that the Browns were winning beyond the handicappers' expectations because of Hornsby's get-tough training program. But in June the excitement subsided. So did the Browns. Hornsby quit the job. He quit, officially, because of temperamental differences with his boss, Bill Veeck, but temperamental differences would not have mattered if the team had gone on winning. It stopped winning because it was not fundamentally a good team.

At this point it can be argued that the Browns, though they finished in seventh place, did better on the whole than they would

have done without the jump that their intensive training gave them.
As Bill Terry, a famous manager and a tough spring trainer of
Hornsby's type, used to say, all games count alike; the ones you
win early are bound to help you later on. But other managers—
Casey Stengel, of the Yankees, among them—disagree. It is nice,
they say, to win the early ones if you can. A basically strong team
will sometimes break fast and lead the race all the way. But it does
so because it is a basically strong team and seldom because it is a
hard-trained team. A team, these experts say, can be too lean at the
start. It will leave some of its vital juices in training camp; exhausted
and brittle, it will lose games in the stretch drive just because of its
stern training.

There is no doubt about the way many of the Browns of 1952
felt toward Hornsby and his methods, including his training methods. When he broke with Veeck last summer, they threw a celebra-
tion and awarded Veeck a trophy as the greatest liberator of slaves
since Lincoln. The trophy was a put-up job rigged by a club official,
but the celebrating players were childishly sincere. Hornsby, a great
player in his time and an honest manager, deserved better. He
proved, as manager of the Cincinnati Reds later in the season, that
he can win the late games as well as the early ones. How well he
will do with the Reds in 1953, if he drives them as intensely in the
early spring as he did the Browns, is something else again.

It has been repeatedly shown that older ballplayers resent over-
training because they feel they are better judges of their own condition than any manager can be, while young players resent it just
because of the general circumstances of their rearing and education.
For better or worse, the young modern athlete, once he has got past
the stimulus of the old college try, is a hard man to train. He dis-
likes the treadmill. He wants recreation, especially at times when
he is drawing no pay checks. There is evidence that the Browns
enjoyed themselves more in the training period of 1951, when a
New York psychologist named Dr. David F. Tracy was hired to
brace their egos by hypnotism, and they could sleep off and on in
the daytime, than they did under the harsh calisthenics of Hornsby.
The effect, in the end, was about the same. The 1952 team, with

slightly more talent, finished one place higher than the basement Browns of 1951.

There is doubt, therefore, whether getting a jump on the next man in training is useful in the long run. The competitors might as well start even. And if this is true, it raises the second great doubt that gnaws at the roots of baseball's policy. Granted, well-conditioned teams will play better ball than poorly conditioned teams. The quality of the game, at the start of play, will be better because of training. But will the fans notice this for the little time it lasts? In other words, is the big spring-training program—with its enormous expense, with its risks and headaches, with its squirrel-cage system of spending a dime to chase a dime—is it necessary? Or could the competing teams just as well start cold as even?

Cold was the way they started in 1944 and 1945. Those were the peak years of war restrictions and travel cut-backs. The teams trained, for the short while they trained at all, in places like Bear Mountain, New York, Asbury Park, New Jersey, and French Lick Springs, Indiana. True, when the season began, the quality of play was subnormal. But the fans knew that this was mainly because of the absence of good players called into service. If they spotted short-comings in physical condition of the players they saw, they never mentioned it. The races were close, as seldom before. And, as never before, the box office boomed and attendance records were broken.

In the light of these facts, there is serious reason to suspect that baseball, in many respects the most successful, powerful, and neatly organized industry in all professional sport, is dragging a white elephant along at the wheels of its chariot, and that the shrewdest baseball people know it. As long as the present national atmosphere of big, easy money prevails, there probably will be no important change in today's spring-training system. But when times get even a little tougher, the elephant is pretty sure to be cut loose or cut down to the practical size of a coach dog.

Expense and complications mushroomed enormously in the course of the physical-conditioning steeplechase—a race based, as we've seen, on doubtful logic—that followed Pope Anson's small gesture in the '80s. The cost of transporting a platoon of men to and from

far corners of the country, and of feeding, lodging, dressing, doctor-
ing, and coaching them for even a few weeks of camp exercise and
intraclub games, appalled the owners. They sought, as they still seek,
to squirm as far out of the red as possible by arranging exhibition
games among their clubs. This involved further travel expense. In
order to find new audiences for whom the bloom of seeing exhibition
ball had not yet worn off—and the bloom wears off quickly, for a
preseason exhibition, in which it is necessary for as many men as
possible to get into shape by playing, is a travesty of a ball game—
the teams must now range all over the country. The route home
from camp today is long, winding, and tedious. For the players,
asked to spend every night in a train, to play on rough fields in ram-
shackle ball parks, often at night, and to perform in steaming heat
one week and in cold, whistling winds the next, the home trek is
purely an ordeal.

It was on the way home that Monte Irvin, outfielder and slug-
ging star of the New York Giants, wrecked himself—and very likely
the Giants' pennant chances—last spring. The Giants and the Cleveland Indians, barnstorming together, had paused to tax the city of
Denver for training expenses incurred back in Arizona. Irvin slid
into third base awkwardly in the second inning of the game and
broke his right leg at the ankle—so badly that he did not play regularly again until late August. Correspondents bewailed the fact that
the slide was unnecessary—there was no play at third base. The
truth is, of course—and the players, managers, and owners had the
next five months to reflect on it—that nothing about the game was
necessary except the gate receipts, which were necessary in the
sense that the price of a mustard plaster later may be needed by a
man who jumps through a hole in the ice.

The training plant and program of the Brooklyn Dodgers, National League champions, sum up the galloping elephantiasis of the
system. The Dodgers, with hundreds of players from their minor-
league farm clubs, gather at Vero Beach, on the east coast of Florida,
in February. It is a "super" plant. The fields, dormitories and mess
halls teem with players, wives, and children. The place abounds in
gadgets, mechanical pitchers, and sliding pits. It crawls with coaches,

secretaries, and strategists. Winning teams come out of the place—also, losing teams. The Dodgers' fairly consistent success brings us back to the old question: Do they win because of their training camp or because of their knack—conceded on all sides—of scouting and signing up good player material? The training period at Vero Beach, as it happens, is brutally brief. By early March the Dodgers are off to Miami for an exhibition series, already trying to retrieve their owners' money. They scarcely see Vero Beach again till next year.

One of the players' major complaints against spring training is night games; they dislike night ball at all times, but especially when they are meant to be acquiring health and strength in the winter and early spring. The Pittsburgh Pirates, for instance, scheduled no less than twenty-five night exhibition games for this spring, despite the fact that after last season two player representatives of the combined big-league teams obtained a "sort of promise" from the club owners that there would be no night ball in spring training in 1953. Dominic DiMaggio, one of the representatives, walked away from the conference in November rubbing his hands in relief—the players, he said, had got their way at last.

But there was an escape clause, having to do with financial need. Later in November, the Brooklyn club published its exhibition schedule. There were no night games listed. The pleased surprise of the Dodgers lasted almost a month. Then, in December, the club announced that six exhibition games in Miami would, in fact, be played at night. "It's a difference between a seven-thousand crowd and a two-thousand crowd each time," said. Buzzy Bavasi, the Dodger vice-president. "How else are we going to get the money to pay these boys' expenses?" The players were not bold enough to say so, but a sensible answer would have been, By staying right at home till April first or thereabouts.

A further way to try to get money back, for Brooklyn, is to seek out towns where Jackie Robinson has not been seen before. This spring there is a game scheduled in New Orleans, 1,000 miles out of the home-bound line, to pick up exploited Robinson dollars from Negro fans there. Robinson is the great single baseball drawing card of the last five years, as Babe Ruth was before him. It never increased the happiness of Ruth, or Robinson, or their teammates, as their clubs wandered about the land beating the bushes for virgin funds, to reflect that neither the "gate attractions" nor the other players were paid, in salary or percentage, for those wearisome and sometimes physically dangerous junkets. Ruth or Robinson independently might try to get something to show for it when they negotiated each year for their over-all salary, which is paid between April and October. But such considerations somehow do not seem to weigh heavily in the negotiating room.

Last year Eddie Sawyer, a firm, scholarly man who then managed the Philadelphia Phillies, laid a heavy hand on one of the few player compensations in spring training. In the old Anson tradition, Sawyer—or someone higher up; at any rate, Sawyer got the blame —thought it well to get his men trained hard and thoroughly and to keep them undiverted. So he ordered them to leave their wives and families at home when they came to camp at Clearwater, Florida. There was no open rebellion among the Phillies over the no-wife rule. One player, at least, broke curfew and was disciplined when he came home late after what the boys described as a tomcatting expedition. But unhappiness was general. The results? It is hard to weigh them exactly. The Phils, well trained or not, floundered deep in the second division for most of the 1952 season. They did not begin to pick up ground till after Sawyer was ousted. It is not sensible to hang the rap entirely on Sawyer, a sincere, intelligent baseball man. But the ban on wives will not be in force this year. That will leave the Phillies discontented only in the standard ways of all ballplayers in spring training from Miami to Catalina Island —discontented over night ball, lack of salary, physical risk, Pullmanitis, and the length of the training season. It adds up to a very deep degree of discontent indeed.

For a lot of us it will be too bad when the club owners come to see eye to eye with the players about the general folly of long spring training—as they probably will someday soon. The years have been crowded with fun, adventure, and pleasant customs for the observer. The teams have trained in hundreds of places over the map of the southern United States, and nearly all of them were good, comfortable places to be in if your own work and private problems were light. To be sure, owners and players have found that it can rain inconveniently even in sun-kissed St. Petersburg, which Al Lang, a long, lean, eager citizen of the town, has helped to build into one of the most famous of training bases; and that the wind can make ballplaying difficult for long spells at a time in Texas and the Arizona desert.

There was a fine camp, from a special point of view, in Marlin, Texas, where the old-time New York Giants used to sweat, and their leaders and the writers to revel. There was Sarasota, Florida, in the days when John McGraw, the Giant manager, used to struggle to keep a real-estate boom going at times when he was not trying to watch all the doors at once for playboy players after hours in a hotel that had too many entrances. For that matter, there still is Sarasota, and the other traditional camps in Florida: Clearwater, Tampa, Bradenton, West Palm Beach, Orlando—the nation's cock-fighting capital—Lakeland, and Fort Myers.

There are the warm California camps: Pasadena, San Bernardino, and Catalina. There are Tucson and Phoenix. There is Havana, where Pittsburgh trains this year, where Van Lingle Mungo, a playful Dodger, once rocked a Havana hotel to its foundations—a lady dancer, her angry partner, a knife, whiskey, and many policemen were involved—and where Leo Durocher, then the Brooklyn manager, almost got himself thrown out of baseball for life for pointing out that Memphis Engelberg, a well-known horse handicapper, was sitting in the field box of Larry MacPhail, president of the Yankees.

This correspondent will miss, if things change, the memoirs of Casey Stengel rambling on through the warm night, and Casey's brooding over the perils his players might run by betting on the dog races in St. Petersburg, if he let them behave as loosely as he used to try to behave as a player. He will miss the Tampa Terrace bar, in Tampa, where writers and former players hang out. But there is not much gold left in those Southern lodes, as the baseball owners are learning. There are few towns left that have never seen Jackie Robinson; fewer every year. The circus grows more expensive all the time; the cost of one modern spring-training program would freeze the tips of Pop Anson's mustache stiff, if he heard of it. It doesn't make sense any more. And Pop would be the first to agree that it doesn't make sense.

Cockfighting Is Here to Stay

1950

THEMISTOCLES, moving against the Persians twenty-five centuries ago, stopped his Greek army along the road to watch a couple of roosters fight to death. "Get a load of that," he told the troops, in effect, "and follow suit." It was known then, it had been known long before, and it is known now that practically nothing in the world is so chronically mad at the rest of the world—especially at its own kind of people—as a game cock.

Shortly after discovering this proposition, men began to promote cockfights. Then they began to bet on them. Then, to make sure that the birds would not come to like each other some day, which would have been very bad taste indeed, they began to breed some of them exclusively for murder. The instinct which makes a game rooster fight to kill is the same, basically, as the one which makes a gentleman buy a five-pound box of chocolates for a blonde. But it is more apt to be fatal among pedigreed birds than it is among mashers.

The breeding process is not surefire. Once in a while a drop of "cold blood," a barnyard strain, will find its way into a game cock, and then he acts much as you or I do when someone comes at us with a piece of sharp steel. He runs like a burglar. Such conduct in a game cock is repulsive to cockers, or cockfight fanciers. I have seldom seen a man so disgusted as a veteran witness at a cocking main I watched on Long Island some years ago, when the bird he had bet on took to the hills.

"I should of known he had donkey in him," he snarled. "Donkey," in those circles, means prudence. In the prizefight game it is called "geezer."

Donkeys will crop up in the best of game breeds, which include Pyles, Claibornes, blues, reds, grays, cyclones, roundheads, toppies (topknots), warhorses, doms (Dominiques), travelers, and white-hackles. But the inclination of a carefully bred fighting cock is to kill every other cock in sight; and man has helped him out by building him special weapons, steel gaffs, to express himself with.

An innocent sheriff in Ohio once broke up a cockfight, fined the spectators, and threw all the birds who were still conscious into a jail cell together. It was the last time he ever tried to collect jailbirds, in the literal sense of the word. In the morning, he found them all dead but one. The one happened to be the winner of a bout that had ended just before the sheriff made his pinch. He still had a gaff on. But even he was not in very good shape.

Man, as I said before, moved in on cockfighting soon after he discovered it. The law did not move in on the cockfighter until a long time after that. Among the civic leaders who fought their rooster stables in a free and open way were Washington, Jefferson, Jackson, Van Buren, Clay, and Calhoun—and, setting them up in another alley, Henry VIII, James I, Charles II, and Sir Walter Raleigh. The game began to get somewhat illegal in England in the time of Queen Victoria. Most states in this country acquired anti-cockfight statutes at about the beginning of the present century. The status of cockfighting today is roughly what the status of liquor was during the Volstead act: You could get it (they tell me) if you looked for it.

The cockfighter has the same sort of genial resistance to statutes as the barfly, though he figures himself more respectable because he is improving a breed, he says, while the barfly, at best, is getting a draw. In 1949 the British House of Commons took note that there was still a great deal of austere cockfighting going on in its territory. So it tightened the law, making a man liable to arrest if gaffs were found in his possession or if he owned a rooster whose feathers and comb were trimmed for fighting. Then Sir William Darling, M.P., rose to his feet and expressed the spirit of cockers in a bit of verse that was popular in taverns in the last century:

> To keep game cocks and hunt the fox,
> To drink the punch and whisky,
> We fear no locks, we'll train the cocks,
> And care not if it's risky.

"We must make it more risky all the time," said Sir William. "Those chaps have great stamina."

In this country the chaps with stamina are often arrested, but they keep right on operating every day, over a wide piece of ground. You have only to read one of the trade publications—*Grit and Steel* or *The Feathered Warrior*—to find the box scores, and also bargains in cocks, gaffs, trimming or dubbing shears, cockers' scales, and feed cups. A party in Ohio, an ex-blacksmith, does a world trade in hand-tooled gaffs, which he sells to order as far away as South Africa and Australia.

You can tell from the play-by-play reports in *Grit and Steel* that the law is taken a little more lightly in the South and West than it is in, say, New York or New England. A few Southern states have no anti-cocking laws. The fights that take place in the South are called by name and place: a $10,000, 17-cock main at the Tallahassee Pit; a 60-pit tournament at Ruleville, Mississippi; a main or a derby at the Goose Creek, Texas, pit, or the Bodcaw Parish, Louisiana, pit, or the Volunteer Club, of Clinton, Tennessee, or Tidewater Pit, at Driver, Virginia. A fight in New York, though, just happened "somewhere in northern New York State" (around Rochester would be a good guess). New York has a law on its books which says you can be fined $10 to $1,000 for cocking, or get ten days to a year in jail. It makes things difficult for cockers, but it does not deter them.

A cockfight on Long Island was raided recently and seventeen cocks valued at $2,000 were among those apprehended. The experience of the Ohio sheriff had proved that you cannot put seventeen game chickens in jail unless you have seventeen cells to spare, so the prisoners were thrown in a soup pot instead.

In Cheshire, Connecticut, one night last year, there being eighty-six men and sixty live roosters in the law's bag, the judge came to the cockpit himself, to save time and trouble. He was impressed by what he saw. The pit was a portable job, twenty-five feet in diameter. The grandstand seated four hundred people. There were betting windows, and there were refreshments.

You get the same thing at the national tournament, but you get it in safety. The national takes place at Orlando, Florida, in January. Sixteen of the country's top breeders enter their birds. The law turns out just to keep order. The man who goes home with an Orlando winner gets the highest price in the country for his cocks, from then on.

I am taking it for granted that, what with the law and other impedimenta, such as a kind heart or a taste for chicken fricasseed in the kitchen only, a great many readers have never seen the breed of game cock improved.

As noted above, the game cock is bedbred to be full of hell. He is angry in the egg, and comes out of it even angrier. He is fought, as a rule, at the age of one year or two. He seldom lives longer than that, unless he is a donkey or a runner—in other words, unless he knows the percentages. But a good game cock is not meant to know any such thing as that.

Until his summer molt of the first year after his hatching year, he is known as a stag. After that he is a cock.

Though born in a state of congenital annoyance, the bird cannot be sure of killing anything with the spur that nature gave him. So his own spur is sawed off, leaving a nub on which the gaff socket is placed and held firm by leather taping and waxed string. Before he is ready to fight in earnest, he spars with muffs, or leather gaffs. Then he gets the true steel gaff, and his span of life from there on depends on how well he uses it.

The gaff is something that would have been outlawed by The Hague Convention, if they'd thought of it—even the "regulation" gaff, which is only one inch and a quarter long. The regulation gaff, or short heel, is used mainly in the Northeastern part of the country, where they fight by what are known as the Eastern (or Fair Play) Rules. In the South and West the cockers prefer a longer spur, from one and three-quarters to two and a half inches. A good pair of gaffs costs twenty-five dollars.

In formal combat the gaff must always be rounded, or cylindrical, right down to its point. For informal use, however, there is a gaff known as a slasher, honed to a razor edge on one side.

An Eastern cock like the whitehackle tends to use the single-stroke style which is also called "sparring." Meeting the enemy in midair, he aims a single jab with his gaff and repeats the policy as long as is necessary. Elsewhere, although he may go into the air for the first punch, the cock usually winds up shuffling. A shuffler is a bird working on the ground, getting a grip on the wing, throat, comb, or some other useful section of the party of the second part with his beak and holding him in position for the steel. To make a cock less vulnerable to shuffling the owner trims out his wing and body feathers and bobs his tail.

Pits vary in size, but the idea is generally the same—a low board fence enclosing a circle or octagon of earth—and so is the cocking procedure. Cocking has its Hoyle, a man named Sol McCall. In most parts of the country the fighting is under McCall's Rules. Two parallel lines, or scores, are marked in the floor six feet apart. The referee (a good, solvent club will pay him twenty-five or fifty dollars a day) tells the pitters, or handlers, to "bill" their cocks, which they do by holding the roosters face to face and letting them click bills, to increase the homicidal instinct.

The referee then tells the handlers to get ready. After five seconds, he says "Pit them!" and the cocks are set down on the opposite lines. From that point, it is every fowl for himself. The men move six feet back from the scores. The birds move forward, unless, to the intense irritation of the crowd, one of them has too much sense to do that. A cock which obviously will not fight can be withdrawn by his handler, or he can be counted out by the referee.

As soon as either bird's gaff becomes hung or fixed—in the enemy, in himself, in the wall, or in the floor—the referee says "Handle them!" The handlers disengage and pick up their roosters, and the first pitting is over. A single fight may have as many pittings as there were rounds in the Sullivan-Kilrain fight, which, if memory serves me, was seventy-five. It may even have more. It usually has fewer. Death, for one contestant and sometimes both, is the characteristic result in the pit. In the seats, the result is redistribution of the wealth. Without betting, as even the most respectable cockers point out, where would the game be?

There are two varieties of rooster war: hacks and mains. A hack is a pickup fight between any two matching cocks whose owners happen to be at the pit, spoiling for action and a side bet. The rule for matching is "give or take two ounces": A cock weighing five pounds six ounces, say, must be matched with a cock weighing somewhere between 5.4 and 5.8. An able cock, however, can be asked to give as much as four ounces if his opponent is a "stag" or a "blinker." A blinker is a bird with one eye disabled or missing. You meet with blinkers frequently in this business. After all, why leave them home? They're still sore, aren't they?

A main is a more formal kind of battle than a hack. It is a series of bouts between two rival stables, arranged in advance. Nine, eleven or fifteen cocks from one side will meet the same number from the other side, in turn, at matching weights. The owners may put up as much as $5,000 apiece for a purse, winner take all, plus a $100 bet on each single fight. That is big money in cocking.

Betting is not confined to breeders. Most of the spectators bet on every fight. There are $5 and $10 bettors, there are $50 and $100 bettors. It frequently happens at the less respectable pits that those who bet highest are the ones with a friend in the loser's corner—for the loser in a cockfight is sometimes doped to the wattles.

It might be a little monotonous if all cocks were either dead game or 100 per cent donkeys. But the birds have their eccentricities. A veteran breeder from North Carolina tells me of a cock he raised and fought which baffled him all its life.

"This ——," said the breeder affectionately, "was game as a pebble most times. He could lick any red cock he ever saw. But put him in there with a gray rooster and he'd throw up his hacks and hide. Every time. Reminded me of a fella I used to know who always got sick on bourbon. Just bourbon. He could drink his weight in rye."

So game cocks can have their separate personalities. But, in the main, they are pretty much all of a piece—hot-blooded once, hot-blooded and mean-tempered always.

They are shrewd operators with the weapon man has given them, the gaff. They aim it for the heart, or the brain, or in such a way as to "couple" their opponent—paralyze his legs. There is even a little dash of Frankenstein monster in the game cock. I am thinking of a case in Honduras a few years ago. A cock flew up above the pit, looked around, and suddenly went for one of the spectators. His two-inch gaff struck the man in the heart and killed him.

That may seem ironical to you, but to the people in Honduras it looked like revolution. So they took the cock to court for trial. He was sentenced and hanged the same day.

Babe Herman

1952

FLOYD CAVES HERMAN, known as Babe, did not always catch fly balls on the top of his head, but he could do it in a pinch. He never tripled into a triple play, but he once doubled into a double play, which is the next best thing. For seven long years, from 1926 through 1932, he was the spirit of Brooklyn baseball. He spent the best part of his life upholding the mighty tradition that anything can happen at Ebbets Field, the mother temple of daffiness in the national game.

Then he went away from there. He rolled and bounced from town to town and ball club to ball club. Thirteen years went by before he appeared in a Brooklyn uniform again. That was in the wartime summer of 1945, when manpower was so sparse that the desperate Dodger scouts were snatching beardless shortstops from the cradle and dropping their butterfly nets over Spanish War veterans who had played the outfield alongside Willie Keeler. In the

course of the great famine Branch Rickey and Leo Durocher lured
Babe Herman, then forty-two, from his turkey farm in Glendale,
California, to hit a few more for the honor of Flatbush. A fine crowd
turned out to watch the ancient hero on the first day of his rein-
carnation.

"It looks like they haven't forgotten you here, Babe," said one
of the players, glancing around the grandstand.

Mr. Herman shook his head. "How could they?" he said with
simple dignity.

And he went on to show what he meant. In his first time at bat
he was almost thrown out at first base on a single to right field. The
Babe rounded the bag at a high, senile prance, fell flat on his face
on the baseline, and barely scrambled back to safety ahead of the
throw from the outfield. The crowd roared with approval. Fifteen
years earlier they would have booed themselves into a state of
apoplexy, for that was a civic ritual at Ebbets Field—booing Herman. But this was 1945. You don't boo a legend from out of the
past, a man who made history.

Before he went home to California to stay, a few weeks later, the
Babe gathered the younger players around his knee and filled them
with bloodcurdling stories about his terrible past.

"You know that screen on top of the right-field fence," he said.
"They put that there on account of me. I was breaking all the windows on the other side of Bedford Avenue."

Looking around to see if this had sunk in, he added, "There used
to be a traffic tower on Bedford Avenue there. Once I hit one over
the wall that broke a window in the tower and cut a cop's hand all
to pieces. Wasn't my fault," said the Babe philosophically. "When
I busted 'em, there was no telling where they'd go."

It's beyond question that Mr. Herman could bust them. He always admitted it. He used to be irritated, though, by the rumor that
he was the world's worst outfielder and a constant danger to his own
life. He was also sensitive about his base running.

"Don't write fresh cracks about my running," he once told an
interviewer, "or I won't give you no story. I'm a great runner."

He proceeded to tell why he stole no bases in 1926, his first year with Brooklyn, until the very end of the season. It seems that the late Uncle Wilbert Robinson, then managing the Dodgers, came up to Mr. Herman one day and said sourly, "What's the matter, can't you steal?"

"Steal?" said the Babe. "Why, hell, you never asked me to."

So then he stole a couple of bases, to prove he could do everything.

One talent for which Babe never gave himself enough public credit was making money. He was one of the highest-salaried players of his time, year after year. He got these salaries by holding out all through the training season. Other players, starving slowly on the ball club's regular bill of fare in Southern hotels, used to go down the street to the restaurants where Herman, the holdout, ate, and press their noses against the window like small boys, watching the Babe cut huge sirloin steaks to ribbons. It wasn't just the food that kept Babe from signing early. Holding out is a common practice with good-hit-no-field men like Herman, Zeke Bonura, and Rudy York in his outfielding days. The reason is obvious. The longer they postpone playing ball in the spring (for nothing), the less chance there is of getting killed by a fly ball.

Mr. Herman had such ambitious ideas about money that one year, returning his first contract to the Brooklyn office unsigned, he enclosed an unpaid bill from his dentist for treatment during the winter. The ball club ignored the bill. After all, Herman didn't hit with his teeth.

The Babe, as a player, was a gangling fellow with spacious ears who walked with a slouch that made him look less than his true height, six feet four inches. He was born in Buffalo in 1903. Leaving there for the professional baseball wars in 1921, Mr. Herman worked for eighteen different managers before he met up with Uncle Robbie, and for nine more after that. It is said that he broke the hearts of 45 per cent of these gentlemen. The rest avoided cardiac trouble by getting rid of the Babe as fast as they could.

He came up from Edmonton, in the Western Canada League, to Detroit, in the year 1922, and was promptly fired by Ty Cobb, the Tigers' idealistic manager.

"The Detroit club," said the Babe, his feelings wounded, "has undoubtedly made some bad mistakes in its time, but this is the worst they ever made."

He was fired from the Omaha club later in the same year while batting .416. A pop fly hit him on the head one day, and the Omaha owner lost his temper. The owner and the manager began to argue.

"Much as I would like to," said the manager, "I can't send away a man who is hitting four sixteen."

"I don't care if he's hitting four thousand!" yelled the owner. "I am not going to have players who field the ball with their skulls. Fire him!"

The Babe explained later that the incident was greatly exaggerated.

"It was a foul ball," he said, "that started to go into the stands. The minute I turned my back, though, the wind caught the ball and blew it out again, and it conked me. It could happen to anybody."

Just the same, Mr. Herman was fired.

The Babe tried baseball in Boston briefly, when Lee Fohl managed the Red Sox. He never played an inning there. Studying his form on the bench, Mr. Fohl fired him. The Babe was just as well pleased. He said the Boston climate did not suit him. He went to Atlanta, where Otto Miller, later a Brooklyn coach, managed the team. Every morning for five days in a row Mr. Miller resolved to fire Mr. Herman. Every afternoon of those five days Mr. Herman got a hit that drove in runs and changed Mr. Miller's mind for the night. On the fifth day, playing against Nashville, he had four hits in his first four times at bat. He was robbed of a fifth hit by a sensational catch by Kiki Cuyler. After the game Mr. Miller told the Babe that they might have won the game but for Cuyler's catch. He meant it kindly, but Mr. Herman took it as a personal criticism of himself. He was hurt. He began a loud quarrel with Otto, and was traded to Memphis on one bounce.

The Brooklyn club bought the Babe for $15,000 a couple of years later, while he was causing nervous breakdowns and busting up ball games in Seattle. Then Brooklyn tried to get rid of him for nothing, and failed. This gross insult to the name of Herman occurred as follows: The Dodgers wanted a Minneapolis player, of no subsequent consequence, named Johnny Butler. They traded Herman and eight other men to Minneapolis for Butler. Minneapolis took the eight other men but refused to take Herman. Brooklyn was stuck with the Babe, and history began to be made.

Jacques Fournier, the Dodger first baseman, hurt his leg one day in the summer of 1926. Herman replaced him. He had a good season at bat that year and the Brooklyn fans began to take to the Babe, wide ears, chewing tobacco, and all. Uncle Robbie took to him some days. Other days gave him pause, like the day famous in ballad and prose when Mr. Herman smote a two-base hit that ended in a double play.

The bases were full of Brooklyns, with one out, when the Babe strode to the plate on that occasion, swinging his bat like a cane in his right hand. Physically, he was a phenomenon, a left-handed hitter with most of his power in his right arm. Scattered around the landscape before him were Hank DeBerry, the Brooklyn catcher, on third base; Dazzy Vance, the Dodger fireball pitcher, on second; and Chick Fewster, an outfielder, on first. Mr. Herman swung ferociously and the ball hit the right-field wall on a line. DeBerry scored. Vance, however, being a man who did not care to use his large dogs unnecessarily, hovered between second and third for a moment on the theory that the ball might be caught. When it rebounded off the wall, he set sail again, lumbered to third base, and made a tentative turn toward home. Then, deciding he couldn't score, he stepped back to third. This move confounded Fewster, who was hard on Vance's heels. Fewster started back toward second base. At that moment, a new character, with blond hair and flapping ears, came into their lives.

Mr. Herman has described himself as a great runner. What he meant was, he was a hard runner. He forgot to mention that he ran with blinkers on, as they say at the race track. He concentrated on running and ignored the human and animal life around and ahead of him. Passing Fewster like the Limited passing a whistle stop, the Babe slid into third just as Vance returned there from the opposite direction. Herman was automatically out for passing Fewster on the baseline, though nobody realized it at once but the umpire, who made an "out" sign. The third baseman, not knowing who was out, began frantically to tag Herman, who was already dead, and Vance, who stood perfectly safe on third base.

"What a spectacle!" observed Vance nonchalantly to Herman, as the third baseman looked in vain to the umpire for the sign of another out. Fewster, confused, stood a little distance away. His proper move was to go back to second and stay there, but Herman's slide had destroyed his powers of thought. Finally the third baseman caught on. He began to chase Fewster, who ran in a panic and did not even stop at second, where he would have been safe. He was tagged in the outfield for the third out of the inning.

Cheap detractors may say what they like about Herman's merely doubling into a double play. It's obvious that what he really did—the rule book to the contrary—was triple into a double play.

It's also obvious that Vance and Fewster were as much at fault as Herman. That is the old, true spirit of Brooklyn co-operation. But Vance regarded Herman as the star of the act. A few years afterward, when Chicago officials announced that they expected a Chicago pennant in 1933 to make things complete for the Century of Progress exposition, Vance announced his counterplan for that year in Brooklyn. Instead of a Century of Progress, said Dazzy, they would feature "A Cavalcade of Chaos; or, the Headless Horsemen of Ebbets Field." Herman was to be the star. Unfortunately, by the time the year 1933 rolled into Brooklyn, Herman had rolled out of there to quieter pastures.

Uncle Robbie's comment on the celebrated double play of 1926 was "————." However, that was Robbie's comment on practically everything, and he meant it in a friendly way. He was tolerant of Herman, for he understood that criticism or scolding drove the Babe crazy. When 30,000 people booed him in unison—and that happened often enough in 1927, when his batting average slipped to .272, and 1929, when he led the league's outfielders in errors—the Babe would sulk for days. It took Robbie a little while, at that, to learn patience with Herman. He asked waivers on him in 1927 but changed his mind and kept the Babe when John McGraw, of the New York Giants, refused to waive.

"If that crafty blank-blank McGraw wants him," reasoned Mr. Robinson, "there must be something in him."

As time went on, the Brooklyn crowds became more sympathetic, too. That's understandable. After 1927, Herman hit for averages of .340, .381, .393, .313, and .326. In 1930 he had 241 hits for a total of 426 bases, including 35 home runs. He scored 143 runs and batted in 130. The fans barbecued him one moment and cheered him the next.

"Not only is that fellow a funny-looking blank-blank-blank," said the manager, "but he is blankety-blank unlucky. Other men, when they're on third base, can sometimes beat the outfielder's catch when they start home on a fly ball. But not this blankety-blank Herman. He always gets called for it."

The wailing and the keening were great in Brooklyn when the Babe, called by Rogers Hornsby "the perfect free-swinger," was traded to Cincinnati in December 1932, in a six-player deal. It was not a bad deal for Brooklyn, in a strictly practical way. Herman never hit in high figures again after that year, while some of the players from Cincinnati helped the Dodgers into the first division. But the fans, in the main, never forgave Max Carey, who had replaced Uncle Robbie as manager, for sending Herman away. They didn't care about being practical. They wanted salt in their stew.

Removed from the choice Brooklyn atmosphere where he had flourished, the Babe began to bounce from place to place again as he had in the days of his youth. Managers resumed the practice of firing him to save their health. He went from Cincinnati to Chicago to Pittsburgh to Cincinnati to Detroit to Toledo to Syracuse to Jersey City, and finally, with a strong tail wind, clear out to the Pacific Coast. The slower he got as a player, the more money he asked, and the more loudly he asked for it. The Babe, however, did not like the word "holdout." Once, in the early spring of 1934, he denounced the press of Los Angeles, near his home, for using that term to describe him.

"You got the wrong idea entirely," he told the reporters sternly. "I am not holding out. I just don't want to sign this ——— contract the Cubs have sent me, because the dough ain't big enough."

On his second time around in Cincinnati, in 1936, Mr. Herman came into contact with baseball's leading genius, Leland Stanford MacPhail, who was the Reds' general manager. They were bound to get together sometime, even though the Babe left Brooklyn before MacPhail was ripe for that city. It was also inevitable that Mac-Phail should some day fine Herman, and some day fire him. They were not made to be soulmates. MacPhail fined him and Paul Derringer, the pitcher, two hundred dollars each, one day in July. It was a true Herman episode. With hostile runners on first and third, Derringer made a balk, the runner on third went home, and the runner on first went to second. Herman, communing with nature in the outfield, missed the play completely. He thought there were still men on first and third. When the next hitter singled to the Babe on one bounce, he studied the stitches on the ball and lobbed it back to the infield. The runner on second scored standing up. MacPhail turned purple and levied his fines on both the pitcher and the Babe.

It's a matter of record that Derringer got his fine canceled by throwing an inkwell at MacPhail, which impressed the great man. Mr. Herman was less direct, and therefore less successful. He waited a few weeks after being fined; then he demanded from MacPhail a cash bonus over and above his salary. It was an ill-timed request.

"A bonus!" yelled the genius. "Why, you're not even good enough to play on the team!" He added that Herman was fired. And he was.

Right to the end of his playing days the Babe retained his fresh young affection for cash money. He was farming turkeys at his home in Glendale by the time he landed with the Hollywood club of the Pacific Coast League in the twilight of his career. One day in 1942—just a short while before that final, nostalgic, wartime bow in Brooklyn—he arranged to have his turkeys advertised on the scorecards in the Hollywood ball park. He then announced that he was holding out. The holdout kept him home in comfort among the turkeys, but not so far away from Hollywood that he couldn't drive over from time to time to negotiate. When he finally got his price and signed up to play ball, the Babe was fat and his reflexes were slow. So he made his season's debut at a disadvantage.

Hollywood was playing a game with Seattle. The score was tied going into the tenth inning. Seattle's young pitcher, a kid named Soriano, had already struck out ten men. Hollywood filled the bases on him, with two out, in the last of the tenth, but the boy was still strong and fast. The manager asked Mr. Herman if he was in shape to go in and pinch hit.

"I may not be sharp," said the Babe, reaching for a bat, "and maybe I can't hit him. But I won't have to. I'll paralyze him."

He walked to the plate. He glowered at the pitcher and held his bat at a menacing angle. He never swung it. Five pitches went by —three of them balls, two of them strikes. Then Mr. Herman pounded the plate, assumed a fearful scowl, and made as though his next move would tear a hole in the outfield wall. The last pitch from the nervous Soriano hit the ground in front of the Babe's feet for ball four. A run was forced in, and the ball game was over.

"That's a boy with an education," said the Babe, as he threw away his bat. "I see he's heard of Herman."

WAR CORRESPOND-ENCE

The Rangers' Beachhead Alamo

1944

IN THE THICK of the winning attack in Italy last week our troops moved into and past Cisterna, a little town that sits beside the Appian Way on ground inland and slightly raised from the coastal level of Anzio and Nettuno. This time Cisterna looked easy. But before we had tried like hell for it without getting it, and around its shell-torn, bomb-battered approaches from the southwest, one of the true, brave, and lonely last stands of the war was fought: the beachhead Alamo, the death fight of the Rangers.

Two of the three battalions of the First Rangers, nearly a thousand men, were wiped out there in a German trap. The Germans claimed six hundred prisoners, but these were taken where they lay, too badly wounded to fight further. You could count on your fingers the men who got back to their own lines alive.

Toward noon of that day, January 29, I found Colonel Bill Darby, founder, trainer, and leader of the Rangers, squatting against a farmhouse by the gravel road which leads up to Cisterna from Nettuno and the sea. We had just had our first inkling of the catastrophe. Darby, who was giving some orders and drawing his thumb across a map, shook his head as I came up.

"Please, I can't talk about it now." His eyes were rimmed with red; his strong round chin wore two days' growth of beard. He was like a shell, a man suddenly emptied of life and warmth. "Maybe later."

The cluster of houses where he sat at work is called Femina Morta. From there, that same morning before dawn, the two doomed battalions, Darby's creation and the pride of his professional life, had moved forward to attack. They went off cheerfully and alertly and silently, conscious of the reputation they had gathered in Africa and Italy as the best-trained and bravest soldiers in the Army.

The First Rangers had spearheaded the beachhead landing, going ashore at 2 A.M. on January 22 against the central point of Anzio harbor, with American infantry following on their right and British on their left. Now, a week later, Germans had begun to collect from all over to drive us off, but we did not know their full strength and dispositions yet, and we were offense-minded. We wanted Cisterna, astride the Appian Way. The Rangers were sent after it.

With the plan there was nothing wrong that could have been righted beforehand, once the command decided to attack the town frontally. But it was a natural point of attack; the Germans expected us there; and they had crept up in strength to snare us.

The first two Ranger battalions went first, according to plan, with the third held in reserve and support. They moved along the line of the gravel road in the dark hours of morning and met no trouble on the way, not even at certain farmhouses that made a natural defense point. There they met shooting but nothing strong enough to delay them. The two battalions moved into the edges of the dark town.

Later, when the third battalion moved up, the strong point of the farmhouses had suddenly become a fence of steel. The Germans had loaded it. The third battalion was stopped and held off. Inside the steel fence, in the town, in the jaws of the trap, the first two battalions fought without hope of retreat or victory against tanks and 88s and waves of locking automatic fire concentrated there in secret and abruptly sprung on the victims in the dawning.

The lost battalions took cover where they could, all surrounded, and fought out their fight. They fought all the morning. Till nearly noon Darby, grim and helpless outside the fence, was in touch with some of his forward men by hand radio. The last man to speak to him was a first sergeant who said, "They're closing in. But they won't get us cheap."

Then the contact broke.

To the rest of the beachhead force this dark and sudden and mysterious disaster came as a shock out of proportion to the number of men involved. The Rangers were the Rangers. And we had high hopes of the offensive in those early days before the great German counterattacks of February.

Darby, unanimously considered one of the best officers in the Army, has since been given command of a regiment in an infantry division in combat. Our reinforced Army on the beachhead has rolled over Cisterna and wrecked the German defenders and in some degree rubbed out the memory of the lost battalions that fought and vanished there. But the beachhead Alamo will live on in the history of this war.

D Day, Iwo Jima

1945

Two DIVISIONS of Marines made the landing on Iwo Jima. These Marines were frankly apprehensive before the landing. I did not see a man, either in the staging areas before we boarded ship or on the journey north to Iwo Jima by transport, who expected anything but a bloody and disagreeable time of it. Iwo was far closer to the Japanese mainland than any enemy possession we had attempted to storm before, and our air observation showed that it was heavily fortified. Moreover, as officers kept pointing out to one another, Iwo was too small to provide room for maneuver, being only five miles long and, at the widest point, two and a half miles wide. Frontal attack was the only possible course, and the southeast beach, where we planned to land, was the only possible landing place. "You can't run the ends up there," one major said over and over again. "Every play is between the tackles." Another officer liked to say that we would have surprise on our side like a burglar with whooping cough. This, if it meant anything at all, may have been a reference to the sinking of some minesweepers and LCI gunboats of ours which had gone close to shore during the preliminary naval shelling of Iwo. Even a Japanese broadcaster had said that we would land on the southeast beach, but that, as I said, was the only possible landing place. Even so, the Jap announcer's remarks reinforced the cynical mood of the younger Marine officers.

The forebodings of these officers—all of which turned out to be perfectly justified except in one or two minor particulars—were uttered humorously, as a rule, but there were also cases of serious gloom among the officers and many gaudy premonitions among the enlisted men. These were examples of that detached professional pessimism which is ordinarily confined in war to intelligence officers, whose minds are top-heavy with knowledge of the enemy, his strength, his dispositions, and his potentialities. The Marines bound for Iwo spoke more flatly, and with less whimsical wood-rapping, of the expectation of death than any assault troops I had ever been with before. There were reasons for this apart from the special nature of the Iwo Jima operation. The number of Marine divisions is not large, and nearly all of them have been badly mauled in the course of the past three years. Their work calls for it. All but two or three of the Pacific bastions attacked by Marine forces were strongly held and bitterly defended, and even when this was not the case, the mere fundamentals of amphibious landings and assault caused them damage. In the Army, shock troops are a small minority supported by a vast group of artisans, laborers, clerks, and organizers. In the Marines there are practically nothing but shock troops. For such troops, no matter how well trained and competent, a saturation point is bound to come in time. The Marines in the Pacific point all of this out themselves at the slightest provocation, and it's difficult, in the circumstances, to see what else they could do.

As it happened, the Marine division I went with to Iwo—the Fifth—was a new one, activated about a year ago and now engaged in its first combat mission. Most of its officers and many of its enlisted men, however, were veterans of earlier campaigns with other units. One of its enlisted men, Gunnery Sergeant John Basilone, had won the Congressional Medal of Honor at Guadalcanal. He was killed by mortar fire on Iwo Jima shortly after the division hit the beaches. Officers aboard our transport, especially those with large responsibilities such as getting artillery ashore or conditioning am-tracks and their crews for the first assault landing, stood on deck for two or three days before D Day, succumbing to bleak despair whenever the ocean swells ran high or the wind changed direction.

"My God!" said Lieutenant Colonel Rose, a very young man from Toledo. "Imagine if that wind is blowing from the south when we hit!"

"I'll tell you a couple of things that can happen to my artillery," said Lieutenant Colonel Duryea, not much older, "if it's rough like this at Iwo." And he did. It was gruesome.

Also unhappy for technical reasons was an officer known in his regiment—our passengers were mainly from the Twenty-seventh Regiment of the Fifth Division—as Purple Heart Louis, a high, broad, hulking man who presented an excellent target and invari-ably got hit in combat. He anticipated a great deal of bloodshed on Iwo Jima, but aboard the transport he was bothered chiefly by the fact that the cook for the commodore of our transport division fried everything he cooked, and Louis ate at the commodore's table. One of Louis' Purple Hearts had involved the loss of his gall bladder, and fried foods were poison to him. He relieved his misery by looting the junior officers in wardroom poker games at night. Ships in the Pacific are hot at night, with doors and blackened portholes closed and all air shut out, and Louis stripped to his gleaming torso when he played poker, revealing a cicatrix across his belly and abdomen that looked like the mother and father of all Caesarean scars. He was hit in the right arm about an hour and a half after landing on Iwo Jima.

D Day was Monday, February 19, and H Hour was 0900. On D-minus-one, the regimental surgeon reported a hundred and twenty-five cases of diarrhea among the men and officers aboard. This had come from something they ate, but that evening the Navy cooks did better and served everyone a turkey dinner with ice cream.

At the last meal, breakfast at 0500 the morning of the nineteenth, there was steak and eggs. Everyone had dressed in his green combat blouse and trousers and had strapped on his pistol belt, with a long knife, ammunition, a bandage roll, and one or two canteens attached, and had checked his carbine. After breakfast everyone put on his helmet, which had a camouflage cover simulating sand, and went out on deck and over to the ladder nets. The sun was just coming up, so Iwo Jima was visible from our line of debarkation, which was several miles out at sea. There the larger transports halted, to keep beyond the range of shore batteries, and put off their cargoes of Marines into small boats. On Suribachi, the volcano at the south end of the island, we could see bursts of fire and smoke from our naval shelling, which continued till H Hour. Some of the men stared at the island. Others remarked that the wind was running in our favor, from the northwest, and that the sea was calmer than it had been, though still difficult. Many could think of nothing but the immediate necessity of climbing the slick, flaccid web of rope down the ship's side without looking silly or getting killed. Even young Marines have been killed on these descents when the sea has been rough, and for those over thirty-five, the endless sequence of nets, Jacob's ladders, bouncing gangways, and lurching boats is a hazard and nightmare which can occupy their minds to the exclusion of all other dangers. Admirals and generals can look ridiculous in these circumstances. They are well aware of it, and their tempers during amphibious operations are correspondingly short.

I got into a small boat with Colonel Thomas Wornham, regimental commander, and some of his staff, his messengers, and his radio operators. We chopped and splashed through the ocean swells to Wornham's control ship, which was anchored nearer the shore, at the line at which the first assault troops formed up in their amtracks and began their long, slow, bobbing run for the beach. They went in in ragged waves which left the departure line at intervals of a few minutes, coached hoarsely by a loudspeaker from the bridge of the control ship. The men in the amtracks were a fierce and stirring sight as they passed us to disappear in the valleys of water between us and the beach. I stood watching them as well as I could from the rail of the control ship beside a regimental messenger, a

Navajo Indian named Galeagon, and we spoke of how most of the troops we could see, their hands and faces greased dead white for protection against possible flame barriers, sat up very straight and looked intently ahead. The first wave struck the beach approximately at the appointed hour of nine, and simultaneously the Navy shellfire, which had been raking the shoreline, jumped its range to the ridges and pillboxes farther inland. The central ridge was in our sector of the island. We could see the wreckage of Japanese planes piled at one edge of the plateau. We knew that an airfield lay just beyond this junk—one of the two airfields for which the Marines were beginning the dogged battle of Iwo Jima.

After a while, I walked to the cabin of the control ship where the radioman was receiving reports that were coming in to Wornham from the first radios set up on the beach. The first two hours' progress seemed to be good. The Japs had pulled back upland from the shore, leaving few dead behind them, and Wornham's regiment, which was second in the assault line striking north along the beach near Suribachi, had reached high ground, had crossed the southern end of the first airfield, and was beginning a descent to the western shore of the island, a half mile distant from the point where it had landed. I left the wireless room, where the radioman, earphones over his head, was now reading *The Case of the Caretaker's Cat*.

Wornham's Higgins boat, a rectangular little launch with a hinged landing ramp in the bow, pulled up on the starboard quarter of our ship, and those of us who were going ashore with the Colonel climbed down a ladder and jumped in. It was exactly 1100, or two hours after the first landings, and this was the fourteenth wave. I should say that we were the fourteenth wave. As far as I could see, no other boat was moving shoreward at that moment. As we cast off, Galeagon came to the ship's rail and yelled something at us through a megaphone. Wornham, a short, stocky career Marine of about forty, smiling and convivial on our voyage north but now very taut and serious, leaned precariously over the stern of the boat, clutching at the rail, and cupped a hand to one ear. "Red One now under heavy mortar fire!" shouted the messenger. The Fifth Division's share of beaches was Green Beach and Red Beaches One and Two. To the north, the Fourth Division had landed on Yellow

One and Two and Blue One and Two. We were fifty feet from the control ship when Galeagon yelled another message. "Red Two under mortar fire," he said, the sound of his voice seeming to bounce across the waves. "Heavy mortar fire on both Red beaches." The others in the boat looked with expressionless faces at Wornham, who smiled wryly.

"Head for a point about a hundred feet to the right of the line between Red One and Two," he told the coxswain. Then he turned to the rest of us and said, "All right, be ready to bail out of here goddam fast when we touch that beach."

We all crouched, whether sitting or standing, as the boat moved in. Now and then we wiped spray off our eyes and noses, and we paid no attention to a battleship and a cruiser through whose shadows we passed. I had some trouble crouching, because of my length and because the shelf on which I sat was only a foot or so beneath the stern rail. There was no special need, however, for crouching now, while we were still on water. It was the beaches the Japs were mortaring. We crouched in a sort of instinctive, shrinking alarm at what we were about to meet.

The Japs burst their mortar and artillery shells up and down the beaches for several days thereafter, but my own sharpest memories of this phase of the Iwo Jima battle are of D Day. That sort of shelling is a procedure someone can always use when he is defending a small area against an enemy who must get his supplies by water. At Iwo, as at Anzio, there quickly developed two fronts—the battle front forward and the shelling front on the beaches, where our supply and reinforcement lines were wholly dependent on boats and amphibious vehicles that were being stalled and pounded by surf and wind. And in the case of Iwo, the Marines depended also on motor or human convoys, which were slowed by drifting volcanic sand. The Japanese were limited only by their ammunition supply. As long as they could stay alive on Iwo Jima and keep their guns intact they were all right, for they had observation over our supply beaches and we were within the range of their mortars. The mortar shell, a little bomb-shaped missile, travels in a high, lobbing trajectory and throws its fragments over a wide radius when it explodes. It makes for tearing, disfiguring wounds and for disfigured dead.

Since the mortar fire continued steadily for nearly a week on the crowded shoreline, and hasn't stopped on the front lines yet, our casualties have not only been large but tend to be more slashed and mangled than usual.

We saw puffs of smoke, white, gray, and black, pluming from the beach as our boat came closer. Most of the men in the boat, whose first task was to set up a regimental command post somewhere between the beach and the front lines, were burdened with radio equipment. Alwyn Lee, an Australian war correspondent, and I were also fairly cumbrously loaded. A pack in three light pieces is more trouble than a single heavy pack, and I had, in addition to my Army musette bag, a typewriter and a blanket roll containing a poncho and a small spade, or entrenching tool. I also had a sash-type lifebelt buckled around my waist, in conformance a few hours earlier with a transport regulation. This belt dropped off and vanished that day on Iwo Jima, I don't know when or where.

The landing ramp slapped down on the beach, and the passengers bustled out with their loads and disappeared behind the first low hummock in the sand. I was on the point of disembarking, second to last, just ahead of the Colonel, when I realized that I had forgotten my gear, and in the moment it took to turn and pick it up piecemeal, Wornham whizzed by me and was gone. I slogged up the beach across one wind-made ridge and trench and then another. Loose, dark sand came up to the tops of my high combat boots at each step, and my breathing was sharp and painful. I made it to the third and deepest trench, some thirty yards in from the shore, and fell to my face there alongside Lee and several men of the command-post detail. When you stopped running or slogging, you became conscious of the whine and bang of mortar shells dropping and bursting near you. All up and down Red Beaches One and Two men were lying in trenches like ours, listening to shells and digging or pressing their bodies closer into the sand around them.

We were legitimately pinned down for about forty minutes. That is to say, the mortar fire was probably heavy enough and close enough during that time to make it impractical to go farther. There is, however, such a thing as wishful pinned-down thinking, and it can become a more dangerous state of mind than any other in an area that is being shelled. A man tends to cling to his trench, even if it is in the center of a target, when the sensible thing is to proceed out of the target as quickly as possible, using his own best judgment about when it's prudent to dive for cover again. It seems to take about twenty minutes under shellfire to adjust your nerves and evolve a working formula by which you can make progress and gauge, very roughly, the nearness of hits and the pattern of fire.

Lee and I, by agreement, finally left our gear in a trench near the shore (we planned to salvage it later, if possible) and worked out way up the beach in the wake of Wornham and his men. There were Marines on all sides of us doing the same thing. Each man had a different method of progress. One, carbine in hand, walked along steadily, pausing and dropping to one knee only when something about the sound of the shells seemed to confuse him. Another made a high-hurdling jump into every trench or hole he used. At one point I listened to a frail Nisei interpreter arguing with an officer who wanted to help carry his pack. Again, at a moment when Lee and I were catching our breath, something stirred beside the dune just behind us. A wounded man, his face blackened by sand and powder, had roused himself from the lethargy in which he lay and noticed us. Shell fragments had hit him in one arm, one leg, the buttocks, and one eye. His eye, a red circle in his dark-stained face, worried him most. He wanted to know if there were any medical corpsmen with a litter nearby. He had been so deafened by the explosion of the shell that I had to go very close to make him hear me. There were no corpsmen or litters about. In fact, the enemy fire on the beach made it hard to get help to wounded men for the first two days, and then the process of evacuating them in boats, which had to bump their way through high surf, was incredibly rough and painful. I promised this man to report him and get him help as soon as possible.

The next Marine we passed was dead, and so were a number of others on our diagonal course over the beach to the upland, but I didn't see a dead Japanese soldier until we got near the edge of the plateau. "That's the third one we've found on Red beaches today so far," said a soldier who sat near the mouth of a Jap concrete pillbox, which gave off a faint, foul smell. This pillbox, with walls three feet thick and built on a frame of metal tubing, was a good specimen of the Jap defenses on Iwo Jima, but in the days that followed I saw others even more substantial, with walls four to five feet thick, revolving gun turrets, and two or more approaches lined with neat stairs.

By mid-afternoon, Lee and I were ready to send our first dispatches. We decided that the only way to get them off quickly was to make for the flagship, several miles offshore. We did not feel very good about the prospect. The mortar fire on the beaches was as steady as ever, and the surf was running higher than it had been in the morning. We reluctantly started down toward the shore, threading our way through a column of silent, apologetic-looking reinforcement troops climbing uphill with boxes of ammunition from the beach. Occasionally a soldier stepped out of line and asked us if we knew where this column was bound. I don't know why the people going downhill inspired more confidence or looked better informed than the leaders of the column moving uphill, unless it was that the very direction of our progress suggested that we were Iwo Jima tenants of long standing—five or six hours, perhaps—possessed of sweeping oracular powers and the ability to speak words that would restore confidence and banish fear and confusion. This was certainly untrue. Lee and I paused in a hole halfway down the beach to argue about where we had left our packs and typewriters. I thought it was somewhere to the left, but every time I pointed, a shell was dropped on the exact spot I had in mind. Shells were now also chasing amtracks, ducks, and other craft some little way out from the shore.

It seemed clear by the time we reached Wornham's command post, now at least several minutes old, in a broad shellhole above the beach, that the Japs had quickly abandoned the beaches after losing a few men, and had taken most of their dead with them. This worried Wornham, because he figured that it meant heavy counterattacks in the next night or two, and he was also worried, as regimental commanders are everywhere in battle, by the problem of keeping his combat battalions in communication with each other and with him. Sitting in his shellhole, along with a couple of dozen staff men, medical officers, messengers, radio operators, and stray visitors who just wanted to be in a hole with other people, we followed, by radio and courier, the adventures of three battalions a few hundred yards away.

The battalions were known in Wornham's shellhole by their commanders' names: Robbie, Tony, and Butler. "Tony says he's ready to make his turn up the west beach," Wornham said fretfully, looking at a message in his hand. "I gotta get him." Now and then he looked around his hole and said plaintively, "Come on, let's break this up. Let's have some room here." At these words, a few of the strays would drift away in one direction or another, and a few minutes later others would take their places. The shells dropped more rarely in that neighborhood, but they were close enough. Tanks began to rumble up from the beach, at long intervals, and angle and stutter their way through a gap at the top of the ridge nearby. Purple Heart Louis came to the edge of the command post and had his right arm bandaged by a doctor, to whom we had already reported the position of the wounded Marine on the beach.

"I knew Louis would get it again," said a young captain. "Right where he deals the cards, too. I hope it will be a lesson to him."

We heard of death after death of men we had been with on the transport. One divisional surgeon had been killed, and another had already had a breakdown from overwork. Visible Japanese dead were still scarce, even though one company had found a nest of Japs and killed a hundred. "Here's a report from FFF Company colonel, sir," said an aide. "He says the presence of a lot of flies in a trench suggests the Japs buried some dead there."

There were live Japs near enough, for whenever the Navy's Grumman fighter planes dived at a point just to our right, near the airfield, they drew machine-gun fire. Looking around, I had the leisure for the first time to think what a miserable piece of real estate Iwo Jima is. Later, when I had seen nearly all the island, I knew that there were no extenuating features. This place where thousands of men of two nations have been killed or wounded in less than three weeks' time has no water, few birds, no butterflies, no discernible animal life—nothing but sand and clay, humpbacked hills, stunted trees, knife-edged kuna grass in which nits that carry scrub typhus live, and a steady, dusty wind.

Presently Lee said he thought that if we were going to file our

stories we should head toward a place where we could see some
boats bunching and where there might be a chance of our getting a
ride. We started off, and a few minutes later we tumbled into a
trench practically on top of our gear. There were a lot of men in
this refuge now. Two Negro soldiers carrying supplies had stopped
to give some water to a pair of Marines who were lying quietly at
one end. The Marines had been hit by shrapnel and were waiting
for litter bearers. After they drank the water their only movement
was a slight, mechanical stirring of their heads each time a shell
burst close by. By now almost everyone on the beaches, even those
not killed or wounded, had had some sort of direct contact with
Japanese shells, if only to the extent of having tiny spent fragments,
still burning hot, drop onto their clothing or into the sand right
beside them.

By the time we reached a hole by the water's edge near where we
had landed, we had lost our sense of urgency and entered that stage,
which comes after a certain amount of time in a shelled area, when
you can no longer bring yourself to duck and run constantly, even
when you are moving in the open. But the men in the boats along
the shoreline immediately re-aroused us. Since they came into the
fire zone only at intervals and remained as briefly as possible, they
had no time to lose their awareness of danger. It suddenly seemed
to us a matter of desperate importance to get out of there at once.
An ammunition dump was beginning to grow up around us, and
the shelling did not abate.

We went up to a boat whose ramp was slapping the waves a few
feet out from the shoreline and whose coxswain was trying to hold
her to shore by keeping her engine running. There we encountered
a Marine named Connell, who for the next half hour gave the most
spectacular demonstration of energy I have ever seen. Though he
moved with great speed and fervor, there seemed to be no fear in
him. He had been helping moor and unload supply boats all afternoon. He was stripped down to his green Marine shorts, and he
spent as much time in the water as out of it, his lank, blond hair
plastered to his skull. When he wanted to salvage a piece of equipment from the water, he made a long, flat power dive over the surf.
His problem at the moment was to make this boat fast, so that the

ammunition aboard her could be unloaded. With the coxswain's permission, we got into the boat and stowed our packs in the stern. It was quickly obvious that the crew of the boat, though they remained calm, were of no help to Connell whatever and considered the odds against unloading at this time overwhelming and the situation irremediable. Connell shouted orders or suggestions at them, but they simply stared at him and then stared up and down the beach at the shellbursts. Connell got hold of a rope, made it fast to the boat, then darted up the beach to tie the other end to a tractor, whose driver surveyed him curiously from the top of the vehicle. Connell persuaded the driver to start his engine and try to pull the boat in. The rope broke. Connell tied it again, and it broke again. He swam out to get another rope, but by the time he returned to the beach the driver and tractor had disappeared. Swimming furiously, he then approached Lee and me, at the stern of the boat, and called out the courteous suggestion that we get ashore. "This is going to take a long time," he shouted over the sound of the surf, "and you fellows will do better somewhere else!" He never once showed the slightest sign of temper or desperation. He appeared to regard the wild scene and his own mighty efforts and constant frustrations as wholly rational and what was to be expected. He was wrong about the boat's being there a long time. A few minutes after Lee and I swam and struggled to shore—Connell made three personal amphibious trips to help us with our gear—the boat withdrew to sea with its cargo still aboard, possibly to try a landing somewhere else. The last we saw of Connell he was racing down the beach to grasp a mooring rope on another boat thirty yards away.

It was getting dark and our clothes and equipment were nearly dry again when we finally boarded an LCT bound for the general neighborhood of the flagship. Five sailors returning from a shore job were grouped in a corner of the hold aft, where the boat's sides rose above their heads. As the vessel pulled out, we saw that four of them were trying vaguely to soothe the fifth, who was in the throes of shock from a near miss by a shell. He was a small young man with an underslung lower jaw. His head lolled back against the bulwark and his eyes rolled violently. "They can't get you here," said one of his colleagues, pointing at the boat's high sides. "Look. They can't even see you." By the time we were a couple of miles out, the sailor had recovered to the point of asking questions about the battle, but these and the answers he himself supplied only had the effect of returning him to a state of shock. The four others stopped looking at him and talked listlessly among themselves.

We made the flagship that night, but my typewriter sank to the bottom of the sea during our transfer from the LCT to a smaller boat that could go alongside the gangplank of the flagship.

The nature of the Iwo Jima battle did not change much in the days that immediately followed. The Marines made slow and costly gains in ground as they fought northward—gains that struck me then, and still do, as very little short of miraculous. A week or so after D Day, in a little scrub grove halfway across the island, I recognized behind his whiskers a staff officer in our transport group who used to surprise me a little by the passion and complete engrossment with which he could discuss for two or three hours at a time such a question as whether or not certain items of battalion equipment should be distributed divisionally, or whether a brother officer of his named Logan, thirty-five hundred miles away, stood eighty-sixth or eighty-seventh on the promotion list. It now seemed to me that such preoccupations were useful indeed if they contributed to the professional doggedness with which this man and the troops of his unit moved forward against such overpowering intimations of mortality. "I hear that the mortar fire is easing up on the beaches," he said seriously. "That's good. There's no reason why everybody on the island should get killed."

The Frontier Down Under

1942

AT AN ADVANCE BASE IN AUSTRALIA—Taking a shampoo and a backward glance in the order named, your correspondent eliminated a shovelful of Darwin's red dirt from his coiffure the other day and estimated that he has now traveled nearly 10,000 miles over and through the great island continent which lies for better or worse on Japan's left flank.

I don't want to be one of those Instant Postum historians who spend a week on Fifty-second Street in New York and knock off a book entitled *The Real America,* but it is possible to see and know Australia more quickly than other places its size—especially now that the whole country has taken on the simple form and flavor of an armed camp. Wherever habitation is possible—in the busy southern cities, in the green fields and groves of Queensland, in Darwin's sun-baked bush, and even in way stations along the barren, red-splotched central desert—there are soldiers, fliers, planes, guns, camps, airfields, barracks, mess rooms, hospitals, and supply depots, all prepared for serious business at little more than a moment's notice.

It doesn't take a big army to fill Australia's scattered bases, but even the most skeptical observer can see that there is too much here now to answer the description of a token force. What is here now is the skeleton and vital parts of a strong force.

There is no purpose of bogus tact or holy humbug to be served by saying that American soldiers and Australian diggers are soulmates. They are perhaps more natural allies than most military combinations, but, as an Australian nurse was explaining to your correspondent this week, much of this country stands socially where the United States stood eighty years ago. An American living with Australian soldiers is apt to feel as Dickens did when he visited the states and returned home with his sensibilities wounded to write *Martin Chuzzlewit.*

This brings about a comical turn of events which Americans here are still trying to get used to. It's a straight reversal of Sinclair Lewis' *Dodsworth* formula, wherein American gaucherie is contrasted in a woman's mind with courtly European grace and manners. American boys here are considered marvels of breeding and politeness, and Australian diggers are amazed and revolted by the number of times Americans say "Thank you," which is a phrase almost unknown in the bright digger lexicon. "Don't you blokes ever say any bloody thing but bloody 'Thank you'?" a local soldier asked your correspondent recently. Apart from this, of course, the American soldier is a well-fed, well-washed dandy by comparison with our ally. His clothes are better quality, his mess is better, and his camp sanitation is better.

Remember, however, that these differences are superficial, and friction caused by them is also superficial. The American soldier is regarded here not as a dude but as an efficient fighter and workman accustomed to higher and richer standards. The digger, once you've got to know him well, is a provocative combination of boldness, shrewdness, acquisitiveness, ingenuity, and frontier humor, corresponding in many ways to the nineteenth-century Americans who offended Dickens.

There are some surface physical distinctions. A surprising number of Australians have bad teeth, which often, in the case of soldiers, are yanked out and replaced. Australians, on the other hand, are startled by the number of Americans wearing glasses. In some localities diggers break out with skin trouble, possibly owing to mess conditions. Despite this the average Australian soldier is probably the finest-looking physical specimen in any of the world's armies. The digger's qualities of strength, shrewdness, and roughness are fostered in the bush and in the far-flung cattle and sheep stations. But even the cities partake of the same rude freedom. Brisbane, for instance, is a wide-open town in all respects, with the rough cordiality and vigor of an American frontier city. It was there, incidentally, that your correspondent, trying to check a Bible quotation, had to send out to the Methodist Mission for a Bible, there being none in the hotel.

DRINKING

IN

AMERICA

An Unfinished History

WHY A BOOK ON AMERICAN DRINKING at this time? And why by this writer? Well, why was *Umwandlung der Schenken* written when it was? And why by Lammers? Certain forces act on certain men at certain moments—as they must have acted on the two of us, the thirsty, apple-cheeked German aristocrat from Weimar (or wherever the hell Lammers came from; the name is new to me), and the thirsty, hard-eyed kid from the streets of south-side Chicago. Speaking for myself, maybe it would be enough to say that I feel there's been no really strong writing done in the liquor field, in America, since *God's Clock Strikes, and the Hour Is at Hand for the Dram-Shop to Die,* by Pentecost (who called it as he saw it), in 1886—unless you count *Chattel Mortgages on Saloon Fixtures in New York City,* by Graham, in 1888.

But the reason for this book goes deeper. I believe that in the years since the Second World War, American drinking has proved itself. Now, at last, a time has come when its friends and critics can relax their efforts and review the past. For three hundred years the going was tremendously hard. Americans were under constant pressure from the idea that drinking is dangerous, not to say evil. The enemies of drinking were many and sinister, and tireless to the point of indecency. (So were its fans. In 1850 three drinkers in ten regularly drank themselves stupid.) But now, following Prohibition (the last of a series of humiliations and purges), and a short, tricky period of adjustment to honesty, America has shown that she can handle liquor. In 1950 less than three drinkers in forty were chronic alcoholics. Granted, there is still in this country some misunderstanding of the facts and a scattering of innocent hysteria. Undeniably, a number of Americans today—mankind being in as nervous and clinical-minded a state as it is—are too conscious of alcoholism. So are their doctors, who tend to see an alcoholic behind every set of red eyeballs with slightly twitching lids. Here is the substance of five hundred preliminary interviews between patients and general practitioners that took place in New York, Cook, and Los Angeles Counties, in 1953:

> PATIENT: Is there any chance of my becoming an alcoholic, Doctor?
>
> DOCTOR: Yep.

And, here, the gist of two hundred exchanges between patients and psychiatrists, in the same year:

> PATIENT: Doctor, may we discuss what alcoholism *per se* means to me?
>
> PSYCHIATRIST: Damn right. Lie down.

But the truth is, the roughest and wildest of America's drinking days are now over. Though drinking in America is more widespread today than ever before—a little more than sixty million people use the stuff at least occasionally—it's a milder, and smarter, kind of drinking that it ever was in the past. The enemy—the spirit of Volstead, Carry Nation, and Parson Weems, who was an anti-booze man as well as the inventor of the story of Washington and the cherry tree—has shifted ground: the idea that drinking is dangerous has been replaced by the idea that thinking is dangerous. In another few years, if books are still being printed, I'll let you know how that one came out.

CHAPTER 1

The Broad,
Philosophical Picture

MOST OF THE EARLY SETTLERS of America had never touched water unless for hygienic or theological reasons, or because they'd fallen off a bridge. So they lost no time, once they were here, in rounding up as much liquor as possible and in forming rules and customs for disposing of it. Americans have worked along the same lines ever since, while varying the materials and changing the rules ad lib. The world at large is rich in drinking culture. American drinkers have borrowed certain ideas from this great body of thought. Other ideas they have left right where they were.

For instance, among the Masai of East Africa, the tribal supply of honey wine is brewed by a man and a woman who have had no sexual intercourse with anyone for two days previously. After the brewing, the man and the woman stay together in a tent for six days and six nights with the wine, until the latter is ready for use. It's believed that if the couple succumbs to love during that time the wine will be undrinkable, and the bees that produced the honey will fly away. No such reasoning as this has ever caught on in America, as far as the record shows. Not, at least, among the whites. (The Indians of ancient Mexico did prefer that their pulque— fermented century-plant juice—be made by men who had been celibate for four days or more. The Mojaves also correlated liquor and chastity.)

But primitive modesty rites, as opposed to purity rites, have had some influence on drinking in the United States. In Dahomey, an assistant holds a curtain in front of the king when the king drinks.

The chiefs of Pongo drink behind curtains, too. In Loango, when the royal cup-bearer rings a bell, everybody present kneels down and hides his face, and the king takes a drink. There used to be a variation of these rituals in high-caste American saloon life: unobserved pouring. Andrew Jackson made it a point to look away when a friend poured a drink from a bottle on the bar, so as not to see how much was taken. Then the friend looked away while Jackson poured. The bartender seldom looked at all; not so much from delicacy as because whiskey in those days wholesaled at from fifteen to thirty cents a gallon.

The primitive drinker's shyness is akin to his modesty about sex or defecation. He wants to hide the actions of certain private parts: in drinking, the throat and the belly. Among American drinkers in Jackson's time, it was the action of a certain private motive, greed, that was thought likely to cause embarrassment, unless it could be hidden, suppressed, or ignored.

In New England, up to Prohibition, polite drinkers serving themselves at bars considered it in poor taste to pour above the "church windows"—the panels in the big shot-glasses of that time—or to watch the next man's pouring. Then came Volstead, attrition, high prices, the end of self-service, and a swing to the law of fang and claw. It was every man against the house. The bottom fell out of modest drinking and *noblesse oblige;* not that these had been in general use, to begin with.

Many Tatars ruin their stomachs with kumiss, or ariki—a liquor distilled from mare's or camel's milk. Kumiss serves as a sort of international stoplight, or Plimsoll mark, for other drinkers. The service has been particularly useful to Americans, who have a tendency to dip their bills inquisitively into tough drinks such as vodka, tequila, and white mule. Kumiss, the world's foremost liquid man-eater, is 160 proof, or four fifths alcohol. Every other nation—Russia, Mexico, America—keeps its drinks safely below that point. Under close watch by international science, the Tatars in their sporting way milk mares and grow ulcers that the rest of us may profit. They are the first line of defense of the Western stomach.

Among the Hindus, at one time, the laws of Manu required that any Brahman who touched liquor commit suicide at once, or as soon afterward as he conveniently could. One Brahman, after thinking over the decree, worked out an alternative to killing himself— he sucked lozenges instead, to purify his breath. The idea caught hold and replaced suicide on a wide scale. Obedience to dry laws has followed similar patterns ever since, in every part of the world.

Only once, in recent centuries, has any race or nation come close to being totally dried out. That was the doing of one man, the most successful single-handed, short-order prohibitionist of modern times. From 1838 to 1842, Father Mathew, a Capuchin monk, went through Ireland like a dust storm, levying pledges, parching palates, and sending phantom snakes to join the real ones expelled by St. Patrick. By the time Father Mathew's crusade had ended Ireland was no longer big enough for drinking men and him. But drinkers found a way around the difficulty. They emigrated and resumed drinking in New York and Boston.

The drinks of primitive peoples are apt to be sweet, or thick, or both. The trend of civilization in drinking, anthropologists say, is toward dryness and thinness. America, in her short history, has summed up the course of evolution in record time.

In the beginning, the settlers made honey drinks (as the Feloops and Hottentots do). They were desperate. They also made thick, pasty beers (like the *tuwak* of the Dyaks). Then they began to import liquor from civilized Europe: gin and schnapps from Holland, gin, ale, and whiskey from England, brandy and wines from France and Spain. For mass consumption, Americans went as far as they could with rum made from West Indian sugar cane—and by the time the sweetness of this had palled somewhat, they had evolved dry, duty-proof American whiskey. In the late nineteenth century they began to take the thickness and warmth out of beer (and the flavor and everything else that made it drinkable, by non-American standards).

From then on the surge toward civilization gained speed, at all levels. Even among women (who had got a late start at calling their shots), pink drinks, green drinks, white drinks, and fruit-salad drinks lost ground quickly. The advance from the pre-Repeal old-fashioned cocktail, like a floating orchard, to the so-called "gag," or naked old-fashioned, was brutally swift. The vermouth in martinis became vestigial. And, while racing to the peak of progress, America added a third factor to the formula for civilized drinking: polar coldness.

Americans live under conditions that make them hotter-throated and thirstier than the run of progressive peoples in this era. Being unwilling to revert to syrup, except in their soft drinks, they have brought off a novel parlay in liquor: austerity, nudity, and chill. They have produced civilization on the rocks.

"On the rocks" was an American contribution to American drinking language. So were "red" and "red whiskey," for rye, though these are not often used any more. One of the first legitimately American slang terms in drinking was "one yard of flannel"—which referred to a certain recipe for flip, a sweet, hot colonial drink. Prohibition tossed up a few uncouth underworld expressions that were native.

But most of the key words, like booze, lush, and rum, came from England. (Rum, till recently, was the commonest generic word for liquor in America, especially in politics and prohibitionism.) In spite of what H. L. Mencken and others have said about the superior ingenuity and freshness of American low language, many Englishmen insist that we've always had to go to England for our best low-life stuff; and that much stuff that we call ours was theirs originally.

A British pedant once admitted that "drunk as a boiled"—or "biled"—"owl" was an Americanism, and an early one. But he ruled that "drunk as an owl" came from Lincolnshire and was earlier. In a report of an American murder trial in 1855 that involved considerable low life, the New York *Times* quoted witnesses as testifying to various degrees of intoxication as follows: "He had cut his oats, I think; he was a little tight." "He was pretty well corned." "She was tight as a brick." Thackeray, who was visiting in New York at about that time, claimed that all those phrases were British.

It's the feeling of British scholars that since Americans are mopping up the best part of the liquor Great Britain distills today and are making powerful music with it, Britain may as well have credit for its share of the lyrics.

Only in France, where reason is queen, has a mathematical formula for drunkenness ever been worked out. In 1912, Pierre Germain, a psychologist, after a close, cleanly fought investigation of *"l'ivresse"* in general (including the lifts that come from alcohol, hashish, and opium), set it down that $XM = F(M)$.

X, in this equation, Germain said, represents the stimulant, the *excitant*. *M* is the *moi*, the thinking, feeling system, the essential "me" in the drinker or drug-taker. What is *F*? From Germain's description, it's hard to tell. It may be the *fonctions*, the actions, of the temperament (M) that undergoes the *excitant* (X). Germain beats around the bush a good deal here. He talks about a girl he knew who threw a couple down and then took a dislike to her own body. His writing becomes feverish and erratic.

France has forgotten this step in science. At least, you seldom hear it discussed there. America has steadily ignored it. The author himself, toward the end of his announcement in the *Revue des Idées*, admits that there are several flaws in the formula. Still, it's the only one there is.

CHAPTER 2

Drinking Is Probably Not Un-American

SHORTLY AFTER THE UNITED STATES had been founded, reformers in Philadelphia denounced drinking as "anti-Federal," which was the contemporary way of saying "un-American." (The term was invented while the ink was drying on the Declaration of

Independence. It filled a need that had lasted several seconds and came, in the opinion of some, none too soon.)

Human experience shows that if drinking is un-anything, it is unavoidable. Whenever early man left a mess of fruit or berries around for a while, uneaten, and forgot about it, there was fermentation. When he left it near a fire, there was also distillation. In both cases, alcohol (C_2H_5OH) resulted. Whether you like the result or not ("I hate it with a perfect hatred," said Billy Sunday, a well-known evangelist of some years ago), these processes are worldwide natural ways of life—if you allow that it's natural in man to leave fruit around. In America, they won a continent for the whites by knocking the previous owners over on their faces—and then, in time, produced a rum age (roughly, 1650–1800), a whiskey age (roughly, 1800 to the present), and gin, wine, and beer, in cans and bottles.

It's true that liquor has caused a lot of trouble, and still causes a lot of misunderstanding, in America. But that has been its tendency everywhere at one time or another. Scotland, a couple of centuries ago, went overboard for liquor at practically all social levels. "Sir," an English visitor said to a Scottish host, "your hospitality borders on the brutal." But you don't hear drinking spoken of today as un-Scottish—that is, as something the Scots couldn't handle, in the long run. The tendency of man, if he's given time, is to snap out of his liquor difficulties by reducing or diluting his ration. In the South Carolina colony, in the eighteenth century, men died like flies from overdrinking; women had to take over many of the plantations. Today, South Carolina men outlive flies. The state is one of the three or four least damp in the country, with an annual consumption of less than a gallon of alcohol per capita of drinking age (over fifteen years old).

There's an idea around today that women and teen-agers in America are drinking more than they used to. The truth is, the alcoholic rate among women was far higher in 1910 than it was in 1950. As to children, they drank much earlier in colonial times than they do now—from scratch, in fact. Almanacs recommended to mothers that babies' beer be heated. In Massachusetts, at one time, adult drunkards were forced to wear a big *D* around their necks, and it's possible that juvenile drunkards had to wear a small, lower-case *d*. (But I know of no source that says they did.) In the nine-teenth century there was a temperance magazine for boys and girls called *The Juvenile Abstainer*. It was published in England, but it had a loyal following among American urchins.

Nowadays, women alcoholics and child alcoholics turn themselves in for cures sooner than they used to—to hospitals or to Alcoholics Anonymous. This leads to fuller publicity and to more extensive records, and may account for the false notions people have today about boozing in those groups.

Another idea is that Democrats drink more than Republicans do. But, in 1954, a year after the Republican party had returned to power in Washington, statistics showed that alcoholic consumption in the District of Columbia had reached a new high. In fact, con-sumption of alcohol in the D.C. exceeded consumption of milk. (Considering that the D.C. almost always leads the national list in liquor intake, it's surprising that people there find time to drink as much milk as they do.)

Probably the main reason why drinking, in America and else-where, is misunderstood and misrepresented is the emphasis given to abnormality in drinking. As with television dials, nobody thinks anyone else knows how to handle liquor. It's a kind of by-condition of the use of alcohol that every nondrinker suspects that every drinker is abnormal. Every drinker suspects that all drinking but his own is abnormal. A few scientists admit that there is such a thing as normal drinking, but they don't pretend to understand it or to be interested in it, so science studies nothing but abnormal drinkers. (Much of this study is done at Yale, which is a hotbed of tables of alcoholic rates.)

Doctors spend an unwholesome amount of time trying to frame definitions of alcoholism, as children try to frame breakfast-food slogans to win a space pistol. Wilfred Funk, in a book on drinking, quotes "top-drawer doctors" as stating that a normal drinker is one who takes no more than thirty cc.s of alcohol—which amounts to two two-ounce drinks—a day. He doesn't say how the doctors ar-rived at this gloomy and insulting estimate, or what, if they were sober themselves, they were doing in a drawer.

Unfortunately, seven out of twenty Americans accept as fact the superstition that the country today is going to hell through drink. (The statistics are my own. They are based on heart-to-heart talks with twenty Americans, who co-operated eagerly in the belief that they would sooner or later be asked to tell about their sex habits. They never were.)

CHAPTER 3

Highlights of American Drinking

A Short, Chronological List

1608—HENRY HUDSON served liquor to a party of Lenape Indians, on what is now Manhattan Island, and the Indians passed out, to a man. Afterward they called the place (it had had no formal name, before then) Manahachtanienk, which meant, in their language, "The island where we all became intoxicated." In time, as one hangover led to another, even the Lenapes had trouble pronouncing the name, and it ended up as Manhattan. According to the best information, the liquor Hudson served was gin.

1633—John Josselyn, an English tourist, went into a tavern in Boston to refresh himself. After he'd had a few drinks, a stranger who was sitting near by told the landlord not to give him any more. Josselyn said, "You take care of yourself, friend, and I'll take care of Josselyn," but his supply was cut off just the same. What Josselyn had run up against was Boston's human drunkometer system, by which drinkers at that time were protected against themselves by grog sleuths, or public eyes.

Circa 1700—Drinking having become the most popular indoor sport in the colony of Virginia, in all walks of life, the home office of the Church of England wrote the following ground rule for Virginia clergymen: Any clergyman who sat drinking in company for one hour, without missing a turn, would be found guilty of intemperance.

1769—An English trader named Williamson paid a Kaskaskia Indian one barrel of rum to kill Pontiac, the great Ottawa chief, who was his race's leading citizen. The assassination took place in Cahokia, Ill., across the river from St. Louis. The assassin stole up on Pontiac from behind and buried a tomahawk in his brain.

1775—Ethan Allen prepared himself and his men for the capture of Ticonderoga by taking on New England rum (which was sometimes known as "kill-devil") at Fay's Tavern, in Bennington (in what is now Vermont).

Circa 1776—Baron von Riedesel, a Hessian general, made observations of American life which caused him to write later, as though he meant it, "Most of the males have a passion for strong drink."

1778—George Washington, at Valley Forge, complained that he could offer a French guest nothing better than "stinking whiskey." He may have been talking about Old Monongahela, a Pennsylvania rye that was the best-known brand of red liquor of the eighteenth century. Washington himself was partial to imported wine, especially Madeira.

1780—General Marion, the "Swamp Fox," a strict teetotaler, attended a wine supper at which the rest of the company threatened to force him to drink his share. The general held true to his principles by jumping out of a second-story window, but he sprained his ankle in the process.

Circa 1825—Cuspidors came into use in many drinking places. Previously, floors near bars had been protected by rubber mats.

Circa 1830—Sam Houston, while doing valuable work developing the frontier in Oklahoma, was nicknamed "Big Drunk" by the Cherokee Indians.

1837—Nathaniel Hawthorne, who knew nothing about public drinking, went into a bar in Concord, Mass., the brainiest town in the country, home of Emerson and Thoreau, to find out what was going on. He saw a bartender mix cocktails by tossing liquor from one glass into another in a high, wide arc.

1838—What was said to be the first free lunch was served in saloons in New Orleans. It included gumbo, barbecued meat, potatoes, and oysters.

1845—John B. Gough, the most famous temperance lecturer in the United States, disappeared one morning soon after leaving his hotel, in New York City. He was found several days later in a room in a brothel a few blocks away, in a state of alcoholic collapse. He admitted to his followers, "I have fallen," but charged that the fall had been induced by an agent of the liquor interests who had spiked Gough's raspberry soda in a soft-drink parlor near the Bowery.

1850—Sportsman's Hall, a New York bar, advertised in the newspapers: "Rats constantly on hand." The claim, which might strike readers as unusually frank, but probably true, if it came from a New York bar owner today, referred to rats kept for the use of dog fanciers in the sport of ratting.

1854—"Ten Nights in a Barroom," by Timothy Shay Arthur, first hit the bookstalls. As a novel and later as a play, it panicked its customers and bedeviled the booze trade in America and England for the balance of the century. The key line of "Ten Nights," "I'll never drink another drop of liquor as long as I live," was spoken by Joe Morgan, a rumpot, at the deathbed of his little daughter Mary, who had been hit between the eyes by a glass thrown at her father, a difficult target at best, by a barkeeper.

1855—Charles Cora, a gambler, shot and killed General W. H. Richardson, a U.S. marshal, in the Blue Wing saloon in San Francisco. The shooting occurred a few days after an outburst of class consciousness at the opera, when the general had objected to his wife's being seated near Cora's mistress, Belle Ryan. The Richardson murder shook San Francisco to the ganglia. The jury at Cora's trial disagreed, but as soon as the trial was over, the town's vigilance committee laid hold of the gambler, tried him again, and convicted him. At his own request, Cora was hanged from a front window of the committee's headquarters. He had thought that this might give lynching a bad name. To some extent, it did.

1855—In Lafayette Hall, a New York City saloon, Tom Hyer, former prizefight champion of America, pushed the face of Lew Baker, a policeman, into a gas-jet cigar lighter. The gesture led indirectly to the murder of a friend of Hyer's, Bill Poole, also a fighter, by Baker, in another saloon, Stanwix Hall. At the time of the killing Pole was drinking champagne and Baker "brandy" (there was a cheap, uncolored whiskey that went by the name of brandy in America and England then). As half the city's drinkers loved Poole dearly, his funeral was the biggest and best attended in New York history, up to Rudolph Valentino's in 1926. Hyer was a pallbearer.

1864—General Grant and General Sherman mapped out Sherman's march through Georgia over drinks at Barnet House, a Cincinnati oasis.

1865—At a wake for Abraham Lincoln in Chicago, Ill., state legislators drank four hundred sixty-nine dollars' worth of liquor. Lincoln's death had left open a question that was to be argued for years afterward: whether he was for drinking or against it—and the legislators gave themselves the benefit of the doubt.

(Notes on Lincoln and drinking: In 1856, Stephen A. Douglas said that Lincoln as a young man "could ruin more liquor than all the boys in the town put together." Lincoln, in reply, said that when he'd sold whiskey in his grocery store in New Salem, Ill., Douglas had held up the other side of the counter buying it. In 1909, Cardinal Gibbons said that Lincoln had not been a prohibitionist. In 1923, Evangeline Booth said that he had been. In 1927, J. A. Danielson wrote a monograph on Lincoln and alcohol. It didn't prove a case one way or the other, but it made it seem likely that Lincoln didn't like prohibition and didn't like drunks.)

1866—Murder fans in Chicago were excited but not displeased when Mary Cosgriff, who operated a bagnio there, shot her lover, George Trussell, to death in Seneca Wright's saloon on Randolph Street. In her defense, Miss Cosgriff said that Trussell had wronged her with a harness horse named Dexter, which he had recently bought and on which he had been spending most of his time and money. The jury found her guilty, but she was pardoned after having served a year in jail.

1877—President Hayes's wife got the nickname of Lemonade Lucy around Washington. She was bone-dry. Friends of the administration preserved international good will by secretly needling the refreshments at Mrs. Hayes's diplomatic dinners with gin, and by syncopating the desserts with wine.

1882—Oscar Wilde, during a lecture tour of the United States, outdrank twelve miners in the number-three shaft of the Matchless Mine, in Leadville, Colo. Since Wilde had a worldwide reputation for effeminacy and was believed to eat flowers between meals, his victory was a severe blow to American drinking prestige.

Circa 1886—To offset Wilde and the mine disaster, Western bartenders took to keeping score in drinking bouts and to building up drinking legends. One report had it that John L. Sullivan, the best free-style drinker and fighter in the country, while making personal appearances in the West, walked into a saloon and asked what the house record was, for one man. He was told that it was seventy two-ounce drinks in one day's drinking. Sullivan, in the next five hours, disposed of one hundred drinks. One hundred two-ounce drinks amounts to more than six quarts. By the cold light of reason, it seems like a lot of liquor, even for John L.

1890—Mark Twain, then living in Elmira, N.Y., acquired a local name for tightfistedness, because he never bought a drink for anyone but himself. Only his best friends knew that his closeness was based on principle. Twain felt that the practice of treating, if encouraged, would sooner or later destroy the saloon as an institution. It's a fact that, thirty years later, the saloon, as an institution, was destroyed.

Circa 1900—Carry Nation, a lady who hated booze, stove in a ten-gallon keg of whiskey with a five-pound sledgehammer, in Medicine Lodge, Kans. Soon afterward she performed her first hatchet job, slashing the furnishings and fixtures in a saloon in Wichita. Mrs. Nation's early life had been hard. Her first husband had died partly because of drink. Her mother had thought that she (Mrs. Nation's mother, a Mrs. Moore) was Queen Victoria.

1903—Big Ed Delahanty, the Babe Ruth of turn-of-the-century baseball, who had once hit four home runs in one game, fell off a train as it was crossing a bridge over the Niagara River. He was drowned in the rapids above the Falls. Ed had been drinking. Baseball fans, as they mourned his death, were aware that he usually had been.

1905—John L. Sullivan walked into a saloon, either in Terre Haute or in Grand Rapids (historians differ), ordered champagne, and astonished potential scorekeepers there by pouring his drink into a cuspidor. He explained the anticlimax by saying that he had suddenly decided never to drink again. He never did.

1910—Signs increased that legal drinking, for the time being, had had it. *The Saturday Evening Post,* with its ear to the grass roots, swore off liquor advertisements and illustrations that showed wineglasses and other inflammatory apparatus.

1920—Billy Sunday, the dry evangelist, who a few years earlier had promised that he was going to make the country "so dry that you'll have to prime a man twice before he can spit," preached John Barleycorn's funeral sermon in a street in Norfolk, Va. The date was January 16, three days before all bars were legally shut down by the Volstead act. "Goodbye, John," said Sunday, addressing a two-foot coffin on a cart that was hitched to two horses. "Hell has frozen over," he added, in part.

1920—On the advertised day, one hundred and seventy-seven thousand saloons closed their doors for alterations. Later, fitted with peepholes, the doors swung open again, on a new hydraulic principle based on the words "Sid sent me."

1927—The national death rate from alcoholism had risen by 150 per cent since 1920. In Kansas, which had been dry before Prohibition, the rise was only 60 per cent, indicating that two laws are twice as good as one.

1929—Vivian Gordon, a beautiful underworld financier, tore a leaf out of the book of Queen Isabella of Spain by backing three explorers with $1,500 to cross the sea and crack open the Bank of Oslo, Norway. The expedition reached the bank but found that the guard there had been doubled. Its members then cruised about Europe, trading with the natives, and brought back a load of ancient liquor, which Miss Gordon sold at a profit.

1930—Flint Rhem, a pitcher for the St. Louis Cardinals, disappeared for forty-eight hours during a crucial series in Brooklyn. On reappearing, Rhem said that he had been kidnaped by gunmen, held incommunicado in a hotel room, and forced at the point of a gun to drink "large quantities of liquor." The story was accepted by Branch Rickey, Cardinal general manager, who said that you couldn't disprove it by the way Rhem smelled.

1935—Dutch Schultz, New York gang chief, became the first

important casualty of the post-repeal era. His killer, Charlie the Bug Workman, followed Schultz into the men's room in the bar of the Palace Chophouse, Newark, New Jersey, and shot him while he was washing his hands. Among Schultz's last words were these: "Now listen, Phil. . . . Fun is fun. . . . What happened to the other sixteen? . . . Mother is the best bet. . . . And don't let Satan draw you too fast."

1938—Robert Joyce, a post-office clerk, got into an argument about the Brooklyn Dodgers in Diamond's Cafe, Brooklyn. When his opponents became malicious and abusive toward the Dodgers, Joyce left the place. He returned with a gun, and killed one man and seriously wounded another.

1949—People in the United States spent $9,640,000,000, a new high, on liquor. But the rate of chronic alcoholism per capita of population was down almost one-third from what it had been forty years before.

CHAPTER 4

The Lay of the Land

BEFORE THE WHITE MEN CAME, America was a garden of peace and prudence, with respect to drink. Reading from north to south, the population was divided into the following groups:

1. Nondrinkers.
2. Reformed hard drinkers.
3. Light-wine-and-beer drinkers.

North America, above Mexico, was alcoholically virgin. The Indians drank water and fruit juices. (The Eskimos had a soft drink of their own, a sort of arctic Moxie, made of hot blood and melted fat.) Liquor, when it finally arrived with the white men from Europe, was a shock to the tribes in what is now the United States. "Unspeakable are the mischiefs which arise from rum," an Iroquois chief said, not long after the Indians had begun to give the country away at a rate of roughly an acre a drink. He spoke as much in surprise as in anger.

The Aztecs in Mexico were less startled by the effects of alcohol, when the Spaniards turned it loose there. Though they drank the white man's liquor as fast as the northern Indians did and lost their shirts even faster, they had reason to know what they were doing. The Aztecs, when the whites found them, were a race of reclaimed alcoholics. Long before Columbus they had learned to drink—and then almost to forget drinking. Such memories as they had of their drinking past were, officially, painful. A native hymn said, in part:

> "Alas! . . .
> This creature in the home of our ancestors
> Was a fearful thing."

The creature had been pulque, a solid potion brewed from the juice of the maguey, a cousin of the century plant. The Aztecs often had spiked their pulque with peyote. Peyote is a strong drug obtained from the buds, or buttons, of the mescal cactus. It has stimulated Western American Indians for centuries; recently, it stimulated Aldous Huxley into writing a book called *The Doors of Perception*. Pulque, laced and unlaced, had raised so much hell among the Aztecs that the ruling classes had passed control and prohibition laws for the lower classes. This pattern has been seen in many civilizations; the nobles feel that drunkenness is characteristically a weakness of commoners, and a dangerous one, which can lead to insubordination, and they legislate accordingly, relying on God and good taste for their own guidance.

The anti-pulque laws were directed mainly at younger commoners, who were thought to have higher capacities for hell-raising. The penalties were crisp, along the following lines:

In one city, first offenders were jailed, second offenders had their brains clubbed out.

In another city, first offenders were enslaved, second offenders were killed as above.

In another city, a two-time loser had his hair shaved in the market place and his house burned down.

The laws made certain dispensations: pulque could be used medicinally; women could use pulque just before and after childbirth; Aztecs over fifty could have small rations of pulque; Aztecs over seventy could have all the pulque they wanted.

It can be seen that the rules were sounder and milder than Volstead's, and that the punishments exceeded the fondest dreams of Carry Nation or Billy Sunday.

Possibly while right-thinking, pro-administration Aztecs were singing of their luck in putting pulque behind them, other Aztecs were praying for rain. In the cloudburst of young, cheap brandy that came just after Cortez, prohibition in this semi-paradise was washed away and forgotten forever.

The light drinking in America in pre-white times was done in South America. The Mayas drank a little *zaca* (fermented corn) and a little *chicha* (fermented pineapple juice, to which chocolate was added). The Incas drank their own gentle kinds of vegetable beer. Some South American Indians put the ashes of dead friends and relatives or powder ground from the bones of the departed into their drinks. These rites resembled Irish wakes in the sense that—no matter how hard a stranger might find it to believe—they were based on loving good will. The Indians reasoned, "It is better to be inside a friend than to be swallowed by the cold earth."

Innocence in the north, austerity in the south, were the conditions that ruled drinking in America before the palefaces came. There's a parlor joke which says that the white settlers first fell on their knees, and then fell on the aborigines. The Europeans brought gunpowder, tuberculosis, smallpox, measles, syphilis, and distilled liquor with them, and liquor proved to be the most influential of these among the Indians; to some extent, it paved the way for the application or distribution of all the others. In North America the virgin drinkers, like the virgin trees, went down in rows, and the swift progress of tuberculosis, for instance, was due partly to the progress of the custom of passing out, in the open, on the cold ground.

There's no hard, scientific support for the idea that the Indians were "natural" bad drinkers, handicapped physiologically as well as by inexperience. But there's a quasi-expert theory that people whose diet is mainly carbohydrate—which would include potatoes, yams, and starches and sugars in general—have a low resistance to alcohol. This is said to be the reason why Indians, Norsemen, and Irishmen have more trouble with liquor than do, among others, drinkers in Mediterranean countries, who fortify their stomachs with oils and fats. The racial approach to drinking has produced a considerable body of back-room ethnology, especially in connection with redskins and Hibernians. Maxims include "Indians can't handle it. Look at Jim Thorpe," and "Irishmen and alcohol don't mix."

A more civil way of putting these things would be to say that it's the poetry in a man, rather than the carbohydrates or the bloodlines, that exposes him to defeat by alcohol. One Indian said about liquor, soon after his first experience with it, "It is made of tongues and hearts, for when I have drunk it I fear nothing, and I talk like an angel."

CHAPTER 5

Manifest Destiny

IT TOOK THE INDIANS no time to speak of to realize that drinking, in spite of the bold, gay feeling it gave them, was, in their circumstances, a bad idea. It caused them to lose their self-control and their property, and they had more of both to lose than most drinkers have. Their d.t. visions were abnormally substantial: live white men going through their pockets, instead of spurious reptiles crawling down their bedroom walls.

It was only the Indians' leaders, however, who tried to resist the trend. As among the Aztecs of unlimited-pulque times, the ruling classes worried about liquor, while the common people (or the common braves) drank it. A Delaware chief stated the problem with eloquence, to William Penn, one day in the seventeenth century. His people, the chief said, were well aware that liquor was bad for them; but they loved it so much that they would take it anyway, whenever it was available. "It makes us mad," he said. "We do not know what we are doing; we abuse one another; we throw one another into fire." Penn, in response, had an Indian prohibition law passed in Pennsylvania. Anyone convicted of selling liquor to an Indian was to be sentenced to serve time in a seven-foot-square cage. This was the same as the penalty for selling watered liquor to a white man.

In general, the pattern in the colonies with respect to Indian protection, alcoholically, was as follows:

When the settlers had some of the land, they began to pass laws. When they had it all, they began to enforce them.

Once, toward the middle of the eighteenth century, Moravian missionaries in the New York colony, having decided that drinking was doing the Indians no good, attempted to interfere with bootleg sales there. This raised the question of which group was more valuable to the government, bootleggers or missionaries, and the Moravians were run out of the colony.

It was officially illegal to sell liquor at trading posts, but an Indian who knew a beaver and brought his skin to the door could always get a drink. According to *Ponteach* [Pontiac]: *or, The Savages of America,* a play that was published in London in 1766 and was said to have been written by Major Robert Rogers, of Rogers' Rangers, the traders prepared the Indians for business with rum "more pow'rful made by certain strength'ning drugs" and paid them off with watered rum—"The cooling draught well suits their scorching throats." The going price was a quart of liquor for five pounds of beaver pelts. The scales, the major said, were rigged to score one pound for each three pounds of fur.

War also stimulated the alcohol traffic. The French on one occasion delivered a shipment of a hundred and sixty kegs of new-mown brandy to an Indian tribe (the Senecas), to buy help in driving the English off Indian land in behalf of the French. The English bought Indian help with rum, to make Indian land safe for the English. The English were not above suggesting in the consumer market that French liquor was poison. The French considered it redundant to apply this word to English liquor.

It became clear to Indian statesmen, in time, that bootlegging, that, is to say, pioneering, was in the white man's blood. It was bigger, pending alterations in the ownership of North America, than any white prohibition law. So the Indians began desperately to make their own laws. The Iroquois, an advanced people with a working acquaintance with shell games, had noted that white men found in possession of liquor on Iroquois land were apt to claim that they were just passing through to supply Algonquin clients up the way, or to relieve an outbreak of snakebite among the Delawares down the road. On top of a prohibition law the Iroquois wrote a transportation law, which forbade the whites even to carry liquor through their territory, en route to other territories.

In self-defense against alcohol, Indian antiliquor squads in several different tribes staged public demonstrations with axes. The Creeks smashed many barrels of rum, though they continued to empty others drink by drink. The Shawnees of Pennsylvania, having voted to "break and split" every keg brought into their country, did a certain amount of breaking and splitting, when the chiefs were looking.

Just as white laws against selling liquor to Indians created white bootleggers, Indian prohibition laws created Indian bootleggers. The Indian bootlegger was a lean and hungry man. He was as low on the economic totem pole as the kind of paleface race-track tout who, two centuries later, hand-prints his tip cards in the shrubbery just after the day's racing is over to show the crowds going home that he's had six winners. The Indian bootlegger worked with barrel scrapings. His goods were so thin or so noisome that only a very desperate Indian drinker just out of the forest from a three-month trapping trip would buy from him.

Almost on the day that the last acre of America passed into their hands, the white men foreclosed on Indian drinking. There had been a broad interchange of cultures. The Indians had learned drinking from the whites. The whites had learned prohibition from the Indians. In the last two hundred years, no men on earth, including Mohammedans, have found it so hard to become stimulated as American Indians have.

Even drug taking is uphill work for an Indian today. For centuries, Indians in the West, for certain sacramental purposes or merely to soothe their nerves, have chewed mescal buttons as tribes in other parts of the world chew betel nut or kola nut. These are the same wild cactus buds with which the ancient Aztecs needled their liquor. Not long ago, Federal Bureau of Narcotics agents swooped down on mescal munchers on a Montana reservation to make what is known in the newspapers as a drug pinch.

At that point, the proud former masters of a continent were pretty much reduced to Coca-Cola, which it has always been legal to sell to Indians.

CHAPTER 6

The Rum Age

RUM WAS THE PEOPLE'S DRINK in America in the days when the people were bunched in the East, and when their need was for a liquor, quickly available in bulk, that would warm a white man's stomach and burn out the lining of an Indian's.

Later, as Americans moved west, they found broad fields to grow grain in. It turned out that one of the best ways to get the grain to market, heavy shipping being a problem then, was to send it in the neat, compact form of whiskey. So whiskey came to be mass-produced, and it soon cornered the drinking trade. But before this happened—and for more than a hundred years of robust American history, from the last part of the seventeenth century to the beginning of the nineteenth—the people's drink was rum. Beer in the colonies was muddy homemade stuff, which might have anything from a pine cone to a Puritan's nightshirt as a base. Imported wines and brandies were for the rich. Water was for witches. Rum could eliminate any difficulty known to colonial man, including the previous tenants, and it sold for less than fifty cents a gallon.

Rum was defined by an early lexicographer as "a strong water drawn from sugar-cane." It was called "kill-devil" in some parts of New England, where it had its greatest success. Among the other things it killed was competition for slaves; used as slave bait, it drove French brandy off the African coast. In the eighteenth century one hogshead of rum brought one African or one healthy African woman.

A beauty of rum was that it came, like a dozen other precious panaceas in human experience, such as soup and penicillin, from leftover or waste materials. The main ingredient of rum is molasses, which is a waste product of the manufacture of sugar. The first rum, like the best today, was distilled in the West Indies. But Americans, especially New Englanders, took the process to their bosoms, imported the molasses, and distilled their own duty-proof rum at home. It's well known that New England rum helped to found Dartmouth college. Dartmouth in turn produced Daniel Webster, who is said to have been one of the champion rum drinkers of New England in his younger days. As he grew older and spent more time in Washington under softening influences, Webster came to favor Madeira wine.

At the price, rum gave the colonists efficient, low-cost stimulation. But the thirst of many New Englanders was so great at the time (as Baron Riedesel said, in his notes on the Revolution), that they were able to run up large bar checks, anyway. In one case, which has found its way into several record books, a party of guests at an inn in Newburyport, Massachusetts, was presented with a bill for about $300 for a night's drinking.

The tab listed:

Three bowls of punch [the punch had lemon or lime juice, shrub, and other elements mixed in with the rum].

Seven double [two-quart] bowls of punch.

One mug of flip, and a thribble [three-quart] bowl of punch.

One bowl of egg toddy.

Six and a half pints of spirits.

Etc. [a Newburyport expression meaning "We won't go home until morning"].

Flip, which is mentioned in this list, had a foundation of home-brewed beer sweetened with sugar or dried pumpkin. A liberal measure of rum was added. The mixture was stirred in a mug or a pitcher with a hot iron that was called either a loggerhead or a hottle, which made it boil and foam and gave it a burnt flavor.

The occurrence of any prodigy of nature, or, for that matter, the occurrence of anything from scattered showers to a noticeable tendency of Wednesday to follow Tuesday, set early Americans to thinking about rum. When an unusually big block of ice was washed up out of the Connecticut River at Lyme, Connecticut, one winter, a Lyme liquor dealer put advertisements in newspapers as far away as Boston urging drinkers to come and drink rum punch made with ice chipped off the superblock, while the supply lasted.

Rum was drunk mainly in a gregarious way, by people going out to bars or to parties. At home, at the table, the colonists drank home-made cider or, in some neighborhoods, peachy (peach cider), or perry (pear cider). A lot of love, time, and energy went into cider making. Among the more conscientious farmers apple juice was first purified by frost, then colored with Indian corn, then laid away in kegs for three months or more, after which it looked and tasted a good deal like Madeira—or so its makers liked to say. Visitors from England spoke of cider, which was all they got to drink at meals in most American private houses, as low, disgusting stuff. John Adams drank a tankard of cider every morning at breakfast. Cider and beer were served at table at Princeton College, though Princeton students often packed a barrel or two of rum along to school with them, for social purposes. George Washington, who had rich, European tastes in some things, drank Rhenish and Spanish wines and French brandy.

Even Washington conceded that for hard drinking, in all parts of the colonies, the people's choice was rum. In his days in local politics in Virginia, he bought the voters rum by the hogshead. Rum was the staple drink in taverns everywhere. Taverns were staple items of colonial real estate. In the middle of the seventeenth century one building in every four on Manhattan Island had a barroom in it. A hundred years later, even after less essential lines of business had begun to take hold and spread in America, the rate in Philadelphia was one grogshop to each ten houses.

Rum taken in therapeutic doses helped women through childbirth and children through colds. Inhaled habitually as a substitute for air it turned the faces of some adult males an intense, permanent blue, as with Captain Flint's in *Treasure Island*. Sprayed over the Indians, it cleared American farm land for the cultivation of whiskey. That last step ended the rum age; a civilization exposed to beefsteak in quantity will seldom use veal again, if it can afford not to, except as a fad or as a change of pace. In the same way, rum became a second-class drink. Its impact had been so strong, however, in the time of its glory that to this day, in the language of politics and reform, the word for liquor as a force in life is "rum."

CHAPTER 7

The Untaxed Whiskey Age

BETWEEN 1818 AND 1862 there were no taxes whatever on American whiskey. A market report in the 1820s—and one decade was like another in this respect, during this period—gave the price of spirits as twenty-five cents a gallon, domestic, and one dollar, imported. In the circumstances, a man who went out without his will power buttoned up to his throat was likely to come home wet, if at all.

As it happened, resistance to drinking was stubborn and fairly widespread just then. There were not so many drinkers, relatively, as there had been in the days of the pioneers with their European habits and traditional hydrophobia. Nineteenth-century life at the middle-income levels abounded in certain kinds of continence. The temperance movement, which had come in with the industrial revolution, was gaining in power. Researchers had stumbled on the use of water as a beverage. Also, impulses toward competitive respectability and social and commercial climbing had begun to set in. Just the same, to Americans who rose above these considerations or sidestepped them, the bargain rate on whiskey was very tempting— and the response to it was enthusiastic enough to give reformers and foreign observers the impression that the whole country was listing slightly to starboard.

A labor feature of the early part of the whiskey age was an alcoholic five-day week, created by the observance of what was called Blue Monday. By unwritten agreement between employers and employees in many factories, shops, and offices, nobody worked on Monday. Workers showed up at their posts, thanks partly to another unwritten rule of the time, which required employers to provide personnel with rations of free liquor daily. But almost nothing got done in the way of business. Monday was devoted to melting down and sleeping off hangovers built up on Saturday night and Sunday.

Sailors ashore were a group especially given to mopping up untaxed whiskey (which included so-called "brandy"—immature, pale-colored, half-processed whiskey). At least it was a favorite argument in temperance circles that sailors ashore were constantly drunk, and polls were taken now and then to support the point. These polls always proved what they had set out to prove:

Q. (asked of sea captains in 1828): "In shipping a crew, how large a proportion of the men have usually come on board in a state of intoxication?"

Some answers:

"About one third."—Captain E. R.

"One half."—Officer, U.S. Navy.

"Two thirds."—Captain G. S.

"One half to two thirds."—Captain J. W.

At sea, the captains dried their men out by restricting them to one to two gallons per seaman per month. Grog rations were no more of an economic strain on employers, on land or sea, than windshield wiping or tire air is on filling stations today. Boardinghouses and restaurants gave hard drink away; at the Indian Queen Ordinary, in Washington, for one, there were decanters of free whiskey and "brandy" on each table. Kegs of whiskey were placed on riverbanks, at boat stops, for the convenience of boatmen. The tin cups used for drinking were chained to the kegs, however; they were harder to replace than the whiskey.

The great, national, dirt-cheap flow of whiskey was composed of varieties made from rye or corn or both, by formulas that were mainly native American and historically new. (The modern legal specifications that define commercial rye whiskey and commercial bourbon whiskey were not worked out till years later.) The best whiskey was made in Pennsylvania, southern Ohio, Kentucky, and Tennessee. At about the time that American ingenuity discovered that straight water was potable, grain farmers discovered the more important properties in a certain kind of water that lay along a vein of limestone running through those states. Whiskey distilled with this limestone-based water, they said—and they sold the idea, apparently, for all time—was the finest American whiskey. The first nationally famous variety was a Pennsylvania rye called Old Monongahela.

George Washington thought of American whiskey, including Old Monongahela, as "stinking" stuff. But shortly after he himself had led a revolution that was touched off, in part, by taxed tea, American farmers led a revolt against Washington's government and its tax on whiskey. Like Washington in his fight with England, they eventually won out. The first President, being a statesman of genius, had realized that you can practically run the business of a Western civilization on liquor taxes. From Lincoln's administration on, for many years, a substantial part of the business of American civilization was so run. Washington, though, as it turned out, had been ahead of his time. Soon after the first excise taxes on whiskey were passed, in 1791, whiskey makers began to shoot and tar and feather revenuers. It was the start of a national sport which has been popular ever since in periods of whiskey taxing, but which has never again been as roughly played as it was in the 1790s.

In 1795, the militia marched out and shot up the farmers who had shot up the revenue men. (Washington, along about then, noticed suddenly that taxes were making it too expensive for him to buy whiskey for his servants and slaves and for local entertainment. So he began to distill his own whiskey at home, from rye mixed with Indian corn.) Taxes remained for more than twenty years after this —but so did moonshining, guerrilla fighting, and public hatred of the excise laws. Once the War of 1812 had been paid for, the Government yielded to pressure and turned American whiskey loose in the open market, unassessed.

This bloody victory for domestic grog made it certain that imported drinks like gin and Scotch whisky would continue to be rare and special in America for another hundred years—till the Government at last drove us to embrace crime and to beg through holes in the wall for gin and Scotch, and so to form new tastes. Beer as a mass drink was set back about fifty years by the manumission of the whiskey distillers. In a representative year between 1818 and the Civil War, the per capita consumption of beer in America was less than a gallon and a half. Today the figure is close to twenty gallons. Whiskey, when it runs like water and is priced like bread, is hard to compete with.

Drinkers also found whiskey hard to compete with, in the whiskey age. Temperance-society statistics, which modern students of alcoholism are inclined to go along with, showed, as noted earlier, that the cheap, high-proof liquor of the first half of the nineteenth century was too much for three of ten of the people who drank it regularly; it wrecked them physically, socially, and economically. Delirium tremens was as common in towns and cities as parking fines are today. Not that the consumer went down without a struggle in his contest with overwhelming supply. He drank with courage and spirit; punishment was inflicted on both sides. The whiskey-fighter drank at all hours. Morning drinking (which is now a slightly sinister term in the vocabulary of alcoholism, more or less synonymous with sneak drinking) was then a social saloon exercise exceeded in popularity only by afternoon drinking and evening drinking. Bill Poole, called Bill the Butcher, a leader of New York City sporting life in the 1850s, often had his first drink of the day, in some Broadway bar like the Gem or the City, at 10 A.M., and his first fight at 10:30.

Drinking cheap whiskey was, in fact, treated in some circles as an extension of athletics; the two fields overlapped curiously in the minds of strenuous men of the period, such as professional athletes. Drinkers like Poole and Tom Hyer (who was the first national prize-fighting champion, and the best-known athlete in New York in the years between 1840 and 1850) took physical conditioning very seriously. They would row across the Hudson to buy milk punches in Hoboken, and then row back. This kind of thing did not exempt them from the actuarial laws of a time when the life span was shorter than it is now, and a drinking man of thirty was middle-aged. Gunplay, an important health hazard in saloons, killed Poole at thirty-three. Dropsy and dissipation killed Hyer at forty-five. To take the case of an athletic whiskey-fighter in Ireland: In his thirties, Dan Donnelly (said to have been the only pugilist to achieve knighthood) drank forty-seven tumblers of whiskey punch one night to test his condition, as an athlete nowadays might do push-ups. He sparred the next day but dropped dead a little while later. His death was attributed by local sports experts to his having taken a deep drink of cold water after the workout, while in a state of perspiration.

Hyer and Poole belonged to the perpendicular majority of American drinkers, the seven tenths who avoided obvious chronic drunkenness. There is no way of knowing in detail what the condition of their bodies was at death. (Poole's was autopsied, but mainly with regard to the chest wound that killed him.) It's possible that a full report would have astonished their friends and enemies, just as Battling Siki's friends and neighbors were incredulous when the autopsy after his murder showed he had been suffering from anemia. Undoubtedly, subversive processes were also at work beneath the hides of the barroom athletes of the untaxed whiskey age.

Some drinkers tried to salvage a little health by desperate application to, and semiscientific study of, free lunch. The ancient Romans believed that hot cabbage was the safest partner for alcohol and the best hangover cure. In American saloons both before and after the Civil War there was a cult of herring. A herring, dry or pickled, in the free lunch was called a black-eyed Susan. It was thought to keep a man sober while he drank and to work so well against a hangover that drinkers sometimes took herrings home with them to eat next morning. Oysters were fundamental in free saloon eating. In the twenty years or so that preceded the Civil War, most first-class saloons had oyster boxes, with hinged lids. Generally the box was set against a wall near one end of the bar, where drinkers had easy access to this kind of protection if they wanted it. Charles Dickens was impressed by American public-house oysters, some of which, he said, were "as large as cheese-plates." It was clear to Dickens, though, as it was to other reformers, that no fish were big enough to check the onset of mass alcoholic poisoning. Free lunch notwithstanding, the bargain drinkers of the whiskey age drank more than they ate.

If American drunkenness shocked Dickens, so did the American temperance movement. He went into a hotel in Ohio one day in 1842, looking for brandy, and was told that the house had nothing stronger to offer as entertainment than the water in the jug on the table and the lithograph of Washington over the fireplace. It's easy to see how a high-strung foreigner might be upset by news like that, especially when you consider the background. Like American hard-liquor drinking at that time, the American temperance movement was somewhat more highly developed than corresponding movements in Britain and Ireland—though British and Irish drys had already begun to take their cues from American teetotalers. Dickens had not been prepared for anything as all-out as the American West was, when he visited there. The Washington Total Abstinence Society, the first important organization of its kind, had been formed in 1840. Within a few years, antiliquor campaigns had seared the Middle West—where living was hard, and women were in the saddle —like a grass fire.

In the East, however, the Washingtonian movement broke down as early as 1844. The Washingtonians, of whom more will be said later, were an outfit of some merit and charm, as such groups go— possibly the most tolerant and tolerable de-juicing apparatus in history up to the time of Alcoholics Anonymous. But they and other temperance groups could make no useful headway against the buyers' market in whiskey in the big Eastern cities or in the small towns. There may, of course, have been differences in the quality of thirst between one town and another. Men drank in Concord, Massachusetts, for instance, but they drank with a kind of chamber-of-commerce concern for the town's best-known product, intellect. At any rate, Nathaniel Hawthorne thought they did. After making a short study of the inside of a Concord tavern one day, Hawthorne guessed that the object of the drinking he'd seen there was "to create a titillation of the coat of the stomach and a general sense of invigoration, without affecting the brain." Perhaps he was right—but elsewhere, generally, stomach coats were not so much titillated as turned inside out, and brains went uninsured. New England, outside Concord, was intense drinking country, even though platforms and pulpits were alive with abolitionist-prohibitionists, and Neal Dow, who got the country's first prohibition act, the Maine Liquor Law, passed in 1851, spent years before and after that worrying Yankee liquor sellers everywhere. In New England, barflies drank local gin and traditional rum, as well as whiskey. It's noteworthy that Timothy Shay Arthur, in "Ten Nights in a Barroom," the *Uncle Tom's Cabin* of the antialcohol crusade, placed his barroom, the archetypal drinking hell, in a New England village.

Boston, Philadelphia, Baltimore, Charleston, New Orleans, and settlements in between—and San Francisco, after the gold rush began—were hotbeds of high-proof drinking. In New York, in the 1850s, in the lively part of Broadway, from Houston Street south, where pigs and other livestock ran wild, it was possible to get raging drunk for a dollar at the City, the Star, the Dexter House, Brady's, the States, Charley Abel's, Jack Wildey's, Phil Maguire's Lafayette Hall, Pete Barlow's, the Gem, Dick Platt's, the St. James, the St. Nicholas, Bill Allen's, the Senate, Johnny Lyng's Sportsman's Headquarters, the Cooper House, Revere House, Abe Florence's The Corner, and Poughkeepsie Jake's. The Bowery was equally wet— "So far," Dickens wrote, after a quick tour in 1842, "nearly every house is a low tavern." Around the Five Points fugitive slaves sold liquor and early Harlemesque entertainment in "juba" ballrooms like Pete Williams' and Almack's.

Samuel Colt invented the revolver in 1836 and patented fresh models in 1839 and 1850. In the atmosphere of the whiskey age, this was like tossing lighted matches into a pool of kerosene. The still smallish town of San Francisco had twelve hundred murders in saloons, most of them committed with revolvers, in the years 1849–51. If the homicide rate was a little lower in Eastern saloons, it was partly because Easterners were poorer shots and serviced their guns less carefully. In one general brawl in a Charleston bar, some twenty drinkers pulled triggers, but no one was hurt. Poole, who was visiting in the South at the time, was one of the baffled marksmen. (On returning to New York, he had his .38 Colt five-shooter checked at a local service station and the cylinder repaired—it had not been revolving.) When John Morrissey, a prizefighter, later a Congressman, tried to kill Poole in a New York dramshop one evening, his gun missed fire repeatedly, and he left the place weeping with frustration. In the circumstances, drinkers with California training formed an elite in saloons in the East—they knew how to make guns go off. A doctor with California training was called as an expert witness on bullet holes in overcoats, in a New York saloon-murder trial in 1855. He could tell whether a shot had been fired from inside a garment or from outside it. "I had charge of coats that had been fired through for the San Francisco police," he said in qualifying himself. "What encounters did you see in San Francisco?" counsel asked him respectfully. The doctor recited a list of them, while crime fans in his audience hung on every word.

In 1862, the Union war effort needed cash badly. Early that year Congress wrote an internal revenue act that included the first tax on American drinking in forty-four years, in the form of a twenty-dollar annual license charge to liquor sellers. The sellers at once passed the load along to the public by raising prices. The new tax did not make hard liquor a luxury overnight. But it did remove it from what might be called, in modern terms, the chewing-gum class. It would be possible for another fifty years or more to drink distilled stuff fairly inexpensively, as in the two-shots-for-a-quarter era that preceded the First World War. But the average steady drinker had to look lower than that for a hobby. After the Civil War, the brewing industry, rising like yeast, gave him what he needed. In short, the tax of 1862 started a trend which was in time to spread and thin out the distribution of alcohol; to dilute its impact on regular users; to promote curious, habit-forming substitutes for alcoholic drinks; and, loosely speaking, to civilize American drinking—if the use of pale, cold beer and tincture of kola nut can be said to comport with civilization.

Ironically, not even its authors recognized the tax for what it was: the beginning of the end of the age of alcoholic gluttony. Temperance workers were shocked and frightened. They saw the new act only as a legal enfranchisement of drinking, as an alliance between the Government and the liquor trade. President Lincoln himself was scared by the legislation he'd asked for. A party of sixty leading drys increased his discomfort by paying an organized call at the White House, one day in April, before he had signed the act, and taking turns scratching his conscience with some of the longest, horniest fingernails in the cold-water movement.

It was an all-star team of teetotalers, including as it did Wendell Phillips, Horace Greeley, Henry Ward Beecher, General Neal Dow, the dry-law Moses from Maine, on furlough from the Union Army, and John B. Gough, the reclaimed drunkard, the cause's champion pitchman and pledge seller. Lincoln told them, according to witnesses, that he mistrusted the licensing act and would work for its repeal after the national crisis had passed. Gently but firmly he stalled, feinted, and straight-armed his guests, one after another. Gough was the last to come at him. The fight against the dragon, said Gough—who had long, black hair, burning eyes, and a voice like a lonesome bugle—had been a hard one for nearly fifty years. "But now, Canaan is in sight. Will you, Sir, close the gates in our faces?" Lincoln, wincing, told Gough that it looked that way. "Though I must call on the very powers of Hades [this is a Goughian version, and maybe a bowdlerized one] for help, I must save the union," he said. He signed the bill on July 1, 1862.

As it turned out, misguided fear of the liquor tax drove the drys to greater efforts after Appomattox. Drinking was generally lower-proofed in the years that followed. Alcoholism was less violent and better controlled. But the temperance movement grew bigger and fiercer, till it became too nervously strong to settle for anything but what it eventually got, the Eighteenth Amendment.

Epilogue

ON A VERMONT HILLSIDE, five months after John Lardner died at the age of forty-seven, Robert Frost mentioned Lardner's name and made a request. "When you get back to New York," Frost said, "tell this fellow Lardner that I think he has a very unusual slant on things. Comical. Tell him I like his stuff. But be careful now. Don't embarrass him with praise."

Frost was eighty-five then and still too youthful, too concerned with the issues of life, to devote much time to reading obituaries. I could not bring myself to tell the poet that Lardner was dead. Instead, on that high hill, I thought how much this compliment, from one believer in understatement to another, would have meant to John. It certainly pleased his friends. One, who had been a sports writer, heard of it and said intensely, "That's the way it should be. Cabbies and fighters liked my stuff. Robert Frost liked his."

Although most perceptive sports writers accepted him as matchless, sports writing was not the craft of John Lardner. Nor was it profile writing, nor column writing. After the painstaking business of reportage, his craft was purely writing: writing the English sentence, fusing sound and meaning, matching the precision of the word with the rhythm of the phrase. It is a pursuit which is unfailingly demanding, and Lardner met it with unfailing mastery. This is not to bracket him with Sean O'Casey and T. S. Eliot, who also write English sentences. John chose his arena, created his world within carefully reasoned limits. I think it is fair to say that within these limits, in his time, he had no equal.

The world of John Lardner was a place of grace and humor, where no one was evil as Iago or virtuous as St. Joan, and where it always seemed that everyone talked softly. Unobtrusively, in a corner near the bar, house rules were posted in a few lines of small type. They went along these lines: "Living is difficult at times and three out of three people die, but there is not much sense in railing against either. Deal, drink, or read, but do it quietly." It was a pleasant place, without hot tears or strident laughter.

No one was judged explicitly. Even the Nazi criminal Lemick-Emden was accepted for what he was and damned only by his own words, his own actions. The conventionalists, who stamp people and things good or bad and move on to the next person or thing, stamp poised, often became confused in Lardner's world and took the back door out. (This led to an alley which was grimy and more familiar to the conventionalists.)

Heroes in his world were gamblers who fleeced innocents, ball-players whose ignorance sang, and prizefighters who attempted to father a large portion of their country. There was no question of these heroes having feet of clay—the clay ran up to the waist.

The villains, at first thought, seemed very much the same, but there was a fine and unwavering difference. Lardner once explained why he liked an avaricious baseball promoter named Branch Rickey and disliked an avaricious baseball promoter named Walter O'Malley. "They do the same things," Lardner said, "but O'Malley won't admit it."

We never talked about Jack Paar. We never had to. The blank-ness of Paar's intellect would have been forgiven, but the combina-tion of blankness and pomposity could not be. (I wonder if it is coincidence that Paar spent a month attacking *Newsweek* before "What They Did to Jack" appeared, then fell silent and did not again attack the magazine until Lardner was dead.)

Because the world seen through Lardner's writing was such an enjoyable place, great numbers of people pressed to meet its creator. I don't know what they expected. Possibly Lardner entering with a soft-shoe routine, while Battling Siki sparred in one wing and Titanic Thompson booked bets in the other.

What they found was a tall, bespectacled man, black-haired and not very comfortable with strangers. Lardner spoke sparely to people he did not know, and it was amusing to watch editors and others cope with silence on first meeting with Lardner. Commonly they threw a few of their favorite anecdotes, then slipped into banalities. I can think of several austere types, unused to silence, remarking to Lardner that Mickey Mantle was a good hitter, or that battle tested a man's courage, or that yessir, it certainly had been hot and here it was only June. As I say, it amused me and I imagine it amused John, too, because he listened carefully, solemnly, and kindly. The silence itself was a kindness. John's wit, turned on a cliché, struck sparks.

It was a foolish but understandable error to think one could gain entry into Lardner's world by meeting the man. The world did not exist in the places and things John liked: not in the Artist & Writers Restaurant, where John enjoyed himself standing at the bar sipping Scotch and soda, nor in Saratoga, where he enjoyed himself on those days when his horses won, nor in St. Petersburg, where he enjoyed himself when the springtime sun burned bright. The world existed within Lardner's mind.

This is a point which many people who do not write find puzzling. I suppose some burst into the Mermaid Tavern looking for Hamlet or Antony and, finding only a bald, bearded playwright, left disappointed. I suppose some asked Herman Melville, "Where do you keep the whale?" A puzzling point, perhaps, but a critical one. For the writer lives in no special physical world. Before him lies only what lies before everyone else. The writer's art begins with his own interpretation and imagination. It is to take the world that has been thrust upon him and from it to create a world beyond, more enticing and more real.

How? Lardner could not have told you, nor could Freud. One knows only that this creation is a private act of the mind. At its highest, it cannot be achieved in editorial meetings or in story conferences. It is achieved by one man working alone.

For reasons that he did not bother to make explicit, Lardner never worked for any of Henry Luce's magazines. In the course of earning a living, he worked for—or against—several magazines which he did not respect or did not take seriously, but always with the proviso that they not be published by Luce. I think this was an intensely individualistic protest by an intensely individualistic man.

After sparring with Harvard (Harvard by a decison—Lardner's) and living in France briefly, he became a reporter on the New York *Herald Tribune*. While still in his mid-twenties, he left the paper to write a syndicated sports column, and presently *Newsweek* hired him to write a sports column once a week. Then came the war correspondence. After that there was scarcely a magazine in the country that did not want Lardner's stories on Lardner's terms. (The reference is to style here, not cash.)

It was a memorable career, and at the end Lardner occasionally had to beat off editors with bottles of club soda lest he find himself writing stories he didn't like, or didn't have time for, or couldn't afford. Yet, while Lardner grew successful by writing in his own original, individual way, magazines, generally, became less interested in original, individual articles. *Time* and the *Reader's Digest*, edited up or down to a single level, edited to read as though they had been written by one man, came to be journalistic giants. At least they made gigantic sums of money.

Like any careful writer, Lardner took editing badly. Some of the pieces in the book are fourth and fifth drafts, and when someone casually changed a word Lardner had struggled to find, or a viewpoint he had formed slowly, John burned with a quiet, enduring rage. Once an editor ordered him to write that Lew Hoad, the Australian tennis player, was as good as Pancho Gonzales, the American. "Grmmmf," Lardner said but made no further comment until eight months later when Gonzales had beaten Hoad decisively in a 100-match series. He then spoke of the editor more extensively. "I told the son of a bitch he was wrong eight months ago," Lardner said.

Lardner the journalist moved against the tide of the times and, through something very close to genius, triumphed over the tide. By not working for Luce, who had produced the fad for group journalism, he was registering a protest vote on behalf of others who had been swept along. With the advent of *Sports Illustrated,* which would have allowed him ample stylistic range, the protest became costly. Lardner stuck to it as a matter of integrity; he guarded his integrity in a fierce, uncompromising way.

He also stuck to journalism, which troubled some of his friends. "You ought to write a novel," people told him from time to time, and Lardner's answer, when he bothered to make one, was a defense of the essay. One evening three of us argued about the form of writing that is most natural. Two held out for poetry, and having Lardner two to one, we moved in with broad, positive statements. Full-arm blows, fight writers call this sort of attack.

"Let's consider primitives," someone said. "Children are primitives, and what do they respond to? Rhyme and meter."

"All right, consider primitives," Lardner said. "The Rosetta Stone was an essay."

John was an essayist in an era of novel worship, an individual journalist in a time of group journalism. That's two strikes, but until the night he died, no one ever slipped a third strike past Lardner. In any time, under any rules, his craft would have carried him to a unique and solitary place, just as it did in the difficult times in which he happened to live.

This book illustrates some of the range and sweep of a writer looking about with wit, taste, subtlety, and sometimes with horror. The articles were written between 1942 and 1959, all but a handful after World War II. Lardner was better after the war than before. He worked at his writing and he learned from it.

I have not written introductory notes to each piece for several reasons, among them that it would be pointless to type and retype, "Here's another beauty." But the circumstances of the book's final section are important. For several years, John had been gathering material for his history of drinking, in libraries and through interviews and correspondence. It was a favorite project, and even toward the end of his life, when he was silently enduring painful heart seizures, he continued, while writing columns for *Newsweek* and *The New Yorker,* to collect historical data. He left notes for twenty chapters and finished, or apparently finished, seven. What we have whets our thirst for more, but Lardner, sick or well, would never permit himself to hurry his writing.

While he enjoyed writing and being read, he could not write easily. It took him a long time to bring each story up to his usual standard and a longer time to build that standard up to what it was. The night he died, he left five drafts of a good lead scattered about his typewriter.

Had he been given a full life span and good health, I think he might have surprised everyone with writing quite different from the rich legacy we have. His mind, his world, never ceased to grow, and in his last months he sometimes mentioned an exciting idea which he was not quite ready to begin. (He mentioned it in confidence, still binding.)

Now, of John Lardner, the writer, I sometimes think of a few lines, not from an essay, but from a poem.

> *The life so short*
> *The craft so long to learn . . .*

I am not going to tell you where that's from. John would have known, and this book is for him.

Roger Kahn

Pleasantville, N.Y.
October 1960